MARTINŮ'S LETTERS HOME
Five Decades of Correspondence
with Family and Friends

MARTINŮ'S LETTERS HOME

Five Decades of Correspondence with Family and Friends

With a Preface by Aleš Březina

Edited by Iša Popelka
Translated by Ralph Slayton

English version edited
by Martin Anderson and Aleš Březina

Musicians in Letters
No. 3

TOCCATA
PRESS

Editor's dedication: For František Popelka

Translator's dedication: For Tereza

English-language edition first published 2012 by Toccata Press

First published as *Dopisy domů. Z korespondence do Poličky*, Mladá fronta, Prague, 1996

British Library Cataloguing in Publication Data
Martinů, Bohuslav, 1890–1959.
Martinů's letters home : five decades of correspondence with family and friends.
– (Musicians in letters ; no. 3)
1. Martinů, Bohuslav, 1890–1959–Correspondence.
2. Composers–Czech Republic–Correspondence.
I. Title II. Series III. Popelka, Iša. IV. Anderson, Martin (Martin J.) V. Březina, leš, 1965-780.9'2-dc23

ISBN: 978 0 907689 77 5
ISSN: 0960 0094

 Toccata Press gratefully acknowledges a grant from the Bohuslav Martinů Foundation towards the production costs of this book.

Typeset by Kerrypress Ltd, Luton, Beds.
Printed and bound in Great Britain by CPI Group (UK) Ltd, Croydon, CR0 4YY

Contents

List of Illustrations

Preface
ALEŠ BŘEZINA

I am delighted that a selection of Bohuslav Martinů's letters to his family and close friends is finally being published in English. In it the editor Iša Popelka – a leading Czech scholar on Bohuslav Martinů and long-time collaborator at the Martinů Museum in Polička (created by his father František Popelka, after renovation in 2009 it was renamed the Martinů Centre) – has made good use of his lifelong experience with the work of this composer. In a courageous political gesture, Popelka's work on Martinů began with a seminar paper 'Poličská léta Bohuslava Martinů' ('The Polička Years of Bohuslav Martinů')[1] in the 1950s, dealing critically with the composer's mythologised relation to his homeland, which was prominently celebrated by the Communist regime in order to avoid questions about Martinů's decision not to return to his native country after the Communist takeover. So the seemingly innocuous title *Letters Home*[2] as conceived by Popelka does not signal another attempt to reduce the last 31 years of Martinů's life only, or mainly, to a cliché about unfulfilled longing to return to his native Vysočina (the Bohemian Highlands). On the contrary, Popelka savours the provocative double meanings coded into the title of his book, which he conceives as referring only to the addressees of the letters, not to the notion of homeland.

Today one can at last rid Martinů of the sentimental accretions and legends through which the Communist state reduced him to something it could accept. Although they identified him as an enemy of the regime immediately after the Communist takeover in 1948 (his works disappeared from the programmes of all Czech and Slovak orchestras and opera houses for five years), the Communists soon recognised they could not long pretend he did not exist and so in the mid-1950s they began to re-integrate him, at least partially, into Czechoslovak musical life. They discovered a useful tool in Martinů's folk cantata *Otvírání studánek* ('The Opening of the Springs'), H354, which shared some external principles with the demands of socialist-realistic music: the use of a folk or folk-like text, a reduced degree of dissonance, the use of tonality and structural simplicity. What the Czech Martinů revival in the second half of the 1950s completely avoided were all his more complex orchestral and stage works, all the radical compositions from the 1920s and early '30s and any vocal pieces based on religious or spiritual texts.

---

[1] Published as František Popelka (Jr.), 'Poličská léta Bohuslava Martinů' ('The Polička Years of Bohuslav Martinů'), in Zdeněk Zouhar (ed.), *Bohuslav Martinů. Sborník vzpomínek a studií* ('Bohuslav Martinů: Collection of Memoirs and Essays'), Krajské nakladatelství v Brně, Brno, 1957, pp. 57–72.

[2] Originally scheduled for publication by Kruh in Hradec Králové (a company dissolved after the downfall of the Communist regime in 1991) to mark the centenary of Martinů's birth in 1891, the original Czech edition of this book, *Dopisy domů: Z korespondence do Poličky* ('Letters Home: The Correspondence with Polička') was eventually published in 1996 by Mladá fronta in Prague.

In Martinů's homeland this large part of his output was fully explored only after the Velvet Revolution in 1989. As in the case of Karel Čapek, whose works were presented to us Czechs in abridged form as an expression of humanity and an anticipation of Communism, the legend of the never-fulfilled longing of the 'great Czech composer Bohuslav Martinů' to return home – for which *The Opening of the Springs* was always cited as proof – attempted to veil the reasons for which Martinů could not and did not wish to come back. The uncovering of this layer (Popelka calls it 'reasons for no return' in the Preface to the Czech edition[3]) is a central topic in this selection of letters.

Thanks to the large number of items here and their wide time-span, covering more than half of the twentieth century – from the time of the Austro-Hungarian monarchy through several democracies (Czechoslovakia, France, the United States and Switzerland) to the era of totalitarianism – this correspondence presents a personal chronicle of its era. Even a quick glance at the Personalia in Appendix One (in which one finds, for example, eight times more references to Martinů's Polička neighbour Bohuslav Šmíd than to Igor Stravinsky) reveals something of the focus and the topics of the entire correspondence preserved in the Bohuslav Martinů Centre. Keeping in mind his addressees and the scope of their experience, Martinů tends to write more about general events than about the development of his opinions on artistic creation, which are mentioned only in association with completion of some work or its performance. An exemplary son, Martinů sent regular reports to Polička about his life, not about his music. The 'dear ones' (*drazi* in Czech) to whom he writes are his mother, his sister Marie and brother František; the letters were generally addressed to Marie, to be passed on by her as necessary.

What image of Martinů does this extensive collection of letters reveal? He is plainly an immensely successful composer. His works are mostly written to commission and are performed immediately upon completion by leading artists and ensembles all over the world. And yet a characteristic trait of the letters as a whole is understatement. Beginning especially in the 1930s, when his music began to be performed in many countries of Europe as well as in the United States, he devotes a single brief sentence to each new performance and each new commission. Also evident from all the letters is the restrained nature of his expression and his unsentimental approach to life. Whether writing about his failures, or about political or economic catastrophes, or responding to news of the death of a close relative or friend, he always writes calmly, with equilibrium, as though addressing something that is a natural part of life. At most – and only when he is really in a bad way – he writes: 'One must never despair; work always pays off somewhere [...]'.[4]

This equilibrium pertains to both successes and defeats, joys and disappointments. Only quite exceptionally – as, for example, in a letter of April 1924[5] – does direct emotion glint through between the lines. At that time his three-month scholarship allowing him to travel to Paris and study with Albert Roussel had long since expired. But Martinů had only just begun to feel a little at home in Paris. He had scarcely had time to come to know some of the important figures in its cultural life and to overcome the language barrier, so it would actually have been absurd for him to leave then and return to Prague. In this state of mind he wrote home: 'Paris is so beautiful

---

[3] *Ibid.*, p. 6.

[4] *Cf.* p. 78, below.

[5] *Cf.* LETTER 3 on pp. 23–24, below.

*Polička, the destination of Martinů's letters – the main square
in a postcard from the beginning of the century*

just now – like a great garden full of spring festivities, lights and flowers, people and pleasures – that I really don't want to leave'. These happy lines conceal the considerable material misery to which he was voluntarily subjecting himself at the time.

Equally rare are the occasions when Martinů drops the mask behind which he hides his political opinions, as in the letter to his family at Christmas 1949, where what seems to be Aesopian irony is directly reminiscent of the po-faced sarcasm encountered in many of Shostakovich's letters: 'I read that everyone there is going to school to be re-educated for the New World, where future generations will be the happiest on earth. We probably won't be here then, so the teaching will hardly help us'.[6]

In recent years several publications have reconstructed Martinů's emotional life based on his correspondence and/or personal knowledge; the most celebrated and artistically most successful of them is *Podivné lásky* ('Strange Loves')[7] by his friend of many years Jiří Mucha. Apparently under the stimulus of these publications, in which interpretation of the composer's emotional life plays a major role, Popelka decided to take the opposite approach. Like a mediaeval monk trying to reach a direct understanding of canonised texts and adding only marginalia, he hides himself from the reader of his book behind its original material. He sees his role mainly in providing information, with brief explanations of the contexts – of which he, as a musicologist and, moreover, a Polička native himself, has a thorough knowledge.

Sometimes his fondness for brevity makes one smile, as for example when he restricts his commentary on something planned or mentioned by the composer to a dry observation: 'They didn't', or 'She was not mistaken', or 'He didn't. He spent that Christmas in Paris'. Like Walter Benjamin, Popelka portrays history only by the appropriate assembly of documents without any kind of commentary. He

---

[6] *Cf.* LETTER 71 on p. 129, below.

[7] Jiří Mucha, *Podivné lásky*, Mladá Fronta, Prague, 1988. A French translation appeared as *Au seuil de la nuit*, Editions de l'Aube, La Tour d'Aigues, 1991.

facilitates this approach also by the arrangement of his selection, which culminates with Martinů's thoughts on the sense and substance of artistic creation in letters to the poet Miloslav Bureš, the author of the text of *Otvírání studánek* and the other cantatas associated with the Vysočina region.

Then, shortly before the publication of this English edition of the letters, a book appeared which offered a radically different interpretation of Martinů's apparent stoicism: F. James Rybka's biography *Bohuslav Martinů: The Compulsion to Compose*.[8] In it, Rybka (the doctor son of Martinů's close friend Frank Rybka[9]) argues that he suffered from Asperger's Syndrome. And that condition, Rybka suggests, was responsible for Martinů's seeming dispassion which, instead, was symptomatic of the lack of empathy typically associated with his condition.[10] Having had access to a version of this translation of Martinů's letters in the preparation of his book, Rybka occasionally sees evidence of Asperger's Syndrome in them. We have added footnotes to draw attention to these points.

Appendix Two: Martinů as Cartoonist on pp. 215–31 offers an element missing from the original Czech publication of these letters: some of Martinů's many humorous drawings, discussed for the first time in English. Since many of them are autobiographical and were intended for a small circle of friends back home, their ironic, even whimsical, view of life complements the relatively deadpan expression of the letters, revealing Martinů as a far more subtle commentator on the human condition than he might at first appear.

The footnotes prepared for the Czech edition have been expanded for an international readership by Martin Anderson of Toccata Press. Kateřina Brádková helped prepare the lay-out and checked the English titles of all of Martinů's works, also adding their 'H' numbers from the standard catalogue of Martinů's music by Harry Halbreich.[11] Lucie Jirglová of the Centrum Bohuslava Martinů in Polička was helpfulness itself in supplying the illustrations, all of which are reproduced courtesy of the Centrum, some of them supplied via Zoja Sejčková and Jitka Zichová of the Martinů Institute in Prague. That on p. 41 is the copyright of Anna Fárová and that of Vítěslava Kaprálová on p. 77 was supplied by The Kaprálová Society. Patricia Breeus of the Queen Elisabeth Competition helped identify some of the faces in the photograph on p. 146. And help with the proofreading was gratefully received from Seth Blacklock and Guy Rickards. The Bohuslav Martinů Foundation has supported the preparation of the English version of this book over several stages of its production.

From 1999 to 2004 I had the opportunity of spending many hours with Ralph Slayton, the translator of this book – hours filled with fascinating discussions about Martinů and his correspondence, but also about a girl he had met years earlier in a hospital and for whom he promised to translate this book. Ralph was a former journalist and a senior lecturer in English literature in the Department of English Language and Literature in the Education Faculty of the University of Hradec Králové. I deeply regret that he did not live to see this publication.

Director, Martinů Institute
Prague

---

[8] Scarecrow Press, Lanham, Maryland, 2011.

[9] *Cf.* note 88 on p. 117, below.

[10] *Ibid.*, pp. 290, 299 and 346.

[11] *Bohuslav Martinů: Werkverzeichnis und Biographie*, 2nd edn., Schott, Mainz, 2007

Editorial Introduction
IŠA POPELKA

This edition – of 115 letters, seven postcards and one telegram – covers half a century of the composer's life and, with the exception of some minor publications in Polička of a few of his letters home, it is the first time any of it has been published in book form. In spite of – perhaps because of – his exile abroad, Martinů never ceased to love his homeland, its history, its traditions and its language, and with time and distance the bond grew even stronger: he remained tied to his birthplace and to the Moravian Highlands which surround it in enduring and tender affection. In his letters to Polička, there is occasionally heard a tone of reminiscence and nostalgia, perhaps especially in those letters in which he knows that his family is expecting him to come home, and this selection reveals those sympathies poignantly. He astutely observed the path on which his country set out after 1945 and prudently put off returning. His reluctance to return was not a matter of intuition alone. He remained well-informed, and his hesitation was determined by his lucid good judgement. So it continued in the 1950s, when only in subtle allusions, so as not to provoke the local censors to obstruct his letters or put their recipients in jeopardy, he managed to write between the lines about his stance toward the totalitarian regime. These letters hint at the reasons for his reluctance to return to his homeland.

His letters to Polička, even though for the most part addressed to his family, reveal very little of his private life. There are no intimate insights, as one might expect from such a reserved man – a true Man of the Highlands. The letters have a different priority; they are, as a rule, selected matter-of-fact reportage of his own accomplishments and, of course, information about the fate of his creative work, rather than insights into the work itself and its making. But the news, though succinct, is a valuable source for the historian and provides the reader with a record of the composer's life in his own words and at least a mention of the more important compositions (far from all of them) and of the persons and personalities who occupied an important place in his life and career (again, far from all of them). It also allows a view of his outlook on life – his refusal to be deterred by its inevitable disappointments; on the contrary, he courageously accepted unalterable, sometimes discouraging realities with calm equanimity.

This volume draws on the 633 letters catalogued (along with several dozen letters from Charlotte Martinů) in the Bohuslav Martinů Centre in the Town Museum in Polička, the composer's birthplace. Some of them are the private property of the addressees[12] or, more accurately these days, of their descendants. An editor –

---

[12] *Cf.* Appendix One: Addressees on pp. 205–13, below. An asterisk at the first mention of a name indicates the presence of an explanatory text there. Similarly, the first reference to any of Martinů's works in the footnotes is accompanied by its 'H' number, from Harry Halbreich's catalogue *Bohuslav Martinů: Werkverzeichnis und Biographie, op. cit.*

*The tower of the Church of St James in Polička with the small apartment
of the Martinů family – postcard from the beginning of the century*

especially one faced with such a large archive – has to make his way between choices. In his Paris years (1923–40) Martinů regularly wrote a letter home every two weeks. Relatively few letters have been preserved from the period before that; perhaps at home his family did not attach much importance to them. From December 1941 until the summer of 1945, Martinů was unable to write home: the United States, where he was living, was at war with the Third Reich, the 'protector' of his homeland. And after the Communist takeover in February 1948, correspondence with his home came to be much less frequent, though fortunately only temporarily.

It needs to be said what this correspondence is not. Until the two letters to Miloslav Bureš,[13] perhaps, it is not a portrait of Martinů's capacity for deep thinking: ever tactful, he did not want to write beyond the intellectual capacities of the addressees. The transient nature of his life meant that he could not keep extensive archives, and so the letters to which he was responding have not been preserved. In any case, the political situation meant that neither side of the exchange would have been able to express itself freely: a genuine *Briefwechsel* would not have been feasible.

Acknowledgements of the Czech Edition

I wish to thank Dr Lenka Chytilová of the publishing house Kruh, Božena Pravdová, who sub-edited this volume and saw it through publication, and those who provided me with letters or gave me advice on Martinů's written communications with Polička and information about people and facts mentioned in the letters. They are, especially, Věra Daňková, Ela Hynková, Blažena Junková, Marie Maděrová, Herberta Masaryková, Anna Trnková, Dr Josef Dvořák, David Junek, Dr Jaroslav Mihule, Dr Jaroslav Michalíček, Václav Rippl, René Slezák, Bohuslav Šmíd, Professor Eduard Vencovský, Zdeněk Vojtek, Dr Tomislav Volek, Dr Zdeněk Zouhar, and most of all my father, František Popelka, to whose memory this book is dedicated and without whose help it would probably not have come into being.

---

[13] LETTERS 111 and 115 on pp. 191–92 and 198–202, below.

Part I
APPRENTICESHIP IN POLIČKA, PRAGUE AND PARIS
1907–29

Born in a small town on the border of Bohemia and Moravia, with parents interested in culture but living in poverty, spending the first ten years of his life isolated in the tower of St James' Church, and having a shy and reserved personality, Bohuslav Martinů certainly was not a very promising candidate to become a strong personal voice in twentieth-century music. In spite of his early success as a violinist in his native Polička, his studies at the Prague Conservatoire ended up with failure and expulsion at the age of twenty. For the next thirteen years, from 1910 to 1923, he lived as a freelance violinist and composer in Prague (except for the war years 1916–18 when he taught music at the music school in Polička). He achieved his first important acknowledgment as a composer when the Czech Philharmonic premiered his patriotic cantata *Czech Rhapsody,* H118, in January 1919. At that time there were already over 100 works in his catalogue, mostly songs and piano pieces; some of his few orchestral works may not even have been intended for public performance. It was therefore highly surprising when Martinů obtained a small grant from the Czechoslovak government, enabling him to go to Paris for three months.

When he arrived there in October 1923, he was leaving Czechoslovakia not only physically but also mentally, since he was breaking the centuries-old tradition of using the German-speaking countries as the jumping point for a Czech composer. Indeed, he was actively seeking a clash: he wrote several articles for Czech newspapers and journals criticising the dependence of living Czech composers on the Austro-German music tradition and proposing the young international scene he witnessed in Paris as a much more appropriate direction. It was an attitude which had made him an outsider in his own country.

The Paris of the 1920s fascinated the young Martinů and soon he found out the 'hot' places for contemporary art and music, sending enthusiastic reports to Czech newspapers and magazines, many of them informing young Czech composers about the music scene in Paris, which was not well known in Prague, and encouraging an alternative group which had been established in 1932 to promote neo-classical ideas. The founding of this association, known as 'the Mánes Group' (after the Mánes Gallery in Prague where they used to meet), can be regarded as a direct result of Martinů's activities as composer and music-journalist. Its principal members were the composers František Bartoš, Pavel Bořkovec, Iša Krejčí and Jaroslav Ježek and the pianist and writer Václav Holzknecht, its spokesman. In the early 1920s, a period of transition for Martinů, it was nonetheless still through Czech musicians, orchestras and theatres in Prague and Brno that some of his major works were premiered and regularly performed. As early as September 1924 his ballet *Istar*, H130, was premiered at the National Theatre in Prague. In December of the same year, with a performance of *Half-Time*, H142, the Czech Philharmonic Orchestra and its chief conductor Václav Talich began a lengthy tradition of performing his orchestral music. Only a month later the Brno National Theatre premiered Martinů's ballet *Who is the Most Powerful in the World?*, H133, which initiated a long line of premieres of theatre works by Martinů in this town. And the String Quartet No. 2, H150, composed for the Novák-Frank Quartet, was premiered in November 1925 in Berlin and one month later received its first Prague performance. It soon became Martinů's visiting card at international concerts and festivals.

After some four years of residence his works began to be performed in Paris and soon he established himself as an interesting young voice. One of his most relevant supporters was his composition teacher (perhaps 'adviser' would be a better term) Albert Roussel, who strongly believed in the qualities of his younger colleague. In the same period Martinů built a close friendship with some of the foreign composers living in Paris. In spite of the vast differences in their approaches to music, they accepted the suggestion of the publisher Michel Dillard and created a group which, at the instigation of the music-journalist José Bruyr, came to be called the École de Paris (the other founding members were the Swiss Conrad Beck (1901–90), Hungarian Tibor Harsányi (1898–1954) and Romanian Marcel Mihalovici (1898–1985); the Russian Alexander Tcherepnin (1899–1977) later joined the group and the Pole Alexander Tansman (1897–1986) became a close friend and associate of the original members). Martinů soon also joined the Société Triton, founded by Pierre-Octave Ferroud in 1932, which was one of the most important forces for new music in Paris. From 1929 on, after many years of real poverty, Martinů began to benefit from the official pro-French political direction of the Czechoslovak government and with the help of Miloš Šafránek, later Martinů's biographer but from 1929 to 1938 cultural attaché of the Czechoslovak Embassy in Paris and his most important supporter, he was officially recognised as a composer by the Czech government in the early 1930s and thus received modest but regular support from the state.

Aleš Březina

POSTCARD 1

To his sister Marie*

[Smíchov, 14 November, sometime in the period 1907–10]

My dear sister!

Thanks for the postcard – but don't write to me at the Conservatoire anymore! I'm looking forward to the holidays! How do you like the card? It's a picture of Kuroki[1] as he always was and always will be! Hide it somewhere! Will Frantík*[2] be coming for the holidays? Why doesn't Dad write? Did my teacher say anything? I'm fine – it's just that I'm a long way from home! I spend a lot of my time walking. What's Junon[3] doing these days? Should I send him a card?

Bye for now!
Boža

PS: And don't call me 'the graduate'!

LETTER 1

To Josef Kaňka*

[Prague, before 11 December 1911]

Dear 'Papa'[4] Josef!

Forgive me for not having written in so long, but I didn't know exactly when I'd take the examination,[5] and I just found out now. It'll be on Monday, 11 December, at 2 o'clock. I'm not nervous about it. I feel well prepared, even if the director[6] gives me a hard time. I'm taking the exams in violin, pedagogy, history and psychology. On Maestro Suk's[7] advice, I'm not taking the examination in piano. I asked him for his

---

[1] The postcard is a colour reproduction of a dog dressed in a Japanese military uniform. Count Tamemoto Kuroki (1844–1923) was a general in the Russo-Japanese War, 1904–5.

[2] Martinů's brother, František. The Czech language uses such diminutives frequently: Martinů later signs himself 'Bohouš', his sister Marie becomes 'Mařka', František 'Fanouš', and so on.

[3] Barely legible; probably the nickname of a friend or acquaintance in Polička.

[4] A form of address used to show gratitude for material and moral support; possibly also a reflection of good manners in old-fashioned Polička.

[5] The state examination taken before an examining board, which allowed the candidate to teach violin.

[6] The pianist and composer Jindřich Kàan z Albestů (1852–1926), the extremely unpopular director of the Prague Conservatoire from 1907 to 1918, because of whose exceedingly strict demands Martinů was expelled in 1910.

[7] The composer and violinist Josef Suk (1874–1935). Martinů studied composition with him in 1922–23 in the Master Classes of the Prague Conservatoire. (The Master Classes were for post-graduate students and became the Prague Music Academy after 1945.)

19

expert opinion of my compositions, and he went over them with me and said I can't continue studying on my own and that it would be a shame to do so and that, if time permits, he'll teach me himself. He asked me about my situation and advised me that if I'm so out of favour with the director I should take the exam later when I'm well enough prepared that I don't have to worry about anyone and said that it would be better to get good grades now in order to get financial aid from the governor's office and that a bad mark in piano would prevent my getting it. Afterward, he said he'd recommend me to Novák[8] for a modest honorarium so that I'd finally have what I've always wanted. Anyway, my work is already being published – some piano pieces – in *Zlatá Praha*[9] – and maybe by Mojmír Urbánek,[10] too, so everything ought to go better. So please, if you happen to come to Prague, come and see how I'm doing! The examination will be in the Teachers' Institute on Panská ulice.

Be well!
Your Bohouš

LETTER 2
To Josef Kaňka
[Prague, after 11 December 1911]

Dear 'Papa' Josef!

I'm sending you the results of the examination. I wasn't expecting anything like this! I'm quite unhappy about it. I don't know what's going to happen now, but it's not really my problem. Somehow I'll manage until the day I can make my own way in the world. But what are they going to think at home? Please, dear 'papa' – be so kind as to talk to them – especially to Mum. I'm afraid to write to them, even though it wasn't my fault. I practised! You saw it yourself, and you were at the examinations, so you know I didn't play badly. And he gives me such a grade! I'd have to be a complete idiot! There are people who take the examinations who don't have the slightest idea what music is and they pass! And I devote my entire life to music and a director like that comes along and makes any further education impossible! All this has left me feeling wretched and like I'm all alone against them and that whatever they say will be believed! But what can I do about it? You know yourself that the one who played before me and played that third-level concerto played miserably, and I played the most difficult concerto prescribed and didn't play badly, but he passed and I didn't! What kind of a dumbbell would I have to be to deserve such a grade! Please, do this for me – speak with my family and try to console them. I'll write to them. Even I was beginning to believe I really don't know anything. They

---

[8] Vítězslav Novák (1870–1949), with whom Martinů was never to study.

[9] The magazine *Zlatá Praha* ('Golden Prague'), Vol. XVI, No. 8, 14 February 1912, published as a musical supplement some songs without words for piano, including Martinů's *Song without Words* in D minor, H46 – his first published composition.

[10] Fr. Urbánek and Sons published Martinů's piano pieces until 1947 and the third suite in the cycle *Puppets*, which appeared under the title *Puppets* I, H137. It still appears under this title.

*Four-sided view of the historic centre of Polička
from the tower of the Church of St James –
lithograph by František Winkler, 1866*

really made a mess for me! But I'm not going to give up so easily![11] I'll find my way and I'll show that director that we have different opinions about what art is! He's no educator! He's a peddler. And it's art that he peddles! I only ask you to go to my family. And write to me!

Thanks for everything!
Your Bohouš

[11] Martinů applied to take the state examination again and took it on 12 October 1912, with the following results: pedagogy and the language of instruction – barely passed, teaching of harmony – barely passed, history of music – barely passed, violin-playing – good, practice-teaching – good.

Martinu with his father,
Ferdinand, in 1911

POSTCARD 2
To his sister Marie
[Switzerland, before 9 June 1919]

Hi, Mařka!

It's so beautiful here it makes my head spin! I think of you often. We're on our way through Switzerland – we'll be in Paris tomorrow![12]

Regards,
Bohouš
Stáňa![13]

POSTCARD 3
To his father, Ferdinand Martinů
[High Tatras] 21 July 1920

A very warm hello! Mařka[14] left today with friends. It's incredibly beautiful here! Lots of people I know are here from Prague. I was at the top of this hill[15] yesterday! Today we're going down to the village. I've already collected some [folk] songs![16]

Bohouš

---

[12] As a participant in the concert tour by the orchestra of the National Theatre, Prague, augmented by players of the Czech Philharmonic (Martinů at the time was not yet a regular member), which took in Paris, London, Geneva, Bern and Zurich. The tour was regarded as an official state cultural visit by the young Czechoslovak nation, and other ensembles and prominent soloists also took part.

[13] Stanislav Novák (1890–1945), violinist, leader of the Czech Philharmonic Orchestra, first violin of the Novák-Frank Quartet, from 1937 professor at the Prague Conservatoire – a lifelong best friend of Martinů from the beginning of their studies at the Prague Conservatoire (1906), and much devoted to the interpretation of Martinů's work. Martinů's letters home refer to him as Stáňa.

[14] Martinů's sister Marie.

[15] The postcard is a picture of Mt Satan and Mt Koprovský.

[16] He probably had in mind his own collections of songs and notes for songs, which he later revised for voice and piano in the form of 30 songs in two series; they were published by Panton in Prague in 1970 under the title *New Slovak Songs*, H126.

POSTCARD 4
To his Father
[Alassio] 6 July 1923

Hello from the road!

We were in Genoa and now we're spending every sunny day swimming in the sea. It's so beautiful here I can't begin to describe it!

Regards,
Bohouš
My warmest regards
to all of you
Your Stáňa

POSTCARD 5
To Václav Rippl⁺
[Paris, 9 November 1923[17]]

Warmest greetings from Paris! It's fantastic here! One day I'll tell you all about it!

Best regards,
Boh. Martinů

LETTER 3
To Vanda Jakubíčková⁺
Paris, 30 April 1924

Dear Vanda!

Your letter was a most pleasant surprise! I kicked myself again and again for having put you in a bad mood with my letter, and I'm very glad that things turned out quite differently than I had said I expected. It seems you can now look forward to your dreams coming true![18] I most heartily hope so! I think everything is going in the right direction now – the way it should have been long ago.

Your letter sounded a little like a reproach that I associated you only with books, but it isn't so. I myself, as you know, will leave everything – or nearly everything – in order to enjoy the sun and the forest, and I'm not a passionate reader of scientific things, but there are so many things like that here – and so many new and interesting things – that I sometimes think I won't manage to take it all in. And I thought you might like to have a list – a long list of books that would be new to you – and that they'd all be at your disposal – although I know you could devote your whole life and all your happiness to flowers and streets and people. Great new horizons have opened for me here, and it seems to me I'm no longer the same person I was half

---

[17] Date of postmark.
[18] To work as a teacher in London.

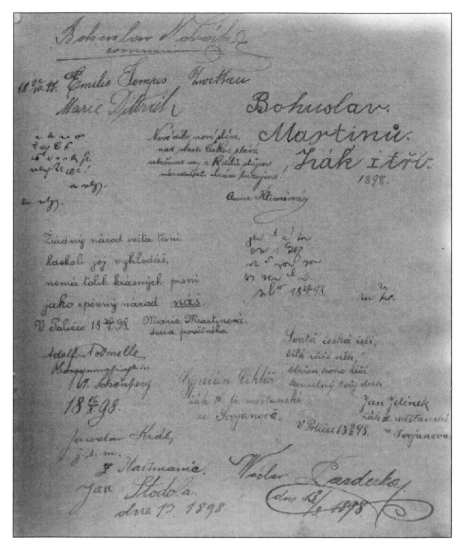

*Signatures of the young Martinů and his sister Marie in the visitors' book
at the tower of the Church of St James, 1898*

a year ago. I keep company with Czechs and Frenchmen and of the Frenchmen mostly with painters and poets, and of these only with the most modern. And the whole world here is completely different from that at home. I can't decide whether it's better or worse, but I like it a lot more. I can see that I'll have to remain here for a few years to absorb all that I missed by being in Prague.[19] Of course, I have happy

---

[19] Martinů obviously has in mind the years 1920–23. He had already been thinking about Paris in Polička during the First World War.

memories of my country, of Prague, and of Polička, but it's just that the tempo of life here is so different – so much more graceful and vibrant! I'm quite well known here after such a short time, and I hope to find plenty of opportunities here to make my way toward the goals I have in mind.

I'm very glad that you'll get to see all your fondest wishes come true, and I know now how happy you'll be! I always had the impression that your destiny lay in another direction and that you couldn't have escaped it even if you had wanted to! I thank you for your lovely letter, and I'm happy that everything that has happened has assuaged a bit the really hurtful things I wrote. The news about Miss K.[20] surprised me, and I'm curious to learn more about what became of her and what she thought about things. I shan't come to your opening,[21] because it seems to me to be a little too expensive – the trip costs a lot. But I'll be there – if only in my work. Now, finally, my interests lie elsewhere, and I think they're more important, and I can't lose much time, although I do regret that I won't be able to come. Paris is so beautiful just now – like a great garden full of spring festivities, lights and flowers, people and pleasures – that I really don't want to leave. I might go home at the holidays.[22] For now, I thank you again for your letter and ask you to accept my best wishes for the fulfilment of all your dreams!

Your Boh. Martinů

LETTER 4[23]
To the Town Board of Polička
Paris, 22 October 1929

Esteemed Members of the Town Board of Polička,

I would like to apply for assistance which would enable me to further my artistic aspirations. The success of my work clearly shows me to be a worthy representative of Czech music abroad and is evidence of the effort I have made to make that music known elsewhere in the world, and I'm happy to have been able to make it known in my native town of Polička, which certainly played its part. My artistic career has only just begun, and I fervently hope that I shall achieve my ambition, which is to make Polička proud of me. Permit me to attest to the esteemed members the fact that performances of my work in America (Boston, New York, Providence) and also here in Paris, London, Leningrad, Moscow as well as in many cities in Germany and even in Stockholm, were for the most part successful and were a big boost for Czech

---

[20] In a letter of 24 December 1923, the name Miss Klofandová appears.

[21] The ballet *Istar*, H130, at the National Theatre in Prague. It was not performed until 11 September 1924; Martinů was present.

[22] He came home, apparently for the entire summer of 1924, among his intentions the regaining of the weight he had lost from his life of poverty in Paris. He speaks of it in his letters to Stanislav Novák, to whom he was able to write more openly.

[23] On p. 3 of the letter there is a note addressed to the Embassy of Czechoslovakia in France, signed by the First Legation Secretary Vladimír Brauner.

*Martinů (centre foreground) in the second-violin section of the orchestra
of the municipal theatre in Kralovské Vinohrady, before 1919*

music generally.[24] I hope that the esteemed members of the Board will show their
confidence in me in the furthering of my work through the granting of my request
for financial support.[25]

Respectfully yours,
B. Martinů
11 bis rue Delambre,
Paris 14e, France

---

[24] *Cf.* p. 36 for a facsimile of Martinů's list of performances c. 1928. A later list, from c. 1935–36, can be
found on pp. 60–61.

[25] According to a letter from the Office of the Mayor of the Town of Polička 'within the city walls' (an
anomaly surviving from the nineteenth century) of 17 April 1930, addressed to the Office of the Town
Clerk in Polička, the Office of the Mayor sent the composer an 'honorary study grant' of 1,500 crowns,
the Office of the Town Clerk 1,000 crowns, and the regional administration in Polička an unspecified
amount.

Kozlov, South Bohemia, around 1920: Martinů with Ela Švabinská-Vejrychová (1878–1967), ex-wife of the famous painter Max Švabinský (1873–1962), who worked in Kozlov for more than two decades), and sister of another painter, Rudolf Vejrych (1882–1939)

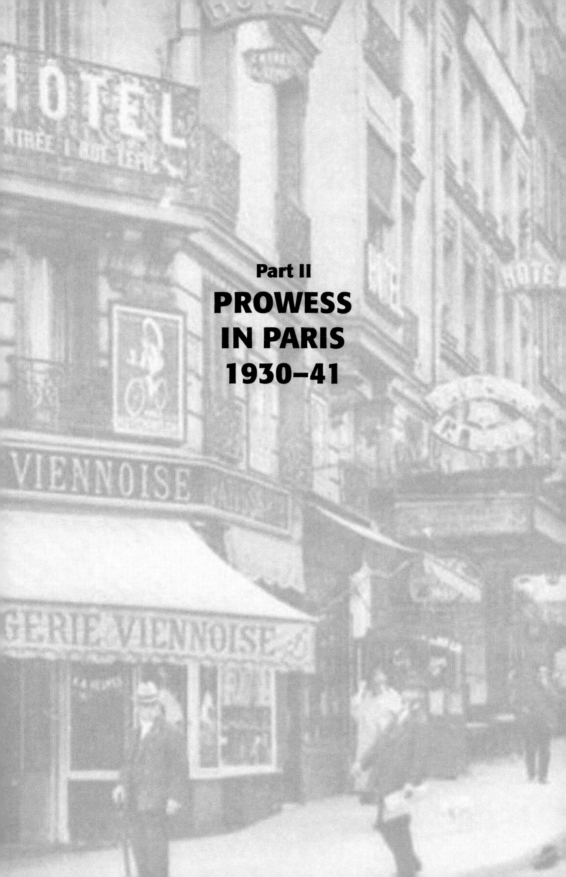

Part II

PROWESS IN PARIS 1930–41

The 1930s marked a period of rapidly growing recognition of Martinů's music. His works were performed by leading ensembles both in Europe and the USA, and he received commissions for new works by a number of artists and organisations. In spite of the deepening economic crisis of the early 1930s Martinů continued to write large operas – not least *The Miracles of Mary*, H236, in 1933–34, and *Juliette, ou La Clé des Songes*, H253, in 1936–37– and was successful in offering them to opera houses, especially in Brno (*The Miracles of Mary* in 1935) and Prague (*The Miracles* in 1936, *Juliette* in 1938). After five years in a relationship with Charlotte Quennehen, he finally married her in 1931, and for almost all the following decade, the partnership was marked by mutual respect and domestic harmony. On the basis of the international accolades for his work he felt ready to return to Prague as a teacher of younger Czech composers, but the failure of his attempts to obtain a teaching position at the Prague Conservatoire undermined Martinů's confidence in the Czech music authorities and from now what he saw as their poor treatment of him became one of the *idées fixes* in his correspondence with his family.

The radical political developments in contemporary Germany very soon had an adverse impact on Martinů. In 1930 the publisher Schott in Mainz offered him a near-exclusive contract but in 1933 it had to stop publishing his works. Five years later, after the *Anschluss* of Austria to the Third Reich, another of his important publishers, Universal Edition in Vienna, was forced to the same decision. In September 1938 the Munich Pact drastically worsened the situation and led for a short time even to a German occupation of Martinů's native Polička.

The period between 1938 and Martinů's emigration to the USA in March 1941 was the most feverish of his entire life. The explosive mix of the deteriorating political situation, a passionate love affair with his talented young composition student Vítězslava Kaprálová, the outbreak of the Second World War, the sudden death of Kaprálová in Montpellier in 1940 at the age of 25 and the nerve-wracking escape from France via Spain and Lisbon to the United States gave birth to some of the most powerful music Martinů ever composed, above all the *Double Concerto for Two String Orchestras, Piano and Timpani*, H271.

Aleš Březina

31

LETTER 5[1]
To his Family
[Paris] 2 October 1930

My dear ones,

I wrote you a few lines from Prague so you'd have at least some news of me. I had a lot of work to do there. You know, of course, that they were furious at me on account of *La Bagarre*[2] – that it was played and nothing of theirs was.[3] It's just a shame that you heard it in that way. It's always better to hear something like that with someone like Ada.[4] He knows how to operate a radio like this. You should have gone to him when the architect's daughter[5] was ill. He'd have been happy to see you! Talich[6] is excited about the work and is going to play it everywhere. In Prague we ate at Stáňa [Novák]'s about five times, and besides that we were constantly being invited here and there. I went out to dinner with Křička,[7] and he sends you his regards. In Prague I got to know quite a few Germans, and they did a lot to smooth the way for me. They liked *La Bagarre* immensely. Now, following the demonstrations, they asked me not to do anything but to wait until things calm down a bit. It's really absurd to create such dissension over a few films[8] – you must have read about it in the

---

[1] Charlotte Quennehen (1894–1978), later Charlotte Martinů, added a postscript.

[2] The symphonic suite *La Bagarre*, H155, composed in 1926 (and premiered by the Boston Symphony Orchestra under Serge Koussevitzky on 18 November 1927), performed by the Czech Philharmonic under Václav Talich on 23 September 1930, at the Prague Congress of the International Federation of Critics.

[3] Martinů was considered by many Czech composers living in Czechoslovakia as an outsider, hence the anger that 'nothing of theirs' was performed at the Prague Congress.

[4] Adolf Klimeš.*

[5] Soňa Šmídová (b. 1927), the daughter of Jarmila and Bohuslav Šmíd;* *cf.* p. 211, below.

[6] The conductor Václav Talich (1883–1961), from 1919 musical director and conductor of the Czech Philharmonic. Martinů helped out in the orchestra – as before – at the beginning of Talich's tenure with the Philharmonic (1918). In the years 1920–23 he worked under Talich's direction as an ordinary member of the orchestra in the second-violin section. In 1938, when Talich conducted Martinů's opera *Juliette ou La Clé des Songes*, H253, at the National Theatre, the artistic collaboration of both personalities began to grow into a close friendship.

[7] Jaroslav Křička (1882–1969), composer, conductor, and music educator, in 1936 the successful competitor with Martinů in the competition for the position of professor of composition in the Master Class of the Prague Conservatoire. *Cf.* also note 144 on p. 59, below.

[8] Anti-German demonstration in Prague, with an anti-Semitic colouring, from 23 to 27 September 1930, initiated by Czech fascist groups under the pretext of showing German sound films in Prague cinemas. The demonstration, with its outbreaks of violence, aimed to damage the policy of the Czechoslovak government toward ethnic minorities – i.e., the Germans.

Karolina and Marie Martinů in front of their Polička residence
at Na Svépomoci 182, around 1930

newspapers. It's hurt us a lot – especially us artists. I was at Vaněk's, too.[9] They weren't far from Polička, but that was in July, and we weren't home yet. We had quite a pleasant journey, except that the train was packed. Where could all those people have been going?

It's beautiful here, but you can tell that winter's coming. The director of the opera in Belgrade was trying to find me – he wants a ballet. I'll meet with him one day soon.[10] Some of my pieces for violin and a new quartet will just be published there.[11] Stáňa will do a festival of only my works in Prague in December with Šolc.[12] I'm going to the legation today to find out if there's any news and anything new about President Masaryk.[13] I'll let you know next time I write.

It was quite tiring for me in Prague – we were constantly being invited somewhere. It's obvious they're starting to take a different view of me, but the musicians were in a fit.

My colleagues at the [Czech] Philharmonic gave me a nice welcome. Talich stopped the rehearsal and they all greeted me warmly. Each of them could feel good about the fact that I had once been with them as a violinist. A lot of my friends from the Conservatoire whom I hadn't seen for years came, too.

Write and let me know how you are. I'll write again just as soon as I can put things in order here.

Be well!
Your Bohouš

LETTER 6
To his Family
Paris, 17 March 1931

My dear ones,

Your letter arrived, and you should by now have mine. You must know that your worries are needless – that if there were something wrong with me I'd write immediately so you wouldn't have to be afraid. I've had so much to do. Things are

---

[9] On a visit to the family of Vladimír Vaněk (1895–1965), at whose home Martinů for some time lived in his early days in Paris in 1924. Vaněk worked in Paris as an official at the Czech Consulate General, and later as Consular Secretary of the Czech Embassy in Paris, his activities being both literary and journalistic. In 1931–37 he served in Stockholm, to which he returned in 1939. Under pressure from Nazi Germany, he was imprisoned for two years by the Swedish authorities for subversive activities. Martinů and he renewed their friendship during the composer's residence in Rome in 1956–57: Vaněk had lived there since 1948. The two friends met for the last time the day before the composer's death.

[10] A few years later, the Belgrade Opera expressed interest in the ballet *Špalíček*, H214 (composed in 1931–32), although no production was realised.

[11] By Alphonse Leduc, the Paris-based publisher of, among other works, the String Quartet No. 3, H183.

[12] Karel Šolc (1893–1985), one of the composer's closest friends, an outstanding pianist, from his youth an interpreter of Martinů's work, and later, until his old age, the composer of a series of arrangements for piano and transcriptions of Martinů's important works. A 'festival' of some works by Martinů was presented in concert at the Prague Mozarteum on 26 January 1932.

[13] Possibly to do with financial aid from the President of the Republic, Tomáš Garrigue Masaryk (1850–1937), the first president of an independent Czechoslovakia.

A page from Martinů's autograph list of 'Works Performed Abroad' from approx. 1928 (from the estate of Marie Martinů)

worse this year because of the financial crisis. Everybody's saving his money. I think you'll agree with the amount that I wrote. It's the price of the piano, and no one will be able to say I wanted to make a profit on it. We could have asked for more, but then it might have seemed to them to be too expensive.[14] Write and tell me what transpires. Mařka will see how they feel about it, especially if she talks about it with Mr Hlavsa.*

I was really surprised that those chaps played the Sonata.[15] It's quite difficult, especially the piano part. I'm glad, too, that it turned out that way with the piano[16] – that now they're taking some interest in me in Polička. What will you do about the radio? Talk to Ada[17] about it and he'll surely take care of it. It'll be fun for Mum, too. Nowadays they transmit theatre plays and operas, and it's not so expensive, and it's a way to spend an evening. Ada will teach you how to operate the radio.

I want to ask Mum about something that's very important to me. It's about Charlotte.[18] I want to marry her, and there's no reason to keep putting it off. I'd like to have it finally settled. It's unnerving for me like this, and I need to have a little peace. I've got to know her quite well since I started seeing her, and I love her, so I don't think Mum will have any objections. I, too, am sometimes a bit strange,[19] and not everyone understands me at first. Charlotte is right for me because she knows me well, and in all that time we've never had any misunderstandings. I think Mum will agree that I've got to make my own decision, and you know I'm not so flighty that I'd take such a step lightly. But I also don't want to do anything without Mum's consent, because it's a serious matter. I'm sure I'll be happy with her, because I know her well and I know she's a good girl and that she loves me in return. I hope that Mum won't take seriously those little misunderstandings which happened during the holidays and that she won't make any difficulties for me. Write soon and tell me what Mum thinks about it. I assure you I've thought it through thoroughly.

Best regards,
Your Bohouš

---

[14] He wanted to sell his grand piano, made by the Kopecký Company, in 1919 and again in 1930. In 1931 he tried to sell the instrument to a local cultural institution, which sale was dependent upon an appropriation by the Mayor's Office of the parish of the Town of Polička (i.e., 'within the town walls'), which found itself in financial difficulties just when Martinů assessed the piano as being worth between 8 and 11 thousand crowns.

[15] The Violin Sonata No. 1, H182, composed in 1929, published by Leduc in 1930 and performed in Polička on 7 March 1931, on the occasion of a musical celebration of the birthday of the president of the Republic, by Polička Gymnázium students František Šauer (violin) and Vladimír Rytíř (piano). Dr František Šauer (1912–89) later – parallel to his career in law – made his presence felt especially as director of the Polička choral ensemble Kollár, and, after moving to Prague in 1945, as a composer, most notably as composer of numerous vocal works.

[16] Premature happiness: the 'town' did not buy his piano.

[17] Adolf Klimeš.

[18] Charlotte Quennehen (1894–1978) married Martinů in Paris on 21 March 1931.

[19] Oddly, although Rybka discusses this letter (*op. cit.*, p. 62), he does not suggest that it indicates an awareness in Martinů of a condition (i.e., Asperger's Syndrome) that might set him apart from others.

Another photograph of Martinů's mother, Karolina, and his sister, Marie

LETTER 7
To his Family
Paris, 20 December 1931

My dear ones,

Charlotte and I wish you a lovely holiday! We'll be thinking about you on Christmas Eve. We'll be at Dr Šafránek's[20] and so it won't be bad. But I wish we could once more spend Christmas Eve at home, and if it's possible next year we'll arrange for me to get home at Christmas somehow.[21] Here you'd hardly know it's a holiday. I thought I'd suggest it for this year, but I didn't want to say anything beforehand. But these are hard times, and it would be risky in these circumstances and with the way things are going. You just don't know what's going to happen next. But next year I'd like to be home for a Christmas with lots of snow – the way it should be on Christmas Eve! You probably have snow there, because even here it's been a real winter.

I'd like to get Mum and Mařka something for Christmas, but I don't know what. Maybe I'll bring something when I come. I'll see about getting some pictures for Fanouš. I look forward to a letter from you telling me how you spent the holidays and that they weren't darkened by sadness. We have to forget all our worries and misfortunes at this time of year. I'm sure there'll be lots of good things to eat. I know those good things are already sitting on the pantry shelves. Will Fanouš have a visitor? It's a shame I couldn't manage to come this year. It would have been wonderful to be with everyone, but I have lots of work to do on the ballet.[22] Ostrčil[23] wrote that he's looking forward to it and that he'll do everything to get it onstage as soon as possible.

Lots of love from me and Charlotte.
I am your
Bohouš

---

[20] Miloš Šafránek (1894–1982) served in the Czechoslovak Embassy in Paris in 1927–28 (among other duties as counsel to the legation). He followed the course of Martinů's life and work for more than three decades, astutely discerning at the beginning of the composer's residence in Paris the merit of his music and of his contribution to Czech modernism. He attempted to ensure Martinů's financial security and importuned for payment for his work in Paris as well as in Prague and later in the USA, where he lived – no longer as a diplomat – from 1939 to 1946. The husband of the pianist Germaine Leroux, he wrote the first monograph on Martinů: *Bohuslav Martinů: Life and Work*, published by Alfred A. Knopf in New York in 1944, by Dennis Dobson in London in 1946, and in a revised and much extended version by Státní hudební vydavatelství in Prague only in 1961. He edited an anthology of Martinů's texts, *Domov, hudba a svět* ('Home, Music and the World'), Státní hudební vydavatelství, Prague, 1966, and *Divadlo Bohuslava Martinů* ('The Theatre of Bohuslav Martinů'), Editio Supraphon, Prague, 1979. Šafránek's papers – containing, in addition to substantial correspondence with Martinů and the composer's diaries, several autographed copies of his works and a large number of documents of the most varied kind – are kept, according to his wishes, in the archives of the Martinů Centre in Polička.

[21] He didn't: he spent that Christmas in Paris.

[22] *Špalíček.*

[23] The composer and conductor Otakar Ostrčil (1879–1935), director of opera at the National Theatre from 1920 to 1935.

LETTER 8
To his Family
Paris, 29 March 1932

My dear ones,

I was in the country at Vieux Moulin[24] over the holidays, and it was quite beautiful, although it was cold on Sunday. On Saturday we went to watch a deer hunt. It was really nice! All the bigwigs were there on horseback and in their hunting livery and there were about fifty hounds, all alike. On Monday there was a wild boar hunt, but we got there late so we only saw them when they brought them back. So I got a bit of a rest.

The ballet is derived from fairy tales and Czech games. It includes *Puss in Boots*, *Cinderella*, the tale about the Magic Sack, and the games 'London Bridge', 'Wolves and Sheep', 'Water-Sprite', and so on, and the Legends of Saint Dorotea and also 'The Spectre's Bride' by Erben.[25] Surely Mum will remember some of these games – perhaps 'The Grim Reaper' from spring in the village. I still don't have an answer from the Ministry.[26] They have to approve all this and that always takes a few days.

I received an award for my *Festive Ouverture for the Sokol Festival*.[27] It will be presented at the opening concert. I should have got first prize. Mr Kunc[28] wrote and said it was the only serious thing submitted, but that it didn't seem festive enough to one of the gentlemen, so they weren't able to give me first prize, even though all the others were for it. The outcome was that no first prize was given at all! I'll find out later who it was! The prize I received is about 2,000 less than it would have been, but I think I'll get it back on the conditions for its performance.

It's annoying about the piano. I'd be glad if you already had the money and if you were already happily settled in. Maybe before the end of the month Mařka could speak with Mr Sommer[29] and ask him to hurry it along. Apart from that, nothing's new. I had a little touch of the flu, but the change of air at Vieux Moulin cured me.

Lots of love! Write soon!

Hello from Charlotte!
Your Bohouš

P.S. Did you get the diploma from Stáňa?

---

[24] Birthplace of the composer's wife, Charlotte, a small town to the north-east of Paris in the south-eastern corner of the forest of Compiègne.

[25] Martinů's *The Spectre's Bride* was cut from the final version of *Špalíček* (1940).

[26] Apparently a reference to the decision to produce *Špalíček* at the National Theatre.

[27] H211, composed in 1931. This performance did not take place, and the score is now missing.

[28] Jan Kunc (1883–1976), Brno composer and music educator, from 1923 to 1945 director of the Brno Conservatoire, followed the artistic career of Martinů for years with friendly interest and, as a member of the Board of Trustees of the Brno Smetana Foundation (in 1928–43 and again briefly after 1945), he supported the awarding of prizes for original Czech compositions.

[29] Karel Sommer (1869–1962), a founding member of the Polička music association 'Mládenecká kapela' (for which Martinů wrote his oldest preserved orchestral work, the little composition *Candlemas* or *Village Feast*, H2), from 1909 manager of the town savings bank and in 1924–48 chairman of the board of the savings bank.

Miloš Šafránek, Martinůs early supporter and first biographer, photographed in 1943, the year before the publication of his first book on Martinů

LETTER 9
To Bohuslav Šmíd
Paris, 16 May 1932

My dear friend,

I had some news from home about the piano and I had to write to tell you that you made me and my family very happy! You probably know how it turned out, and thanks to you I'm very glad that it was resolved in this way and that the piano will be in good hands.[30] It gives me great pleasure, you know, because it wasn't easy to part with. It had come to be something of a friend with whom I worked on my compositions and who in turn created a lot of work for me.[31] I had a lot to do to get it – I had to write a lot of notes! And in that piano are lots of memories, hopes, disappointments, and successes. But because it looked so forlorn there, I decided to sell it, and I know that I'd have been happy to see it remain in Polička, because one day it might call forth pleasant memories for those who come after us,[32] and maybe even for some future composer from Polička, who'll carry on my work and who'll think about it and remember me and also you. I'm glad that it went to such a person. Perhaps you won't play it, which would be a shame, but you'll surely find someone who will enjoy it.[33]

I thank you many times for your decision, and again I assure you that I was very happy to get the news from you and my family, too, as you might have seen. I'm also glad that it will be in good hands. If it hadn't turned out that way, perhaps there wouldn't have been many people who would take care of it. Just now the season is in full swing, but when I get a little free time I promise to write some little piano pieces for Božánek or for Sonička so they might have my manuscript as a souvenir.[34]

I wish you and yours all the best!
Your Bohouš Martinů

[30] The piano, which the composer tried to sell in 1919 and again from around the autumn of 1930, was doubtless bought by the addressee shortly before the date on the letter.

[31] Martinů bought the grand piano in September 1916 from the firm of Josef Brož for 1,000 crowns (the price including its transport to Polička by rail).

[32] In 1973 the instrument became part of the B. Martinů Memorial Exposition (now Martinů Centre) in Polička (until 1976) and again from 1984 to the present.

[33] Šmíd's children – Bohuslav (b. 1924) and Soňa (b. 1927) – also played the instrument.

[34] Martinů produced a small piano cycle, published only in 1992 by the Prague publisher Tempo and Bote und Bock in Berlin under the title *Božánkovi a Soničce*, H221.

On a trip to the Giant Mountains (Orlické hory), 21 August 1932.
From left: Martinů, Charlotte Martinů, his sister Marie, and their Polička friends
Jarmila and Bohuslav Šmíd

LETTER 10
To his Family
Paris, 16 November 1932

My dear ones,

I got your letter at my new address[35] telling me that Mum had a good name-day. We were in the process of moving. Charlotte had a name-day, too, but we didn't do anything because I had a lot of work to do. But now that's all taken care of and there's peace and quiet here. There's a big garden outside my window, and part of it belongs to us. We have a huge rosebush beneath the window and a window-box seat. We'll do a little gardening in the spring. It's like being in the country except that there aren't any hens clucking early in the morning. I hope I'll recuperate properly here – already my work is going better. The place where we are is behind Montparnasse – it's where I lived when I stayed at the Nebeskýs'[36] – about 15 minutes

---

[35] In November 1932, the Martinůs moved into a courtyard bungalow at 172 rue de Vanves (now rue Raymond Losserand) in Montparnasse in Paris 14ème and lived there until January 1935. The painters Jan Zrzavý (*cf.* note 77 on p. 49, below), František Tichý and other artists lived in neighbouring bungalows.

[36] A rented apartment at the home of art theorist and critic Václav Nebeský (1889–1949) at 11bis rue Delambre, Paris 14ème, where Martinů lived from 6 December 1924 until the spring of 1929, when he and Charlotte Quennehen settled into an apartment at 10 rue Mandar in Paris 2ème.

from here. So I feel quite content here and I'm looking forward to spring, when we'll be able to walk in the garden. The only problem is that it's only for two years and then they'll probably tear it down and build a block of flats. But even that isn't certain. Who knows what will be in two years!

Apart from that, there's no news – no word from the theatre. I don't even know if they're in rehearsal yet, but I think they're doing some work on it at least.[37] They wrote to me about the film, saying that they've changed the story a bit[38] and that they might find some investment for it after all. What did that Sr [?] write in *Jitřenka** about *Špalíček*?[39] The weather here is quite nice. It hasn't rained since we got here, but it's been foggy for the past three days. We've got the heat on anyway. It's nice here and everybody likes it a lot. I wrote to Prague about that matter concerning the President,[40] and now I'm waiting for an answer. I still haven't received anything from the Academy[41] – they don't know how to send it. I wrote that they might arrange it somehow with the National Bank, but I still haven't heard anything.

We send our love.
Your Bohouš

LETTER 11
To his Family
[Paris] 22 January 1933

My dear ones,

I got your letter. The year hasn't got off to a very good start. We've both had the flu, and Charlotte had a bad case of pneumonia and suffered a lot. That violinist Dushkin[42] is an American and has a lot of connections, so he found some help for us. There's an organisation among Americans that takes care of artists when they're ill! They arranged for us to take Charlotte to the hospital and they're going to pay for the hospital care and for the entire stay and the treatment! Dushkin really devoted himself to her. He saw that I wouldn't make it on my own.[43] We didn't sleep the first two nights. Charlotte is already better. Her fever has broken, and the doctor

---

[37] The National Theatre, Prague, did not produce *Špalíček* until 19 September 1933.

[38] Apparently a reference to the film *Marijka nevěrnice* ('Unfaithful Marijka', screenplay by Ivan Olbracht and Karel Nový, directed by Vladislav Vančura), for which Martinů composed the music (H233) at his Prague residence from September 1933 until the middle of January of the following year (with a break for Christmas in Polička).

[39] Martinů's abbreviation is difficult to read. The article appeared in *Jitřenka*, Vol. LI, No. 20, 15 October 1932, p. 312, under the title '*Špalíček* by Bohumila [*sic*!] Martinů.' It is signed with the initials M.S.

[40] Apparently to do with financial support from the President of the Czechoslovak Republic.

[41] Martinů was perhaps anticipating some news here: the Czechoslovak Academy of Arts and Sciences awarded him a prize of 2,000 crowns at their meeting on 22 November 1932.

[42] Samuel Dushkin (1891–1976), American violinist. Martinů composed his First Violin Concerto, H226, for him in 1932–33. Dushkin did not perform it. It was premiered on 25 October 1973 in Chicago by Josef Suk.

[43] James Rybka (*op. cit.*, p. 302) offers Martinů's apparent indecision when faced with Charlotte's illness as evidence of autism.

said the crisis is over and we can stop worrying. She's getting excellent care, and she'll be there for two more weeks so as to get back the weight she lost. The poor thing didn't sleep almost the whole week. It came on rather unexpectedly, and even though things are as they are, good people are still to be found in the world! We had a doctor, too, but after all I wouldn't have been able to take care of her myself. I hope that next time I write I'll have better news.

Somebody must have put a jinx on us this month because everything has been upside-down and backward. But now it seems that things have come right. I'm getting good news from all sides. They played three concerts here and they were a great success, especially the Trio,[44] which was played by a trio from Budapest.[45] Everyone was excited and all the composers were there and there was a very nice audience. The Princesse de Polignac,[46] who's been supporting Stravinsky, mostly, left a message saying it had been a long time since she had had such a moving experience as she had on hearing my Trio and sending her congratulations. She's a very influential person in Paris, especially in regard to music. A letter came from Spain requesting the work, so I immediately passed it on to the trio from Budapest, and they're going to play it there. I got a letter from Mr Špaček[47] in Geneva with a great review of a performance there of my *Serenade*.[48] I also got a letter from Antwerp asking if I could come. They're going to do my Partita,[49] which Talich just did in Prague, as a ballet at the opera. So, you see, things are really starting to move. The cheque came,[50] but now it's going to take about another month for it to clear. They have to send it back to America, and then the authorisation will come from there to the bank here and only then will I get the money.

How are you doing? Write soon. Charlotte sends her love and so do I.

Love,
Bohouš

---

[44] The Piano Trio No. 1, *Cinq piéces breves*, H193, composed in 1930.

[45] The Trio Hongrois at the Société Triton on 18 January 1933. The Société Triton, one of several organisations fostering contemporary music in Paris in the first decades of the twentieth century, presented a total of 53 concerts between November 1932 and May 1939 – *cf.* Michel Duchesneau, *La Société Triton 1932–1939*, Observatoire Musical Français, No. 3, Paris, 1997, and Michel Duchesneau, *L'avant-garde musicale et ses sociétés à Paris de 1871 à 1939*, Pierre Mardaga, Sprimont (Belgium), 1997, pp. 133–48. All seven seasons the Société Triton presented featured the premiere of a Martinů work, a sign of his close engagement with the group: he was elected to its executive committee in 1934. The only other foreign composers to be honoured with a work in every season were Mihalovici, Harsányi, Prokofiev and Stravinsky.

[46] The Princesse de Polignac was born Winnaretta Singer, an heir to the sewing-machine fortune of the Singer family, in 1865. She married Edmond, Prince de Polignac (1834–1901), in 1893, and their Paris salon became a centre of new music, the venue of numerous first performances. She died in 1943.

[47] Jaromír Špaček from the Czechoslovak Embassy in Paris.

[48] The *Serenade* for chamber orchestra, H199, composed in 1930, performed on 17 January 1933 by the Orchestre de la Suisse Romande under Ernest Ansermet.

[49] The *Partita* for string orchestra, H212, written in 1931.

[50] For his String Sextet, H224, from 1932, Martinů was awarded a prize of $1,000, worth at that time about 25,000 francs, in an anonymous composition contest held by the Coolidge Foundation.

To his Family
[French Riviera, before 19 March 1933]

My dear ones,

The weather has been gorgeous recently and we've made a few trips. Today we were at the seaside, and quite a few people were already bathing. We also went to San Remo – I sent you a postcard. Everything is well organised here, the trips are by motorcoach – they're quite comfortable and not too expensive – and we profit a lot from it. Yesterday we stopped at a small spa. People were fishing – hauling up nets full of sardines! We were also in Nice for the Battle of the Flowers. It was beautiful! There are so many flowers there that they don't know what else to do with them! I wonder what Dad would have said about it – I think he would have enjoyed it! Just now we're on our way back. We should be in Marseilles on Sunday and from there we'll go directly to Paris.

I got a good rest and Charlotte put on some weight. I think she weighs 60 kilos now, but she'll lose some of that in Paris. I look well-fed, too. It's really lovely here. It's hard to leave, but I must so that I can get to work again. Mrs Coolidge[51] sent me a telegram. She's giving a concert in Paris in May. On the program is my Sextet, which won a prize.[52] I'll write you the news from Paris next week. I don't know anything at the moment, because I'm not getting the mail. I'm not having it forwarded to me, because we're already on the way back. I'll write next week. I probably have a lot of work waiting for me there. I hope that all is well with you and that I'll find a letter from you when we get to Paris.

We both send our love.
Your Bohouš

To his Family
Paris, 27 June 1933

My dear ones,

I got your letter and was glad to hear that things are better at home. I hope you learned a lesson from it – that Mum, especially, has to realise that old age isn't to be ignored and that she can't do all the things she could when she was young. There had already been quite enough of that sort of thing, and as soon as things let up, the

---

[51] Elizabeth Sprague Coolidge (1864–1953) North American patron of composers, soloists and musical events in general. In 1925 she created the Coolidge Foundation at the music department of the Library of Congress in Washington and generously endowed it. The Foundation was oriented – besides collecting manuscripts of contemporary composers – toward organising concerts and festivals and the awarding of prizes for as yet unperformed compositions. Its activities extended to the musical life of the larger cities of western Europe.

[52] The Paris concert with the String Sextet on the programme was not held until two years later, on 21 May 1935.

whole story began again! I hope that it will be all right now and that you'll make the best of it so you'll get a good rest and be able to see the premiere of *Špalíček*, which is set for the end of September.[53] The ballet master[54] wrote me that he has it almost completely rehearsed and that it's going to be sensational. He says the orchestra is excited about it, and I, too, am anxious to see how it turns out. As for a vacation, I don't think I'll allow myself one, because I lost a lot of time this year. I didn't do anything before Christmas, and then there was the illness and then we were away – so I'll probably stay in Paris now, and I'll have to get some other things ready. It's also a matter of that film company that's being set up here – if I'm not here, I might lose a good job. Besides that, I want to see the premiere in Prague at the end of September, and I have an idea rather to spend autumn and a little of the winter in Czechoslovakia until Christmas,[55] so I'd also let myself be seen a little in Prague when people are back from the holiday, which means that again I'll lose three months of work, so I'll have to do it ahead of time. It's almost like being in the country here, so it'll be more bearable this year. We'd also put you to unnecessary trouble, and after the holidays you'll both have had a good rest, and I definitely have to get some new things ready over the summer so as to make some money for later on. The most important thing for you is to get some sun and for Mum to get some rest by working in the garden. She'll probably be sorry I don't come, but these two months will go by quickly. In the meantime, get ready for Prague.

They played my Serenade in Amsterdam. Dushkin wrote to say he's coming back from America in August. He wants to talk to me about the final arrangements for the concert. There's a virtuoso here from Zurich. He's going to play my cello concerto in Switzerland.[56]

I'm working on something new for the theatre – it's an old and well-known Dutch ballad.[57] I hope I'll manage to get it performed in Amsterdam.

Fanouš wrote to say he put on some weight there and that his nerves are better. I hope he gets his strength back. He always takes things too much to heart. Mum's illness caused him a lot of worry. Now he'll be more at ease. Charlotte and I send you our love. She's already beginning to jabber a bit in Czech. She'll be able to talk a little with Mum. I wish you gorgeous weather for the whole holiday and a lot of rest. Mother ought to go with Mařka to some summer place – where there are lots of people – to think about other things – maybe to Poděbrady.

Love,
Your Bohouš

P.S. Write and let me know if I should send some money for the holiday – if you need it – or if I should bring it with me when I come in September.

[53] It took place in the National Theatre on 19 September 1933.

[54] The dancer and choreographer Joe Jenčík (1893–1945), choreographer of the Prague productions of *The Miracles of Mary*, H236, and *Juliette*.

[55] He stayed until mid-January 1934, spending Christmas 1933 in Polička.

[56] The cellist in question has not yet been identified. Pierre Fourner and Gaspar Cassadó (*cf.* note 85 on p. 49, below) had both played Martinů's First Cello Concerto, H196, by this date, but neither was based in Zurich.

[57] *Mariken of Nimègue*, the second part of the four-part opera-cycle *The Miracles of Mary*: *Mariken z Nimègue*, composed in 1933–34.

LETTER 14
To Bohuslav Šmíd
[Paris] 10 September 1933

My dear friend,

I'm going to have a premiere at the National Theatre. The date is set for the 19th of this month, and because you've rather got into the habit of coming to my premieres, I'm inviting you to the first performance of *Špalíček*! Of course, I tell you this only in case you'll be coming to Prague – maybe there'll be a congress of architects there! Otherwise, I know, of course, that you are not used to wasting your time and that it may not be convenient for you to make a trip to Prague. Of course, I'd be overjoyed to see you there! I'm going there this week for a rehearsal. If you do decide to go, I would ask you if you would be so kind as to take my family with you. Mum would like to see the premiere, and the trip would be more fun for her if she were with you.[58]

If you decide to do it, talk it over with my family, because I'll send them a telegram probably on Saturday or Monday. It's still possible the premiere will be put off a few days,[59] and I wouldn't want them to come for nothing. I send you and all your family my warmest regards. I look forward to seeing you again, if not in Prague then in Polička, where we'll be some time in the autumn.

Best regards,
Your B. Martinů

LETTER 15[60]
To his Family
[Prague, before 4 November 1933]

My dear ones,

We wish Mum a beautiful holiday[61] and all the best – especially health and happiness! Charlotte thanks you for your good wishes and adds hers to mine. I have the same hassle at this time and various worries. I got a contract for the music for a film. It's called *Marijka*[62] and it's set in Carpathian Ruthenia. It's sure to be a lot of work, but at least I'll get a little more money for it than I usually do. I'm going to have to find some little room with a piano so I can work in peace. It's going to be a lot of writing. I'll get 15,000 crowns for it and it has to be finished by the middle of December. I also approached the theatre about their playing my work more often,[63] and now I'm

---

[58] Šmíd drove to the premiere in his own car, bringing the composer's mother and sister with him to Prague.

[59] It was not postponed.

[60] Charlotte Martinů added a postscript.

[61] Karolína Martinů celebrated her name-day on 4 November, St Borromeus' Day.

[62] *Marijka nevěrnice* ('Unfaithful Marijka'); *cf.* note 38 on p. 43, above.

[63] *Špalíček* at the National Theatre, Prague.

waiting for an answer. Muzika[64] in Brno created a beautiful set and lots of people are going there to the opening.[65]

All our love,
Bohouš

LETTER 16
To his Family
[Paris, February–beginning of March 1934]

My dear ones,

The premiere of my Sonata for Two Violins and Piano was in London.[66] I had a letter saying that it was a big success and that Minister Jan Masaryk[67] was there and that they say he was quite pleased. The Quintet will have its first performance here next Friday[68] and then they'll play it again in Amsterdam. They also played my Quartet[69] in Sweden, in Oslo and in Bucharest. Now I'm working on the new opera.[70] It has a religious motif and is derived from miracle and mystery plays from the Middle Ages.

The situation here is calmer, except that the drivers' strike has been going on for more than a month, but it doesn't bother me, because I just sit at home anyway. Mrs Osuská[71] came back, and I'll go to see her next week to ask if she can help me in regard to the National Theatre.[72] Stáňa wrote to me, too, to say they're going to play *Špalíček* at Stavovské divadlo [Theatre of the Estates],[73] so I'll ask Mrs Osuská to write to the Minister of Education to let him know something about it. I have an idea to give the new opera to Talich, who'll be guest-conducting at the National Theatre, so I can be sure it will be done well.[74] I want to go to Prague anyway, so I can be there from the start, and if something somewhere bothered anyone,

[64] Painter, set designer, and graphic artist František Muzika (1900–74) designed the premieres in Brno of *The Miracles of Mary* and *Theatre behind the Gate*, H251, and the Prague premiere of *Juliette* at the express wish of the composer.

[65] Of the Brno premiere of *Špalíček*, on 25 November 1933.

[66] H213, composed in 1933 for the London Sonata Players.

[67] Jan Masaryk (1886–1948) was the son of the Czechoslovak president, T. G. Masaryk. At the time of this letter he was Czechoslovak ambassador to the United Kingdom.

[68] The Piano Quintet No. 1, H229, composed in 1933 and presented by the Société Triton.

[69] Either the Second String Quartet, H150, or Third String Quartet, H183, composed in 1925 and 1929 respectively. Both works were then generally obtainable in print.

[70] *The Miracles of Mary*.

[71] Pavla Osuská (1891–1978) in Prague from 1914 to 1919 as soloist (dramatic soprano) at the opera of the National Theatre, in Paris from 1920 to 1940 as the wife of the Czechoslovak ambassador, Štefan Osuský.

[72] He was hoping for more frequent productions of *Špalíček*.

[73] Later the Tyl Theatre, from 1991 reverting to the name Stavovské divadlo, at that time one of two stages of the National Theatre.

[74] *The Miracles of Mary* was directed and conducted in Brno by Antonín Balatka, in Prague by Josef Charvát. It was only with the staging of *Juliette* in 1938 that Talich conducted an opera of Martinů's.

I could immediately straighten it out. And, besides, Prague is impossible – there are too many 'dear friends' there. It's turned a bit colder here, but it's beautiful. It's already like spring. I received 3,000 crowns from the Academy for *Špalíček*.[75] They sent the money here, but I lost a lot of it because of the new law they've made in Czechoslovakia.[76] It may be that Fanouš will make some profit in dinars, if he hasn't already changed the money at the old rate. Zrzavý[77] is probably also complaining. I told him repeatedly to bring the money here gradually and to change it to francs, and he had enough time but now he's going to lose a few thousand. I also bought a lottery ticket. It would be great if something were to come of it. Otherwise, we're fine, and I hope you are too. I don't know if I already wrote asking you to make our apologies to Jindřiška[78]* that we weren't able to stop by, but I had lost a lot of time because of the film[79] and had to hurry back in order to get to work again. Křička[80] wrote to me that my music has already been recorded and that everybody liked it a lot. When the premiere will be I still don't know.[81]

We both send our love.
Your Bohouš

LETTER 17
To his Family
[Menaggio (Lago di Como) after 8 September and before 22 September 1934]

My dear ones,

I haven't had a chance to write until now. There was no time in Venice – there were rehearsals, and there were lots of people there I had to talk to. The concert was lovely.[82] It was successful, mainly with the critics, especially the Swiss and the Germans. The audience wasn't so used to new music, but even they liked it. The conductor was excellent.[83] Stravinsky[84] was there and the whole crowd from Paris – Cassadó,[85] who

[75] From the Czechoslovak Academy of Arts and Sciences.

[76] Lowering of the value of the Czechoslovak crown on the international currency exchange, the result of the reduction of its gold content.

[77] Painter Jan Zrzavý (1890–1977), a friend of Martinů from his first years in Paris. Martinů used to live in his flat in Prague and later put Zrzavý up for a short time in Paris. *Cf.* also p. 84, below.

[78] His sister-in-law, Jindřiška Martinů: she was married to his brother František.

[79] *Marijka nevěrnice.*

[80] Jaroslav Křička conducted the recording of the music for *Marijka nevěrnice*.

[81] 2 March 1934, in the Prague cinema Kotva.

[82] The orchestral work *Inventions*, H234, had been premiered at the inaugural concert of the third international festival Biennale di Venezia, in the Teatro la Fenice on 8 September 1934 (it had been composed in January of that year).

[83] The Italian conductor Oreste Piccardi, graduate of the Berlin Music Academy, was engaged, among other appointments, as an operatic conductor in Buenos Aires and Rio de Janeiro.

[84] The music and aesthetics of Igor Stravinsky (1882–1971) had a considerable influence on Martinů in the early years of his residence in Paris (from October 1923) and left lasting traces on his work.

[85] Gaspar Cassadó (1897–1966), Spanish cellist and composer.

played my cello concerto,[86] the Princess Polignac. We got a very nice reception in Venice, and I think it did me a lot of good. We stayed there until Tuesday, then we went by way of Milan, and we stopped at Lake Como for a couple of days. Venice was quite tiring, but now we're in the mountains, and it's really gorgeous and the weather is magnificent. Such beautiful countryside is hard to find! There are vineyards everywhere, and we've been picking grapes. The conductor Piccardi from Venice is also coming tomorrow. He said he'll show us something of the countryside and the mountains. We'll go back to Milan with him, where we'll go to the opera, which is famous all over the world, and then we'll go back to France. On the way we'll stop in Dijon – so we'll be back in Paris in about a week. So write to me in Paris! I sent you postcards from Venice and from Menaggio, where we are now.

We both send our love.
Your Bohouš

LETTER 18
To his Family
Paris, 19 October 1934

My dear ones,

I'm answering your letter at once so you won't worry. The assassination wasn't in Paris but in Marseilles.[87] Of course, there was considerable alarm here and an alert and a lot of checking of all foreign passports, mainly Czech, because all the gangsters had fake or forged Czech passports. Filipi[88] came right in the middle of it, and they didn't take him into the Legion. They probably didn't believe him either – he has a Czech passport. He's staying here until things calm down a bit, and then he'll try again. A lot of foreigners have been expelled from France.

I can't write well. I've got some sores in one place on my finger. That hand is completely crippled. I had to go to the doctor about it, and I lost the whole week. I couldn't do anything. It's better now, and in three or four days it will be all right. But it's unpleasant. It's a good thing I went to the doctor right away. You never know what might develop from something like that. Just what time the *Rhapsody* will be on the 28th of October,[89] I still don't know, but I'll write – in any case you'll find out easily enough. It will be broadcast on Prague Radio. Someone who subscribed to a journal will tell you – I think it's in the evening.

---

[86] Martinů's Cello Concerto No. 1, composed in 1930, re-orchestrated in 1939 and revised in 1955. Cassadó played the work for the first time on 13 December 1931 in Berlin.

[87] On 9 October 1934, Alexander I, king of Yugoslavia, had not long arrived in Marseilles, on a state visit to France, when he was assassinated by Vlado Chernozemski, a Bulgarian revolutionary.

[88] Prague relative of the Polička family Filipi, owners of a Polička pub; his first name seems not to have been preserved. He wanted to join the Foreign Legion, and he caused problems for Martinů, as is obvious from later letters (*cf.* pp. 52, 53 and 54). Martinů unselfishly helped everyone who came to Paris from Polička or was referred to him from Polička.

[89] *Rhapsody for large orchestra* (*Allegro symphonique*), H171, composed for the tenth anniversary of the oath of the Czechoslovak legionnaire units in Darney, 30 June 1918.

Venda Sommer[90] arrived today, and I'll have to look after him a bit so he'll enjoy himself here. You're certainly going to miss the Šmíds.[91] Today I got an invitation to the opening of the museum.[92] We'll talk about it all when I get home, which won't be long now.

It wasn't so serious about Suk. He'll remain at the Conservatoire. The position, which Hába[93] got, I really didn't want. It's at the rank of full professor, and they might have offered it to me, as well, but then they would have thought that was the end of it, but I thought I want to try for the Master Classes. It's like the university and the salary is appropriate to it, so it would be better to wait a while and later they'd also take into account the years I spent in Paris when they calculate my pension, whereas what Hába has isn't a definite thing, and he could get his notice at any moment.

Stáňa wrote that Fanouš was at his place. Mr Šafránek is making arrangements for a concert of my work here and in London. We've already started to heat the house, and it's raining, so it's rather gloomy. We shan't escape the winter! I don't know where we'll stay in Prague. We could stay at Mr Zrzavýs' again, but if it's going to be for a long time, it would be a bit of an inconvenience, even for him. I think we'll find a little place somewhere in the centre of town so we don't spend so much time and money on trams.

We both send our love,
Your Bohouš

LETTER 19
To his Family
Paris, 1 January 1935

My dear ones,

So here we are in the new year – once again denied a chance to be together at Christmas.

We stayed at home and listened to the radio from all over the world. We wondered whether you got our letter in time – I sent it by express mail. The holidays weren't good – it rained all the time. Yesterday we waited at home for the New Year, and people came to us from hereabouts, and we had an international get-together,[94] although we didn't hold out for long.

---

[90] Dr Václav Sommer (1906–45), theatre historian and radio director, graduate of the Philosophical Faculty of Charles University, son of middle-school teacher Celestin Sommer, who in retirement moved to Polička with his family. Václav Sommer spent his childhood and part of his youth in Polička. He met Martinů not later than the summer of 1929 during work on the Polička staging of Pirandello's play *Six Characters in Search of an Author*, for which the composer apparently wrote incidental music or at least collaborated on it. During his time as a student in Paris in 1934–35, Sommer visited Martinů frequently.

[91] The Šmíd family at that time moved from na Svépomoci Street to their own family villa on (at that time) the southern outskirts of the town.

[92] The museum in Polička was opened on 28 October 1934, in building 112 of the former boys' elementary school and apparently in 1936 (and not later than 1937) the first documents relating to Martinů's life and work were deposited there.

[93] The composer and theorist Alois Hába (1893–1973) was named professor at the Prague Conservatoire (not its Master Classes), effective from 1 October 1934.

[94] With the artists living in bungalows at 172 rue de Vanves.

There might not be much to look forward to, the way things seem. We finally found an apartment.[95] It's a little farther out than where we are now, and again it's the same kind of house, except that it gives us more room. It has two floors, so I'll have a workroom for myself. We have a garden, too, so we won't be without flowers, but we won't get the flat before the beginning of April, and in the meantime we can put our furniture in one room and arrange it when we come back. So at least we have one worry out of the way. Otherwise, it's very nice and the house is quite lovely, and it's quiet there. True, it's rather far away, but it's not too expensive, and there are trams and buses. Now we're waiting to move. It's going to be a lot of work. We'll start moving out slowly this week, so we'll get to Prague around the 15th (of January). It would be nice if the weather were good, at least, and if it wouldn't rain when we're moving.

I haven't seen Filipi in a long time. I don't know what he's doing, and I think that maybe it's going to be hard for him. He had another medical examination and he's quite overweight, and so the commission will perhaps think twice about his being able to stand the climate in the colonies. Not everyone can tolerate the heat.

We thank you for your good wishes and we also wish you all the best for the New Year. What will it bring, I wonder. We will send a card to the Šmíds, too. Otherwise, there's no news. Venda Sommer was here Wednesday evening and Mr Kupka,[96] too. I'm still waiting for news from Brno,[97] but in any case we'll leave by the 15th because we have to be moved out by then. We'll spend a few days in Prague to look over the situation again and to get the visits over with, and then we'll stop at home on our way to Brno. See you soon!

All our love,
Your Bohouš

LETTER 20[98]
To his Family
Paris, 7 May 1935

My dear ones,

We're more or less settled now, but it seems we didn't make a very good choice. All over there's the sound of radios, especially on Sunday, when everyone stays at home. It's like that everywhere nowadays – it's hard to find a place where there's peace and quiet. We listened to *Mary*,[99] but it was hard to hear – we could only catch parts of it. There was a storm, and it caused a lot of interference. Venda Sommer came to listen to it with us. I protested to the radio station about their not having broadcast the work in its entirety. I wrote them a letter that isn't going to please them – I'll be interested to hear their explanation. I asked them to give me specific

---

[95] From January to October 1935 the Martinůs lived at 3 passage Richard, Malakoff-Seine.

[96] Painter, graphic artist and illustrator František Kupka (1871–1957).

[97] This allusion undoubtedly pertains to the production of *The Miracles of Mary* which had its premiere at the Brno Opera on 23 February 1935.

[98] Charlotte Martinů added a postscript.

[99] *The Miracles of Mary*, broadcast on Prague Radio.

reasons why they didn't play the whole work. A critic from *Venkov*[100] – Engineer Šourek[101] – wrote to me that he had heard it and that he liked it and that he already knows where the most successful composer of Czech opera is to be found! They've been playing it in Brno for quite a long time.[102] I don't know what will happen about Prague – Ostrčil is sick.[103]

They played something else of mine on the radio and yesterday I had a great success with the Duo for Violin and Violoncello.[104] Mrs Coolidge is coming and will give a concert on the 21st of this month. They're playing my Sextet, which won a prize. I finished the little opera for radio,[105] but I don't think it will be done now, but in the autumn. It's hot here, but up until the first of May temperatures were just above freezing. Has Fanouš already been at the Ministry in Prague? What did they tell him? Filipi still hasn't shown up – I suppose he's settled somewhere. It won't be long now until Venda Sommer will finish here. He'll be coming back in two months, and he'll probably find some job in radio. Charlotte has already got the garden underway. It only would be nice if it were a little quieter here!

Otherwise, everything is as it used to be – once again I have more quiet for work. When I have my own workspace again, it'll go smoothly. We both came back from Prague awfully tired – next time I won't go for so long – it's a waste of time and costs a lot. If I come in the autumn it will probably be alone.

We both send our love.
Your Bohouš

LETTER 21
To his Family
Paris, 11 June 1935

My dear ones,

I was very surprised by the news of Suk's death.[106] He never got much rest – he was always on the verge of leaving the Conservatoire, which was so tiring for him, and now he's left it for good. It must have been a huge funeral, from what I read in the newspapers. I immediately wrote to Mr Schieszl from the President's Office[107] and he told me that he informed Minister Krčmář[108] and that he'll keep an eye on it and

---

[100] A daily newspaper.

[101] Otakar Šourek (1883–1956), well-known music-critic and columnist, author of a four-volume critical biography of Antonín Dvořák, the basic work in Czech Dvořák studies.

[102] *The Miracles of Mary.*

[103] Ostrčil died on 20 August 1935. Josef Charvát conducted *The Miracles of Mary* in Prague (after its second staging in Brno) on 7 February 1936.

[104] Duo for Violin and Violoncello No. 1, H157, composed in 1927 for Stanislav Novák and Maurits Frank.

[105] *The Voice of the Forest* (*Hlas lesa*), H243, to a Vitězslav Nezval text, premiered on Czech Radio Prague on 6 October 1935. A photograph of Martinů and Nezval together can be found on p. 84, below.

[106] Josef Suk died on 29 May 1935.

[107] Dr Josef Schieszl (1876–1970), at that time section chief in the Office of the President of the Republic.

[108] Dr Jan Krčmář, Minister of Education and Culture from February 1934 to January 1936.

will let me know when the issue is discussed.[109] Mr Šafránek also told the Ministry of Foreign Affairs about it. The discussion will mostly be about who the professorial staff of the Conservatoire suggests. Ostrčil will probably also apply, and he would be a serious competitor, but just now he's ill. In any case there are sure to be big intrigues in Prague, but I'm hopeful that I might get it. I wrote to Talich and also to Stáňa, but I can't count on him much.

Apart from that there's no news. It was cold here and then it got hot over the holidays. Today it's quite cool again. I'm working on the thing for Ballets Russes,[110] and also completing a new piano concerto.[111] Mrs Šafránková – Madame Leroux[112] – will play it here and Firkušný in Prague.[113] The National Theatre wrote me that they're very interested in doing *Miracle of Mary*,[114] and they requested the scores in Brno. Charvát is in charge of all that now. He's the one who conducted *Špalíček*. We're having some problems with the place. The neighbourhood isn't awfully pleasant and there's not a lot of peace and quiet.

Mr Sommer is slowly getting ready to go back. I haven't been to see Filipi yet – I have so little time. There are constant meetings with the manager of Ballets Russes and with the artistic director. Stránský[115] wrote and asked me to send something for orchestra to Polička, but the publisher has them all and they're too difficult to play anyway. It would be more feasible to do something for violin or for mixed chorus.[116] Tell him this, won't you, so I don't have to write to him as well.

We both send our love. Charlotte has a lot of work, too, with the house and the garden.

Love,
Your Bohouš

---

[109] The issue was who should succeed Josef Suk in the Master Classes of the Prague Conservatoire.

[110] The Ballets Russes, working mainly in France, asked Martinů to write the music for a one-act ballet, *Le jugement de Paris*, but it was not produced, and the score is missing. In his catalogue (*op. cit.*, p. 222) Halbreich gives it the number H245 but wonders if the work was ever composed. In 2010 Aleš Březina discovered a short score of the ballet at the Paul Sacher Foundation in Basel.

[111] Piano Concerto No. 2, H237.

[112] Germaine Leroux, French pianist, wife of Miloš Šafránek, played the Second Piano Concerto in Paris on 31 January 1937 (*cf.* also note 160 on p. 64). Martinů wrote the *Sinfonietta Giocosa* for piano and small orchestra, H282, for her in 1940, and she played the first performance in New York on 16 March 1942. She also had Martinů's works for solo piano in her repertoire. She was a considerable help to Martinů in his early days in America after 1941.

[113] The pianist Rudolf Firkušný (1912–94), who later became a close friend of Martinů and his wife. He gave the first performance of the Second Piano Concerto in Prague on 13 November 1935, with the Czech Philharmonic. His name is associated with a number of well-known Martinů works, of which he gave the premieres: the *Fantasy and Toccata*, H281, written in 1940, the Third Piano Concerto, H316, composed in 1948, and the Fourth Piano Concerto, *Incantation*, H358, dating from 1955–56. He remained loyal to Martinů's music until the end of his artistic career, not least in concerts and recordings in his native country after November 1989.

[114] The National Theatre, Prague, produced *The Miracles of Mary* on 7 February 1936.

[115] Karel Stránský, at that time professor at the Polička Gymnázium, devoted himself intensively to theatre as actor, director and dramatist in the amateur group Tyl.

[116] He could have had in mind the *Four Marian Songs*, H235, composed in 1934, which the Vinohradský choir Hlahol performed on 12 April 1935.

LETTER 22
To his Family
Paris, 18 September 1935

My dear ones,

I'm finally getting around to writing. I know you've been wondering why I haven't written in so long. I've had a lot of correspondence with Prague as well as a lot of work, so I didn't have a chance. It's also been mainly because we might have to find a new place to live, so we've been going to see where it might be. It's unbearable here with that radio going all day long without interruption. We don't even go to the garden anymore and it bothers me a lot at work. But the main thing is that we found out, when we came back from the vacation, that bedbugs are creeping in from the neighbouring houses! We immediately made a thorough search for them and disinfected everything, but it wouldn't be worth staying here. They might have settled into the furniture, in which case we'll never get rid of them. It's been a lot of work, but we don't see them anymore. You can imagine what a surprise it was! So, we're looking for another place. Of course, it will again be a big extra outlay and worry, but there's nothing else to be done. It would be foolish to stay here. It also costs me a lot on the tram and the bus from here, so we're going to look for something in town again – without a garden, of course.[117] In any case, I think that from the way things look, my sojourn here is nearing its end, and that I'll go back to Prague. That probably won't be decided this season – things are still up in the air about the directorship at the opera. Those competitors who would rather go to the theatre[118] will withdraw, anyway, and I've arranged to be informed in advance if the issue is discussed[119] – so I might come to Prague alone and earlier than we had intended. I still haven't received a notice about the money, so I can't send anything right now. The thing with Ballets Russes also dragged on without result – they're not inclined to pay. So I'll send you the money when the notice comes from Prague.[120]

I'm sending some pictures of the mountains – in the background is Mont Blanc. I could still use a little more rest, but everything is terribly expensive everywhere. The shoes will probably be what I wanted. Apart from that there's nothing new. The weather is what it usually is at this time of year – there's a constant strong wind, and it'll be cold soon. The season is gradually getting underway here, but it looks like it won't be a great one. There are problems with taxes and with politics, and who knows what will finally come of it all.

We send our love.
Your Bohouš

Pay attention to the radio! I think they're going to broadcast the little opera *The Voice of the Forest* soon.[121]

---

[117] In October 1935, the Martinůs moved back to Montparnasse to an apartment in 31 avenue du Parc de Montsouris (Paris 14ème), where they lived until April 1940.

[118] After the death of Otakar Ostrčil, opera director of the National Theatre, Prague.

[119] The professorship Suk had held.

[120] Most likely an accounting of royalties by The Authors' and Composers' Union from productions of his stage works in Prague and Brno.

[121] The first broadcast of the work took place on Prague Radio on 6 October 1935.

LETTER 23
To the Mayor of Polička
Paris, 10 November 1935

My dear friend,

I thank you with all my heart for your good wishes,[122] and I ask you to convey my thanks to the Board of the Town of Polička for their congratulations on my state prize for this year,[123] which you sent me from the town of my birth. I am very much pleased by your continuing interest in my work and its achievements, and I find it a great incentive to further effort.

With best regards.
Respectfully,
B. Martinů

LETTER 24
To his Family
Paris, 15 November 1935

My dear ones,

Charlotte thanks you for your good wishes and will add a few words herself. I didn't have a chance to write sooner. I've had a lot of work with the Czech Philharmonic tour to be sure that everything is ready. Mr Šafránek has a lot of worries about it, too, so I'm helping him, running here and there, mostly in town and to the legation. Talich will conduct *La Bagarre*. I'm looking forward to it. It might be broadcast from here by way of Prague on Monday, 2 December, from the Opéra Comique.[124] It's clear that a lot of people from Prague will get their finger into it, so we'll have to be on our guard here constantly.

Firkušný played the Concerto for Piano.[125] Perhaps you heard it. It couldn't be heard very well here – only a little bit of the first movement. There was a lot of interference during the other two movements, so we caught almost nothing of it. They also broadcast the Cello Concerto[126] from Vienna, but it was early Sunday morning, so we didn't hear any of it either. Yesterday they broadcast *The Kitchen Revue* from Switzerland[127] I received a programme from America – in Los Angeles they played my Quartet with Orchestra.[128] I think Mrs Coolidge recommended it.

---

[122] Martinů was congratulated 'by resolution of the Town Board of Polička' in a letter of 7 November 1935.

[123] State prize for the year 1935 for *The Miracles of Mary*. He also received first prize (8,000 crowns) for this opera from the B. Smetana Foundation in Brno for the year 1935.

[124] *La Bagarre* was played by the Czech Philharmonic at the concert mentioned with extraordinary success.

[125] The Piano Concerto No. 2, with the Czech Philharmonic, on 13 November 1935.

[126] Cello Concerto No. 1.

[127] Suite from the ballet *La Revue de cuisine,* H161a, composed in 1927.

[128] H207, composed in 1931.

In Pennsylvania they're going to play *Inventions*, which were played in Venice.[129]

Still no word from the Conservatoire and, according to the news, I think that nothing will be decided now – at least not before Christmas – and by then I'll already be in Prague. It would have been a waste of time and money to have gone there before. I have the impression that my chances are better now. The state prize helped a lot. It's not a great sum of money – 5,000 crowns – but rather it's the honour. They sent me congratulations from Polička – V. Rippl and the Town Council and the Mayor, and I thanked them. In Prague they keep arguing now about Talich's appointment.[130] I also sent an article to the magazine *Přítomnost*.[131] I'll surely speak with Talich here. They'll be here for two days, and I'll find out the details about the Conservatoire. I'm glad you had a nice holiday.

The weather is ghastly. It changes constantly. One moment it's lovely – the next moment it's freezing – and the next moment it rains – so that a person is constantly out of sorts. Zrzavý is also going to Prague. He has an exhibition at Umělecká beseda.[132] Stáňa writes more often now and tells me what's going on. I think I'll apply for the position that Suk held in order to keep people from saying that I don't want to return to Prague.

That's about all my news.

Love,
Your Bohouš

LETTER 25
To his Family
[Prague, after 31 January–before 7 February 1936]

My dear ones,

The premiere[133] has been put off until this Friday, the 7th of February. Write and let me know how it would be for you to come and if you'd come with Mr Šmíd. It might not be convenient for him at the end of the week. I'm going to have a lot of work. There are long rehearsals all this week – they always go on until three or four o'clock and then there's not much left of the day. Mr Šafránek writes that I had a great success with the Concerto for Harpsichord and Orchestra, which Mme de Lacour played.[134]

Mrs Šafránek is coming this week. She has a concert at the German Theatre,

---

[129] *Cf.* note 82 on p. 49, above.

[130] On 17 October 1935 Talich was named Assistant Musical Director of the National Theatre Opera (and Musical Director and Conductor from 21 April 1942).

[131] Not the article 'Is Opera an Anachronism?' published in *Přítomnost* ('Presence'), Vol. XII, No. 7, 20 February 1935, pp. 105–7, but rather a polemical article about Talich, which *Přítomnost* did not publish.

[132] An association of Czech intellectuals and artists founded in 1862. Smetana was one of the founding members.

[133] The Prague premiere of *The Miracles of Mary*.

[134] Concerto for Harpsichord and Small Orchestra, H246, which Martinů wrote in 1935 for the harpsichordist Marcelle de Lacour (1896–1997); she gave the premiere at the Concerts du Triton in Paris on 29 January 1936.

so she'll also be here for the premiere.[135] I think that a lot of important people are coming – probably the Foreign Minister,[136] Mr Schieszl and his wife – and lots of others. There's a great deal of interest. Should I write to Mr Šmíd or will you speak with him yourself? Does Mum feel well enough that the trip wouldn't be too hard for her? It'll be performed again Sunday evening. I'm waiting for news about how you'll arrange it and when you're likely to arrive. I'll have a box in the loge again. Write and let me know if Mr Šmíd is coming alone or with Mrs Šmíd. I'd have to take Mrs Šafránek with me. I'll wait for your answer and then I'll write again.

Love,
Your Bohouš

P.S. I'm so much looking forward to seeing Mum again! I only hope she'll feel well enough to make the trip.

P.P.S. If it's not too cold in the attic, perhaps Mařka could bring a book with her – it's in French – maybe she'll know where it is. It's greyish, large and quite thick – *Anthologie Negre*. I think Mařka read it, so she might know where she put it. I think it's by Blaise Cendrars.[137]

LETTER 26
To his Family
[Equihen, Pas de Calais] 23 July 1936

My dear ones,

I got your letter and I'm glad that things are better. The weather is the same everywhere now. It changes here every day and there isn't much sun, but at least it's not cold. It's quite peaceful here – I haven't had such a good rest in a long time. I have my work with me and so, when the weather is bad I write and, in any case, time is growing short – in a week I think we'll go back to Paris. But we won't stay there. We're invited to the mountains again by an acquaintance of ours who has a house there,[138] and I'm going to write a concerto for flute[139] for him there. He has already put it on the programme. He will perform it for the first time on the radio in London.[140] So we still have something to look forward to – if only the weather were better! I can imagine how it must be there. It's a shame that nothing will come of this summer and that then

---

[135] Of *The Miracles of Mary*.

[136] Dr Milan Hodža.

[137] *Anthologie nègre* (Éditions de la Sirène, Paris, 1927), by the poet and prose writer Blaise Cendrars (1881–1961), was the first French, if not European, anthology of oral folk literature of 'Black Africa'.

[138] The French flautist Marcel Moyse (1889–1984), in whose country home in Saint-Amour in the Jura Mountains in eastern France the Martinůs lived after their residence in Normandy in the summer of 1936.

[139] Concerto for Flute, Violin and Orchestra, H252, composed for Moyse in October 1936. For his trio, founded in 1933, Martinů wrote the Sonata for Flute, Violin and Piano, H254, in 1937 and probably also the *Promenades* for flute, violin and harpsichord, H274, composed in 1939.

[140] First performed in Paris on 27 December 1936, and not in London (by the BBC) until 1937.

again there'll be a long, hard winter. The Nováks and the Masaryks[141] are here, too, and they like it a lot – except for the wind, which never wants to stop blowing! We've had a good rest from the stress of Paris, and I certainly needed it!

Talich sent me a message saying he'd like me to give the premiere of the next opera[142] to the National Theatre in Prague and that he promises me he'll do it himself. It disappoints them that I give all the premieres to Brno.[143] Stáňa said that things are much better at the National since Talich began working there. No one writes to me now. It's vacation time and I suppose everyone has left Prague for the country.

Křička[144] is putting an ad in the newspapers, but Mr Schieszl wrote me that there still hasn't been any decision by the Ministry.

Mr Šmíd has some real worries, and he doesn't deserve that. They're just doing this out of spite in order to upset him. I'm glad that Fanouš finds something every now and then. Stáňa promised me he'd ask again at the National Trust and that he'll ask Dr Pečírka[145] to speak with Dr Wirth.[146] Perhaps everything will finally be better. Dr Wirth could help him a lot, but he's an old man, who doesn't like to be disturbed but to be left in peace and quiet. Maybe it would do him good if Fanouš visited him at the Ministry in Prague. Certainly he remembers him from Želiv.

I'll send the pastilles with Stáňa. We send you our best regards and wish you all the best. Write me again at the Paris address. We'll probably be back toward the First of August.

Love,
Your
Bohouš

---

[141] Stanislav Novák with his wife and Bohumila Masaryková, widow of the painter Herbert Masaryk, son of T. G. Masaryk, with their daughters Anna and Herberta.

[142] *Juliette or The Key to Dreams.*

[143] *The Miracles of Mary* in Brno on 23 February 1935, the opera-ballet *Theatre behind the Gate* on 20 September 1936; before that the ballets *Who is the Most Powerful in the World?*, H133, on 31 January 1925 and *The Revolt*, H151, on 11 February 1928, and the opera *The Soldier and the Dancer*, H162, on 5 May 1928. This tradition of Martinů premieres in Brno was revived with the world premieres of *The Tears of the Knife*, H169, on 22 October 1969, *The Three Wishes or The Inconstancy of Life*, H175, on 16 June 1971, and the ballet *Check to the King*, H186, on 11 April 1980, as well as the Czech premieres of the operas *The Marriage*, H341, on 22 May 1960, *The Greek Passion*, H372, on 3 March 1962, *Ariane*, H370, on 23 October 1962, and *Alexandre bis*, H255, on 10 February 1964, and the ballet *The Strangler*, H317, on 30 September 1990.

[144] Jaroslav Křička, professor of composition at the Conservatoire from 1919, appointed professor of composition at the Master Classes of the Prague Conservatoire after Josef Suk in the autumn of 1936 on the basis of a vote by the professors of the Conservatoire. Martinů thus failed in his candidacy for the position, although he was already famous in Europe as a composer. His long-standing reserved attitude toward Prague and toward musical education in Prague was fostered by this decision.

[145] Dr Jaromir Pečírka (1891–1966), art historian, professor at the Prague Industrial Arts School, from 1935 associate professor of art history at Charles University. In 1931 and, especially, in 1932 Martinů spent part of his summer vacation in Hluboká.

[146] Zdeněk Wirth (1878–1961), art historian and activist in the preservation of monuments, head of the Cultural Section of the Ministry of Education and Culture in the years of the First Republic.

Another autograph list of foreign performances listing local premieres in approx. 1935–36: two pages from the collection of Miloš Šafránek

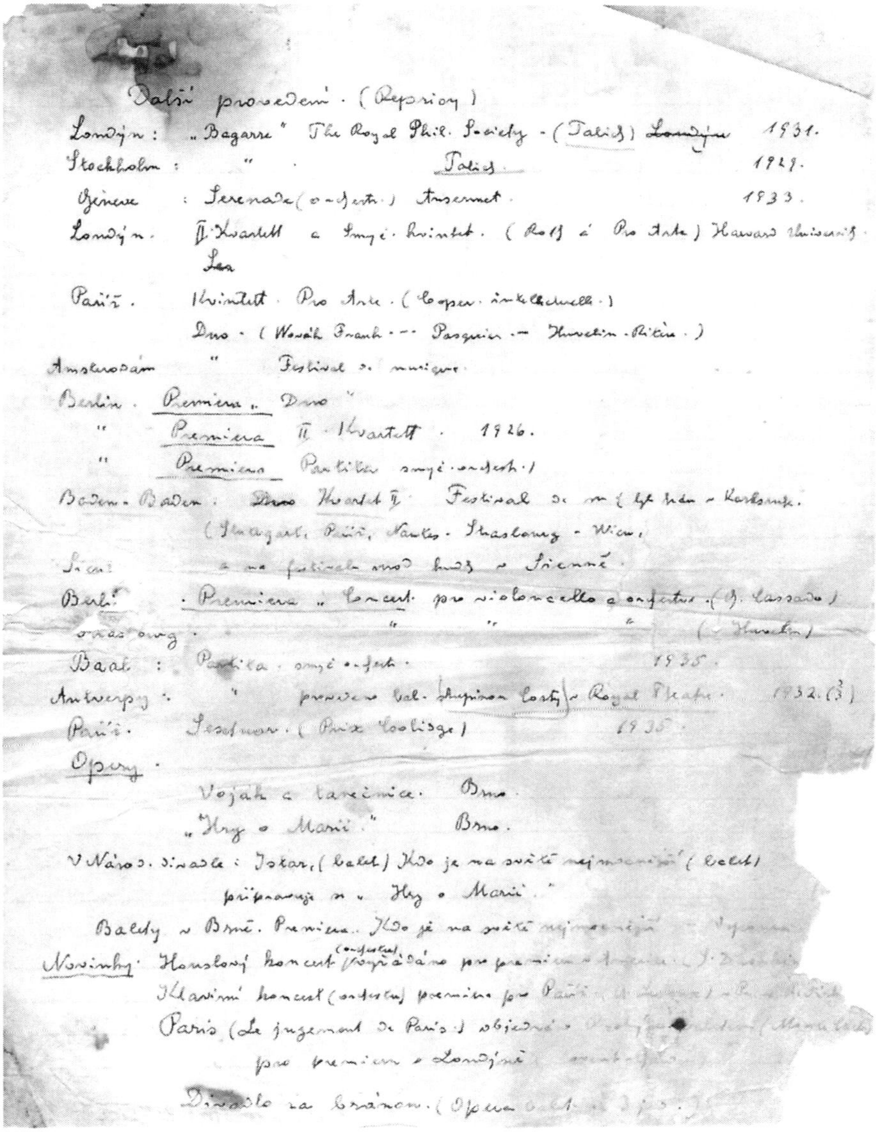

LETTER 27[147]
To Karolína Martinů
Paris, 2 November 1936

Dear Mum,

I wish you all the best on your birthday, and we both especially wish you good health and that you'll be with us for a long time and that you'll be happy and content. It's the wish of all of us, and it's our hope that, now that you have reached a ripe old age, it might be an old age filled with peace and joy. So don't worry about things, especially with regard to me – everything will get straightened out somehow, anyway, and who knows if it isn't better that I stay here.[148] The atmosphere is quite different here, and it would be more meaningful for me to stay – you never know what might come of it. I'd be very glad, too, if it weren't so far, but we can't change that, and once having started on the road I've taken, I've got to stay on it. Besides, they don't like me very much in Prague. After all, there are many influential people there who keep an eye on my work and who can help me by their influence if necessary. Don't worry anymore about my well-being. Things will come right![149]

Your letter just arrived, and we thank you for your good wishes. Charlotte will add hers to mine and thanks you for thinking of her. We were thinking just yesterday that you surely want to visit Dad's grave. I'm happy that you at least heard the broadcast from Brno.

There was a long article about me in a Swiss music magazine by O. Ferroud, a French composer, who met a tragic end in Hungary during the summer holiday.[150] The article was his last work. It's very nice, and I'll ask for one more copy, which I'll send you. It's about how they think of me in America and how much they value my work. I must see to it that it appears at home as well.[151] They'll try to stop it, but they can't change things.

I remembered that I know a high-ranking official in the Catholic Party.[152] He was here and I let him know through Šafránek that I'm sorry they didn't make more of *The Miracles of Mary* at the National Theatre. Who knows whether his influence could be helpful for Fanouš. I'll ask Mr Šafránek for his advice, and then I'll write to this official. Fanouš could see him in Prague and speak with him.

Lots of love,
Your Bohouš

P.S. I'm just now writing to the Writers' and Composers' Union,[153] asking that they send you some money for the winter.

---

[147] Charlotte Martinů added a postscript in Czech.

[148] In Paris, after his failure to win appointment to the position that Suk had held in the Master Classes.

[149] Martinů achieved financial security in the USA only after 1941 thanks, of course, to sheer hard work.

[150] Pierre-Octave Ferroud (1900–36); he died in a road accident. The article appeared first in the *Schweizerische Musikzeitung*, then in a French version in *La Revue musicale*, XVII, 1936, p. 427, under the title 'Un grand musicien contemporain: B. Martinů'. A year later, it appeared in an English translation: 'A Great Musician of Today: B. Martinů', in *The Chesterian*, No. 122, March–April 1937, pp. 89–93.

[151] A Czech translation of Ferroud's article appeared neither then nor later.

[152] Msgr. František Hála, prominent member of the People's Party, from 1945–1948 Minister of Post and Telegraph in the Czechoslovak government.

[153] The Authors' and Composers' Union, which collected and looked after performance fees for his works.

LETTER 28
To his Family
[Paris] 3 December 1936

My dear ones,

I wasn't able to write sooner because of the work on the concert of Rejcha,[154] who also lived in Paris a hundred years ago and was well-known and much appreciated, certainly in Paris, but the Czechs got to know him only a short time ago and are now celebrating him and his work. There has been a lot of talk about how Czechoslovakia thinks of such people and so on – you know my own thoughts about it. They sent Jirák[155] here for it as representative of the Czech Academy. So, I've had to be somewhat friendly with him. He promised me that the radio station will again request an opera like the one I already wrote for them.[156] *The Comedy on the Bridge*[157] will be in the spring – around April. Again they have been intending to present the *Slavonic Dances*, but somehow it hasn't got anywhere.

I don't know anything from Prague, and that's also holding things up. They gave me a lot of empty promises, and when I got out they forgot about it and seem to think that everything is all right – but they're mistaken! I'm just writing a letter to the President in order that he be aware of the situation. Jirák also said that it's scandalous and that the whole Conservatoire looks like some kind of village music school. The one who's supposed to take Křička's place is even less capable. Firkušný told me it's quite possible that Novák will retire sooner than had been expected,[158] so it might not be going to last so long. I spoke about it with the managing director of the Conservatoire,[159] who let me know that I should prepare for my own position by making contacts with the people in high places starting now. It also seems they must have something of a bad conscience, because Stáňa tells me that the professorial staff won't decide on the next appointments any longer, but rather the Ministry of Education directly.

Tomorrow we're going to listen to Vienna and Radio Paris. I'm sorry that Radio Paris is so late for you – sometime after midnight. But on Saturday there's the concert at the Luxembourg [Radio], which we should be able to hear quite well. Miss Šafránek is going to play it for the first time.[160] I was also asked to give a performance

---

[154] The Czech composer Antonín Rejcha (or Reicha, as he later spelled it), born in Prague in 1770 and later, from 1808, permanently domiciled in Paris, where he taught at the Conservatoire, with many of the leading composers of the next generation among his students. In 1936 a hundred years had elapsed since his death.

[155] Karel Boleslav Jirák (1891–1972), composer, conductor and educator, associated at the time with Prague Radio. He lived in the USA from 1947, where Martinů met him again. *Cf.* also p. 121, below.

[156] Prague Radio had at the time manuscripts of two operas by Martinů: *The Voice of the Forest* (composed in 1935, broadcast on 6 October 1935), and the as yet unproduced *Comedy on the Bridge* (composed in 1935), H247.

[157] It was first performed on Prague Radio on 18 March 1937.

[158] Vítězslav Novák taught at the Conservatoire until 1939.

[159] In the academic year 1936–37, this position was held by the piano pedagogue Vilém Kurz, who had been Firkušný's teacher.

[160] Undoubtedly the Piano Concerto No. 2. The broadcast performance thus preceded that in Paris (31 January 1937), which as a foreign premiere is mentioned by Šafránek (*op. cit.*, p. 356) and Halbreich (*op. cit.*, p. 296).

here of *Mariken*[161] at the World's Fair, but they don't have such a big orchestra, so I'll have to revise it somehow. I'd be happy if it turned out well. I'll write to Brno, they had such high expectations but perform it so little.[162] Also, Olomouc wants to do *Mary*, but undoubtedly I won't be able to do without the score, so I'll offer them *Theatre behind the Gate*.[163] Talich tells me that he's really counting on my new opera and that he'll do it himself, and I also think that I would direct it myself so as not to be disappointed.[164] In Prague, the magazine *Smetana* has resumed publication, and they're having a go at Talich. Stáňa wrote me after an interval of three months that he's applying for Hoffmann's position, but he says he doesn't have much hope.[165] It has become warmer here, but it rains a lot and that's unpleasant.

We both send our love.
Your Bohouš

LETTER 29
To his Family
Paris, 7 February 1937

My dear ones,

I haven't had a chance to write until now. There were rehearsals for the concert[166] by Mrs Šafránek-Leroux, first at the Conservatoire Society on 31 January and then on Friday, 5 February – the radio concert with F. Zweig,[167] conductor of the Prague German Theatre. They turned out quite well – Mrs Šafránek had a great success with both concerts. The second concert was broadcast over almost all the French stations and from Strasbourg and all the Belgian stations – so we were all happy. The reviews are excellent both for her and for me. Mr Šafránek was quite pleased, as you can imagine. It's been recommended to London, and we just wrote to America about it. I lost a lot of time with it – rehearsals and meetings – but now I'll continue with my work. Both concerts were sold out and there's been a lot of talk about them. I hope there'll be some mention of them in the newspapers at home.

I have no news as yet from Prague. Melantrich is going to publish the scores,

---

[161] *Mariken z Nimègue* (*Mariken of Nimègue*) from *The Miracles of Mary*. It was not played at the Paris World's Fair in 1937.

[162] The opera-ballet *Theatre behind the Gate* (composed in 1935–36), premiered in Brno on 20 September 1936.

[163] *The Miracles of Mary* was presented in Olomouc on 6 February 1938, but *Theatre behind the Gate* not until 1958.

[164] Martinů got his way with Jindřich Honzl (1894–1953), a leading figure in Czech avant-garde theatre in the 1920s and '30s, as director of *Juliette*.

[165] He succeeded his teacher at the Conservatoire, the first violinist of the Czech Quartet Karel Hoffman (1872–1936), in the following year.

[166] The Second Piano Concerto.

[167] The conductor Fritz Zweig (1893–1984), a Schoenberg student, worked in a number of Berlin opera houses before the Nazis came to power and forbade the employment of Jewish musicians. He was then engaged at the Prague German Theatre from 1934–38, fleeing to Paris in 1938; in 1940 he emigrated to the United States where, based in Hollywood, he taught at the Music Academy of the West in Santa Barbara.

and Mr Šafránek suggested to director Šalda[168] that they secure the rights to all my compositions and especially to the works for theatre – *Špaliček* and *The Miracles of Mary* – and that they pay me a monthly honorarium.[169] While he was in Prague, he spoke with Šalda about it, and he showed a lot of interest. I think I might have to come to Prague on account of it, but not until something is definitely decided, because you know it won't be as if my 'dear friends' in Prague won't care. I'm waiting for the results, and Šafránek is also watching it closely.

Ask how expensive radios are there – I think it's possible to buy them on instalment. It seems to me it would be a nice thing for you if only because you could know what's going on in the world and could listen to good concerts and lectures, and you could learn languages. I don't think they're as expensive as they used to be.

I wrote to Belgrade,[170] and they wrote me from the National Theatre that the theatre in Sofia asked to look at the work.[171]

I read that Talich is sick again and that he's cancelled his concerts in Holland. I'll send the new opera[172] to the National Theatre in Prague one of these days, but again his illness might cause a delay.

Fanouš shouldn't delay in that matter with Mr Hála, if he can remember it. And he should send a letter there when he finishes the work.

> We both send our love.
> Your Bohouš

LETTER 30
To his Family
[Paris] 1 March 1937

My dear ones,

I've had a lot of work lately, so I haven't had a chance to write. I'm working on the opera for the exposition,[173] but I don't know how the performance will be. There are a lot of contestants, and you know that since the French are paying for it, they'll get preference. Still, I hope I'll succeed in getting a place.[174] My librettist is a Frenchman[175] who has a lot of connections, so he's going to try hard, too. At home, no one is lifting a finger for the exposition, and so to all appearances there probably

---

[168] Jaroslav Šalda (1880–1965), director of the Prague publishing house Melantrich.

[169] Martinů made a contract with Melantrich (which, together with the Brno-based publisher Pazdírek, published sheet music from 1936 to 1949 under the brand Melpa) at the beginning of April 1937, during his brief visit in Prague.

[170] The reference is apparently to the performances of *Špaliček*.

[171] More likely *Špaliček* than *The Miracles of Mary*.

[172] *Juliette*.

[173] For the Paris World's Fair of 1937, Martinů was preparing the one-act comedy *Alexandre bis*, H255.

[174] It was not produced. *Alexandre bis* was first performed in Mannheim on 18 February 1964.

[175] The Parisian journalist, essayist and critic André Wurmser (1899–1984). A member of the French Communist Party from 1934, during the Occupation Wurmser was active in the Resistance, publishing the underground newspaper *Le Patriote du Sud-Ouest*; he joined the editorial board of the left-wing newspaper *L'Humanité* in 1954. Wurmser resisted Martinů's request for a singing cat in the libretto for *Alexandre bis*; they compromised on Wurmer's suggestion of a singing portrait.

won't be much of anything – except that perhaps Nikolská[176] will come with the ballet. Other countries will have lots to show – concerts and theatre – so it's obvious that it's important to think about it well ahead of time and take care of everything that might be necessary. Our people in high places don't care much for that kind of thing – they'd rather just calmly draw their pay the first of every month and be done with it. Why should they exert themselves for an exhibition!

With Fanouš feeling the way he does it would be better if he didn't go out until he's really well again. Influenza has to be completely cured, and the best way is to stay at home or else there can be recurring complications. I'll send that article[177] soon. I need it here for now because it will also come out in London in an English-language music magazine and possibly in Hungary as well. It will be published in four languages, but nobody in our own country is interested in it! I sent them a Czech translation, but they never printed it. I'll send it to you in French and Mařka can translate it.

I also sent the reviews. I'll have them typed and we'll send one copy to Dr Alice Masaryková. I hear she asked Mrs Leroux for it – I think she has a bad conscience![178]

The Pasquier Trio[179] played my Trio[180] in New York and had a great success. One of the Czechs with the orchestra also wrote me to say how pleased they were. There are more Czech musicians there, and he wants me to send him the cello concerto.[181] My Trio was also played on radio here, and we listened to it. The cello concerto will be played here on Radio Lugano in Switzerland around the 8th or 9th of March, but we don't get that station very well.

Otherwise, the winter is not a pleasant one – there are floods everywhere. It's been raining incessantly and the rivers are rising. We have to have the heat on all the time. Prices are going up again – it's going to be quite expensive at the exposition.

I'll give Talich the new opera soon.[182] The premiere of the little opera *Comedy on the Bridge* will be broadcast from Prague on the 18th of March. You should listen to it.

We both send our love. If I go to Prague I'll certainly come home for a visit.

Your
Bohouš

---

[176] The dancer Jelizaveta Nikolskaya (1904–55), engaged from 1923 – with interruptions – until 1945 at the National Theatre, Prague, toured in Europe and the USA with the so-called Czechoslovak Ballet. In 1924 she danced the role of Istar in Martinů's ballet of the same name at the National Theatre.

[177] *Cf.* note 150 on p. 62, above.

[178] Apparently a reference to his assumption, justified or not, that Dr Alice Masaryková (1880–1966), daughter of T. G. Masaryk, did not support his candidacy in 1936 for the position which Suk had occupied.

[179] Renowned string trio, founded in 1928 by the brothers Jean, Pierre and Étienne Pasquier.

[180] String Trio No. 2, H238, composed in 1934.

[181] The First Cello Concerto.

[182] *Juliette.*

At Vieux Moulin, 1937

LETTER 31
To his Family
Paris, 4 June 1937

My dear ones,

I'm answering your letter at once, mainly on account of the Šmíds. I think they'd do better if they'd decide to come later because, although the exposition[183] has already opened, it's still not finished. Only about a third of the exhibits are open to the public with the result that everyone is crammed into one place and it's tiring, so they probably wouldn't get much out of it. If they came in September there would be enough time and they'd be able to see the whole fair. It would be a shame to come here now. Tell Venda Rippl that, too – I think he wanted to come in June. It wouldn't be worth it – our pavilion won't be ready until some time in July, and the whole colonial wing is still closed, so it would make more sense to postpone coming until they could see everything, and that won't be before August. Otherwise the exposition will be quite beautiful and will certainly be extended, so it will be at its best at the end. That's why I'm writing back immediately – so that you can tell them this – so that they don't make a decision to come in the meantime. Go to see them and tell them these things.

The weather has taken a turn for the better. The heat wave has passed and it's beautiful here now. The performance of the quartet hasn't come off for the time being. That man is already going on vacation, so we had to postpone it until after the holidays.[184] Fanouš really has bad luck, but surely someone will stand up for him. He should go to see Mr Wagner and Mr Pečírka so that he could talk with them personally. It would be better for his future work if they knew him.

We can't get Prague on the radio now. There's a lot of solar interference until next winter, but the programmes really aren't worth much anyway.

Mr Šafránek doesn't know about the Foundation, but he's going to find out. There are a lot of concerts and theatre here now, and I think you can find the whole gang from Prague at the festival of modern music. Hába[185] has something there, and he's sure to come with the whole delegation, for which there's always money. But the programme isn't up to the mark.

They're already fixing the house at the Vieux Moulin so it'll be nice for us, and I think I'll borrow an upright piano and work there.

Tell the Šmíds right away! And write!

Love,
Your Bohouš

---

[183] World's Fair, held between May and September 1937. It bore the title Exposition Internationale des Arts et Techniques dans la Vie Moderne.

[184] String Quartet No. 4, H256, composed in the spring of 1937, commissioned by the Paris-based Czech Čestmír Puc and dedicated to his wife Helena. A private premiere was given on 13 June 1938.

[185] The Duo for Two Violins (in a six-tone scale), Op. 49, of Alois Hába (1893–1973) was played at the Paris festival of the International Society for Contemporary Music in 1937. Hába was in a position to influence the programming of Czech music at festivals of the Society, especially in the 1930s.

LETTER 32[186]

To his Family

[Vieux Moulin, before 15 September 1937]

My dear ones,

We're still at Vieux Moulin but we're about to go to Paris, though I'm not very happy about it, because it's lovely here and we don't look forward to the noisy streets and the cars. But we can't put it off any longer! I think we'll leave on Wednesday. So write to me in Paris. I really got a good rest here. I wonder if you read about A. Roussel's death.[187] Poor chap! It was a surprise for us – I don't know the details. There wasn't so much as a word of it in that journal we get. You see how it's the same all over the world? Thieves and murderers and even cyclists get a whole page, but a person like that doesn't get a mention! All the same, there are people who will have fond memories of him.

I'm anxious to see what's new in Paris. The Sextet[188] will be played in London in October. What's on the schedule at the National Theatre in Prague? I'm curious to see what Talich will decide.[189] They pester him from all sides, but I hope he also got a rest. I don't think anything is going to come of the visit here by the Czech Philharmonic or the National Theatre, which is better, as a matter of fact. Audiences here are not particularly enthralled by them performing nothing but *Bartered Bride*!

I know it's been hard for you with the illnesses and with the weather. I have to write an article for *Lidové noviny* again – about Roussel,[190] I think. If you read it, save it for me or send it to me, but send the whole page or at least with the name *Lidové noviny* on top.[191] I got some work done here at Vieux Moulin, but now again I'm going to have to work harder.

Love,
Your Bohouš

---

[186] Charlotte Martinů added a postscript.

[187] Albert Roussel (1869–1937), French composer, teacher at the Schola Cantorum, Paris, and Martinů's teacher for two years from 1923 – or, rather, his mentor: Martinů went to him only irregularly as his private pupil. Roussel's music, which Martinů first heard in 1920 played by the Czech Philharmonic (the First Symphony, *Le poème de la forêt*), was one of the incentives for his going to Paris in 1923.

[188] The String Sextet.

[189] Apparently a reference to the dates of planned performances of *Juliette*.

[190] Martinů dedicated a short article expressing undying gratitude to Roussel in *La Revue musicale*, Vol. XVIII, 1937, No. 178. It appeared in Czech translation only in *Tempo*, No. XX, 1947–48, p. 21, and in Šafránek's anthology *Bohuslav Martinů: Domov, hudba, a svět, op. cit.*). There is no evidence of an article in *Lidové noviny* (the oldest Czech daily newspaper, founded in 1893).

[191] Martinů's sister studiously cut out articles on his work from newspapers and magazines but often failed to note their sources.

LETTER 33
To his Family
Nice, 30 November 1937

My dear ones,

Your letter came, and I'm answering it at once. We're already settled in nicely here.[192] I'm working on the commissioned work for Lausanne.[193] Yesterday we were in Monte Carlo for a Sunday outing, and I sent you a postcard. I'm writing as well to the Authors' and Composers' Union asking them to send you 1,500 crowns so you'll have something for the winter. You'll surely need it for coal and other things. I hope they'll send it soon. I also wrote to the radio about their programming and pointed out to them that my work has been broadcast all over the world but not in Prague! I wonder if it's going to do any good. About the manuscripts – I'll take care of it with Melantrich directly. I'd like them to do it at Christmas on Prague Radio and then we could get an engagement in London.[194] Vanda[195] also wrote and said she'd like to settle everything quickly, but of course she doesn't know that these things don't get done so quickly as one might wish.

I had a big success here with the Quartet with Orchestra – Pro Arte[196] played it brilliantly and the conductor from Brussels was excellent.[197] It was generally very well liked – it's a shame you weren't able to get it. I arranged with Pro Arte that they suggest *Mariken z Nimegue*[198] to the theatre in Brussels and they promised that they'd make a big effort to get them to take it and maybe to do it in May. There are some festivals there and Mrs Coolidge will be there and Pro Arte will play my Quartet again and they asked us to come. Pro Arte likes me a lot, and they'll do everything possible to have it performed – they have a lot of influence there. It only bothers me that just in May the Olomouc theatre wants to do it.[199] They have it set for a guest performance in Prostějov, and so on. Somehow I'll have to see to the scores and other materials. It will be good if it's performed. In addition, they're going to broadcast my First Piano Concerto from Paris on the 11th of December with Mrs Lucette Descaves.[200] Maybe you'll get it better through Strasbourg – I think it's going to be hooked up.

It's gorgeous here – there's lots of sun and the roses are still in bloom everywhere. The mimosa is starting to blossom and all the trees are green. I go around without

---

[192] At the Villa Point Clair of painter Josef Šíma at 94 chemin de Brancolar in Mont Boron, by Nice, where they lived from about the middle of November until 10 January 1938, and again from September 1953 until September 1954. (*Cf.* also note 1 on p. 153, below.) Šíma (1891–1972) was an important French surrealist painter of Czech origin. He settled in France in 1921.

[193] *Duo Concertant* for Two Violins and Orchestra, H264, written for Georges and Victor Desarzens, first performed on Radio Lausanne in 1938.

[194] Refers to one of the parts of *The Miracles of Mary*.

[195] Vanda Jakubíčková.

[196] Belgian string quartet, noted in the 1920s and '30s for its orientation toward contemporary music.

[197] Not yet identified.

[198] The second part of *The Miracles of Mary*.

[199] The Municipal Theatre in Olomouc presented *The Miracles of Mary* on 6 February 1938.

[200] H149, composed in 1925. Lucette Descaves (1906–93) had been playing the work since 1928.

a coat. It's beautiful! The evenings are cool, of course, but we don't go out much in the evening. So I think we'll get a rest here even while we work. It's already winter in Paris. Here they have it good – the sun is always shining! It's a different life! We're living in a villa on the side of a hill, and it's completely surrounded by gardens. We have our own bathroom and, to put it briefly, all the comforts, so we've got to take advantage of it. If I could, I'd send you a little sunshine!

Jeníček Jílek[201] wrote, but that project won't come to anything – it's a lot of work. I'd lose a lot of time with it – at least two months. They probably think I have nothing to do – but I have to make a living, too! No one is going to give me something for nothing and the best will in the world won't change that fact! They want to dramatise the sculptured reliefs by Šaff entitled 'The War of the Girls'.[202] I don't think that will work well, either. Perhaps they imagine it differently than it would be, though. I'll send him an answer. About Žalmanová[203] – that's a most peculiar story! I think she's quite off her rocker – best not to answer her – which is what I do. I've already received all her novel-length letters and her 'poems'.

Charlotte and I send our love.

Your Bohouš

LETTER 34
To his Family
Paris, 3 April 1938

My dear ones,

We're back in Paris. It was a good trip – uneventful. Everything here is just like it used to be. I got a lot of work done in Prague.[204] I mostly spoke with the people who have influence at the Conservatoire, and we'll start preparing for that now. The way it looks, I would stay here yet another year and in the meantime it would all be made ready, and then I'd probably go back to Prague after the holidays. A lot depends on whether or not V. Novák retires, and that will most likely be next year,[205] and everything will have been arranged, especially at the Ministry. I spoke with Šafránek about Fanouš and he promised me that he'll ask about it, but he didn't want to talk about it, so we couldn't discuss it seriously. They have their hands full at the Ministry of Foreign Affairs now, so he wasn't even very interested. I talked with him for about a quarter of an hour, but I'll also write to him. I didn't see C. Novotný.[206] There are some changes there, too. Wirth[207] is probably going to retire. He wasn't

---

[201] A friend of Martinů, Polička meat-wholesaler Jan Jílek, to whom Martinů dedicated his 1920 piano work *Foxtrot*, H126 bis.

[202] A large 'epic' work by sculptor Vojtěch Šaff (1865–1923), who was born in Polička and lived in Vienna and later in Brno. *The Girls' War* is to this day in the collection of the Polička Museum.

[203] Olga Žalmanová (1904–94), a friend of Martinů's from the early 1920s. The 'peculiar story' has eluded elucidation.

[204] He was there with his wife for the final rehearsals, the premiere (on 16 March 1938) and the first repeat performance of *Juliette*.

[205] Vítězslav Novák retired in 1939.

[206] Unidentified.

[207] *Cf.* note 146 on p. 59, above.

anywhere to be found – I left a message for him. On Thursday we went to see *Juliette* and it was even more beautiful than at the premiere – a big success! Talich said he won't force it through but that in about two years we'll try again. He also wants to do *Špaliček* again. He said I definitely must go to Prague. I dedicated the score of *Juliette* to him and he was quite pleased.

How was the trip? Good, I hope. The weather has taken a turn for the worse, and we still have to put the heat on. It's quite cool. If we stayed in Prague, we could go on two more weeks of visits. Everyone has invited us. If the situation calms down,[208] we just might come to the rally[209] anyway and spend a couple of days at home during the holidays.[210] Let's hope that somehow things will get a little better. They're afraid here how everything will turn out. It's expensive and prices keep going up. Write and tell me the news and what you and the Šmíds talked about. Say hello to them for us and write soon!

Love,
Your B. Martinů[211]

LETTER 35
To his Family
[Schönenberg] 30 September 1938

My dear ones,

I haven't had any news from you. I think that perhaps you're unable to write, so I'm sending you a letter myself just so you won't worry. We're still in Switzerland[212]

---

[208] The *Anschluss* of Austria by Nazi Germany had occurred a month earlier.

[209] The Tenth All-Sokol Rally, June–July 1938; the main days of the Rally were 3–6 July. Sokol (from the Czech word for 'falcon') is a youth sport movement and gymnastics organisation first founded in Prague, then in the Czech region of Austro-Hungary, in 1862 by Miroslav Tyrš and Jindřich Fügner. Primarily a fitness training centre, through lectures, discussions and group outings, Sokol also provided what Tyrš viewed as physical, moral and intellectual training for the nation. Though officially an institution 'above politics', Sokol played an important part in the development of Czech nationalism, providing a forum for the spread of mass-based nationalist ideologies. The massive gymnastics festivals called *Slet* (plural *slety*, meaning 'meetings of birds', from the verb *slétnout se*, to come together by flying) helped to craft and disseminate the Czech nationalist mythology and version of history.

[210] Martinů returned to Czechoslovakia (without Charlotte) in summer 1938. After the Sokol rally in Prague, he stayed in Polička, before going on to Tři Studně, the estate of Václav Kaprál (1889–1947), father of the talented young composer Vítězslava Kaprálová (1915–40), who studied composition with Martinů in Paris and had an intense affair with him. At the end of July he stayed again for a short time in Polička, whence he went to Paris by way of Prague, as was his custom. It was the last time he spent in his native land.

[211] Martinů almost always signed his letters home with only his given name (his wife's letters were slightly more formal, using both her names). This letter may show force of habit: he was in the habit of attending to his correspondence *en bloc* rather than letter by letter.

[212] As guest of Paul Sacher (1906–99), the conductor of the Basel Chamber Orchestra, and his wife Maja at their home in Schönenberg, near Basel, to which the Martinůs later often returned (indeed, in 1959 he was buried there, at his own request; his remains were returned to Polička twenty years later). It was at Schönenberg in 1938 that he completed his orchestral masterpiece, the *Double Concerto for Two String Orchestras, Piano and Timpani*, H271, dedicating it to Sacher, who also conducted its first performance. *Cf.* also note 254 on p. 82, below.

and we get the newspapers only rarely. We're all alone on a mountain, and we were on the point of going back to Paris yesterday, because things didn't look good. But today it seems that things are much better and that we'll avoid the worst,[213] so we'll stay here as long as we can. Anyway, there's nothing to be done in Paris. Naturally we registered at the legation. In the case of conflict, they would need me for some kind of work – and Charlotte too. Paris seems abandoned – everyone who didn't have something to do there has gone to the countryside. I have no news from home – only the French newspapers and it's mostly foreign politics, but nothing about us. Sometimes in the evening we catch the news on the radio, but we don't learn much from that either. Today the news is much better, and it seems that things have been settled peacefully – but at a cost to us.[214] I think of you all the time – of what you're doing in these difficult times. I'm glad we left Paris. There was all that agitation there – often to no purpose – on the radio and in the newspapers but mostly in the streets – and here at least we can find a little peace and quiet. And in any case – we can't alter the course of events.

I received a request from America to write something based on Czech dances – right away – some kind of Czech suite[215] – and they said they'll perform it as soon as they get it. We have a lot of support there. The violinist Dushkin[216] would play it. They're very interested in us here, too, and everyone is supportive of us even though it's the German-speaking part of Switzerland. If you can at least write a postcard, tell me the news and let me know if you're well. We think about you a lot, and Charlotte and I send our love and our wishes that we'll soon see better times – at least for a while.

Love,
Your Bohouš

LETTER 36
To his Family
[Paris, 22 October 1938]

My dear ones,

Your letter finally arrived today, and you've probably already got mine, which was held up. Let's hope they'll be delivered regularly once again and that everything calms down a bit at least. I got the news of Polička[217] from Stáňa and from the newspapers, and I already wrote you how it was for me and how we came here in a hurry in order to find out exactly what's going on and that I already found better

[213] That is, a war with Germany.

[214] The Munich Pact was signed in the night of 29–30 September 1938.

[215] *Suite Concertante* for violin and orchestra, H276I, composed in 1938–39, revised 1941 in the United States; the second version (H276II) was completed in 1945.

[216] Dushkin first performed the work in the version for violin and piano in New York in 1943. The Suite was first performed with orchestra at the end of 1945 in St Louis, Missouri.

[217] Polička was occupied by the German army on 10 October 1938, although it was a thoroughly Czech town (in 1938 only 30 Germans lived there). The street Na Svépomoci, where the Martinů family lived, found itself in occupied territory for all of two days.

news here, although I still don't know how it finally turned out, especially with regard to Mr Šmíd. According to the news, we lost the Teachers' Institute and the apartment houses behind it.[218] At least it's gratifying news about Mum, if only a little peace and quiet might reign so that everyone could take it easy and get ready to take care of what's left to us. I can't write about it, and it would be very sad, too. Who knows what still awaits us, anyway. Mr Zrzavý saved me a picture of Polička from a Czech newspaper. He was also quite unhappy. We should at least be glad, though, that it turned out the way it did.

The mood here isn't good – people are uneasy. They aren't happy with what's happened and are even more worried about what might happen next. They realise that a trick was played on us, but they have their own worries here. Unfortunately, the mistake has already been made – and to our loss. I don't have cheerful news from Prague, either. All the people I know who had some influence are gone – either into retirement or else they've been re-assigned. It isn't possible to speak with anyone at the legation, and so everything is quite gloomy. I can't send money now – I don't think it would work. But I'll try to get them to send you something from the Authors' and Composers' Union. If worse comes to worst, Stáňa would probably lend you something for now. I could pay him back when I'm able to. Melantrich also wants to change my contract. That means they're not going to pay me anymore or certainly not as much, but I still don't know what their plans are. No one knows what will be, so it isn't possible to make any decisions about the future. We have to wait until something comes of all this, but it most likely won't be anything too pretty. Everything has turned out badly and, at the moment, even I don't know what I'll do.

I'd like to go to Prague – maybe in February if possible[219] – to see how things in fact look for me, but it seems it won't be too pleasant for anyone right now, so for the time being I'm not giving much thought to it. We can't change things. I won't lose my way in the world, but I would have been happy to have come back and worked at home. Now, of course, everything has become quite complicated. The trains still aren't running, so I wouldn't even be able to come, but it should get straightened out soon. So we wish you all the best and we send our love. We think about you all the time, and now both you and I will be more at peace when we have news from each other. It's true we're not able to say much in a letter, but at least we know what each other is doing. We send you all our love. I'll write to the Mayor of Polička and thank him for having succeeded in saving the town.

Love,
Your Bohouš

P.S. I don't know what the Mayor's name is – Vencovský? Take it to him or send it, won't you?

[218] On 12 October the German army withdrew to a new border line which divided the town in two parts. In the occupied territory, there remained a number of homes inhabited by Czech families, the building of the district office, the Gymnasium (formerly the Teachers' Institute) and Masaryk School. Only on 24 November did the German forces leave the town and withdraw to the line which respected the language border. Until May 1945 this line marked the border between the 'Protectorate of Bohemia and Moravia' declared by Hitler in Prague on 15 March 1939 and the territory affiliated to Germany. On that day (24 November) several Czech communities in the Polička district were taken out of the Third Reich and integrated to the Protectorate of Bohemia and Moravia.

[219] Although it was still possible, Martinů did not go to Prague.

LETTER 37
To Eduard Vencovský,
'Esteemed Mayor of the Town of Polička'
Paris, 22 October 1938

Dear Sir,

I'm sure you understand the anxiety with which I followed the course of events that took place in my birthplace – the precious Czech town of Polička. Permit me to thank you with all my heart for your self-sacrificing effort and to tell you of my joy at your having succeeded in saving our town.

To you and to everyone who worked with you and who suffered with you – to the whole town of Polička – please extend joyous and sincere greetings from its native son who is far from his home but who constantly returns – if only in his thoughts – with gladness – to that dear region – the most beautiful on earth. Thanks to all of you! And to Polička – all the best!

B. Martinů
composer

LETTER 38
To his Family
[Paris, 9 December 1938]

My dear ones,

I really don't know now whether I wrote to you or if you're still waiting a letter from me. I had a lot of correspondence, and I have the impression now that it's me who owes you a letter. I had a bit of a cold and lost five days. I stayed at home – I'm better now. I'm working with Dushkin on the violin compositions.[220] He was supposed to have gone to America already, but he postponed the trip for a month. He wants to take the scores with him so he can play them as soon as he gets there.[221] So – I've been frittering away a lot of time. I go to him and sometimes he comes to me and it's making a lot of work for me. A publisher in London wants to bring out the *Ricercari*,[222] which were done in Venice. We listened to them the other day, broadcast from Rome, and we were able to hear them quite well. You don't know whether Vanda has gone home, do you, or if she's still in London? I wrote to her, but she didn't answer, so she might not be in London. Ruda Firkušný was here and said that the concert in London was a big success and that even here a lot of people listened to it, and that abroad you hear something of mine on the radio almost all the time, but nothing at home. Well, I'll let it go until I get back, and then I'll give them a piece of my mind!

---

[220] The *Suite Concertante.*

[221] *Cf.* note 216 on p. 73, above.

[222] *Tre Ricercari* for chamber orchestra, H267, composed in 1938; they were published by Boosey & Hawkes, London, in 1939.

The news from home isn't very happy, and it's even worse here, so who knows what next year will bring – it probably won't be very good. Everything in the world is very, very strange nowadays and it seems it will surely finally lead to some kind of cataclysm. Better not to think about it if there's nothing we can do to change it.

The weather here has been miserable – it's rained for almost two weeks. It's quite a nasty winter and that's not very pleasant, either. I had some news from Prague that quite a few people at the Conservatory are probably going to retire, but for the moment everything is uncertain. Maybe after the New Year it will all come clear. Yesterday – Thursday – I celebrated my birthday.[223] The years are getting away from us!

But what can we do? Otherwise I feel fine except that events have had a bad effect on me. You carry the news around in your head and think about what might happen and how it might turn out, and all that distracts you from your work. How are you all? Are you well? How is Mum? Is she in good health again?

I send my love,
and Charlotte adds hers to mine.
Your Bohouš

LETTER 39
To his Family
[Paris] 3 March 1939

My dear ones,

I'm answering both of your letters at once so that you won't again worry unnecessarily before something is decided. About America[224] – for the time being it's only an idea in the event that things get even worse than they are now and in case they need me there for promotion of the music. But all that is still very unclear. I don't know what Kaprálová wrote to her family, but it isn't so easy to get admitted. You have to have some kind of guaranteed position or employment or an invitation or else you don't get a visa – and they don't let in just anyone. It's only a plan that could be carried out if the situation were prolonged and got worse. I couldn't take such a responsibility upon myself without the consent of her parents.[225] Well, in brief, these are only ideas with a mind to our making a living. You know that I'm never going to do awfully well here, and as far as Prague goes it's still complicated. I could still always come back and surely I'd get a position even if something different than at the Conservatoire and something good. Anyway, now they can and will need me a lot, and as far as the Conservatoire goes, it's still going well, but that's a different

---

[223] He had turned 48.

[224] Martinů was considering emigrating to the USA with his lover, the composer and conductor Vítězslava Kaprálová (1915–40). In his book *Podivné lásky* ('Strange Loves'; Mlada Frontá, Prague, 1988), Jiří Mucha, who married Kaprálová in 1940, describes at length the complicated love-affair of the married composer and his much younger student.

[225] The Brno composer Václav Kaprál (1889–1947) and his wife Vítězslava. Kaprál was a student of Janáček and Vitěslav Novák and composed largely piano music (including four sonatas), chamber music (not least two string quartets) and songs.

Vitěslava Kaprálová, Martinů's gifted but short-lived student – and, in 1938, lover

decision. I don't know whether I could work under those conditions. And, of course, I would be a little dubious after my long stay in France. So I can't decide, which means I would rather stay here because here at least I'm not burdened by other obligations. And who knows how everything will turn out. Things are changing – every day it's different. For the time being I could still manage here for quite a long time, but in spite of that I wrote to America to ask what I might do – whether I'd find a way to make a living. It's the same for Miss Kaprálová. She has a great talent and who knows how she could live at home now after all the time that she's been here on a stipendium. I'm concerned about her. She's in good health – that's one thing she doesn't have to worry about[226] and, as far as her plans go, it's all in the stars. I think she most probably wrote home and gave them a bit of a fright, so I can understand that they're worried. But don't set your mind on it. And live in peace while you can! Lay in some food that can be stored away. And, as for me, be sure that I'd write you myself about what I wanted to do, but not until something is arranged definitely, because for now everything is unclear and it isn't possible to make a decision about anything. I only tell you this so you can calmly wait until time and fate bring what they will bring. Anyway – even if we went to America it wouldn't be forever and, in the meantime – as I write – it's not even a question. At all events it would cost a lot of money that I don't have, and up to now I haven't heard anything from there, not even any news. So just take care of yourselves and don't even think about what will be. We're all in the same situation now. It's even possible I'll be able to go back to Prague.[227] For Charlotte the return would surely be even harder because she's French. But it's all in the stars and what's meant to be will be and we can't change things. Just don't worry! You know I'll think over carefully what would be best for all of us. So be calm! Mum should take care of herself and not worry about what's going on in the world. We can't change anything and maybe the Good Lord won't abandon us and we'll see each other even sooner perhaps than we had thought. My love to Mum! I wish her lots of good health and mostly that she not worry unnecessarily and that she wait to see what I decide.

Love,
Your Bohouš

P.S. If you send a slightly heavier letter they usually look to see if there's money in the envelope, so don't put anything other than a letter in it!

---

[226] Martinů's optimism was wildly misplaced: Kaprálová died only a little over a year later, on 16 May 1940, apparently from miliary tuberculosis.

[227] A comforting word for his mother, brother and sister. In reality, Martinů had no illusions about returning or about the future course of his life.

LETTER 40

To his Family
[Paris] 15 May [1939]

My dear ones,

Your letter of the 8th of this month came and I thought how nice the programme about Polička must have been. There was a mention of it in the magazine *Zlín* of May 10th in the article about the Mácha Festival.[228] That must also have been quite nice. I sent a short article to them. They may want to publish it. Their article was so beautifully written that I had to respond to it.[229] On Monday the 9th were the *Ricercari*[230] which had been played in Venice, and it was a huge success here – an absolute triumph! There was a big applause after each movement and it went on and on when it was over. I had to take a bow again and again and everyone was so excited that they couldn't talk about anything else! In short, it was a lovely evening. We thought of you and we were sorry you weren't able to hear it. It wasn't broadcast, but you'll certainly hear it from somewhere, because it will be published soon[231] and will surely be played everywhere and often. After the slow second movement, people couldn't restrain themselves and started to comment out loud. That's wonderful, except that you usually don't show your appreciation until it's over!

There are a lot of people here too who, when they found out that I want to go to America said they can't let me leave – that I've already done so much in Paris, for French culture, and for their music that I really already belong to the history of music in Paris and no doubt in the most prominent place and that it's not possible that I would leave them now. They're almost envious of my going to America, although I'm not going there yet, but they say they have to find me some position here so I won't have to leave, and that they won't permit me to work anywhere else now. So you see that I wouldn't get lost anywhere and that they would appreciate me more than in my own country. But there, too, it seems they already appreciate what I stand for. The wind has already shifted according to all the news that I'm getting, and now they're sorry, too, that I'd have to go away and teach somewhere other than in my own country. It's only that it's complicated now, of course. But I'm sure that I'd find a career soon enough in America – they say I have even a bigger name there than here. One must never despair – work always pays off somewhere and maybe it will finally turn out well and I could come back to Prague, which I would be the

---

[228] K. T., 'Zač vděčíme Máchovi' ('What we owe to Mácha'), *Zlín*, Vol. VIII, 1939, No. 19, 10 May, p. 4. The article examines, among other things, a radio broadcast about Polička (*Prague Station*, 30 April 1939). Martinů was especially intrigued by the part dedicated to him and to the tower of the Polička. On 7 May 1939, only shortly before the annexation of Litoměřice to the Third Reich, the remains of the most eminent Czech poet Karel Hynek Mácha (1810–36) were transferred from Litoměřice to the Pantheon in Prague. The funeral ceremony turned into a massive demonstration against the Nazi occupation. Václav Sommer (*cf.* note 90 on p. 51, above) directed the broadcast.

[229] He wrote a letter from Paris, dated 17 May 1939, which was published in the weekly *Zlín*, Vol. VIII, 1939, No. 21, 24 May, p. 5.

[230] *Tre Ricercari* was performed for the first time by the Société Triton on Monday, 8 May (not, as here, on 9 May) 1939, under Charles Munch.

[231] By Boosey & Hawkes.

happiest doing, and it would be best to be at home and near to you and so that our people would again benefit from what I can do. We must bide our time until everything is turned around. I think that even if I went to Prague they'd be sorry about it here. If I really wanted to ask for something here, I could certainly have something in the way of a career, and if I had wanted to be naturalised, I would long ago have been professor at a conservatory somewhere and have been well provided for and appreciated. But for all that, my deepest longings remain for my home.

As for the money, I'll be informed by the National Bank. I suppose it's going to be difficult. The next time you're in town, ask at the savings bank if it's possible to transfer funds without difficulty (possibly from a savings bank to the National Bank or to some other bank in Prague) in case they'd permit me, so it could be taken care of in Prague.[232] But that probably won't come into consideration in the near future. It's only for your information, because no one can say now what will be in days to come. I wonder if you've been able to buy anything to store away for the future.

I send my love. Don't worry unnecessarily. There are plenty of real things to worry about, and that's quite enough. Charlotte sends her love, too. We think about you often.

Your Bohouš

LETTER 41
To his Family
[Paris] 1 June 1939

My dear ones,

Your letter came, and we hope that everything is better with you and that Mum is well again. She can't always take such thoughts too much to heart – like never seeing each other again[233] – and, anyway, perhaps things will change for the better. You know that I would like nothing better than to be at home and that a situation like this, which is always strained, can't last long and will perhaps be resolved so I can return to Prague.[234] The most important thing is that Mum get better and that she be able to get a rest. We were at Vieux Moulin for a couple of days during the holidays, so I also got a little rest – even though I'm not doing much right now, but all this would tire anybody out – and there's a heat wave here now. We don't know, either, what we're going to do over the holidays. I think we'll go to Vieux Moulin, except that I'd have to do some work here. About America, it's going very slowly, and in summer I really wouldn't have anything to do there, anyway.

I remember it was just one year ago that I was getting ready for the rally and how beautiful it was and how even after a couple of days at home and at Tři Studně I came back again refreshed. Everything has changed, and it will probably be an

---

[232] He was considering transferring his financial assets, which were in a bank in the Protectorate, to a bank abroad.

[233] She was not mistaken.

[234] Again, as often before, merely a comforting word.

unhappy vacation if not something worse. They broadcast the *Bouquet*[235] from Prague – did you hear it? We don't get much nowadays, and so we haven't heard anything. They're going to play the Trio[236] here on Saturday. The season is in full swing here now – all concerts and guests – they're full everywhere. We get together with Czechs more often now and we tell each other the unhappy news. Was my article in the magazine *Zlín*? We think of you constantly and of all our friends and of what you're doing. I suppose everyone has a lot of worries. Stáňa probably doesn't know either if he's coming or going. Who knows whether they'll separate.[237] We all have something to worry about.

As for the money, I'll write to the National Bank to find out if they could send it there.[238] But I can't promise much. It might be difficult, but I'll try, anyway. We've all had lots of worries. We were all doing quite well, and I was already so much looking forward to arranging things so that everything would be a little calmer, but it seems to me it's not my destiny. If it works out with America, there would be new hopes again, but it's just far away. The news nowadays goes so quickly from good to bad and back and the situation changes with every passing day. Who knows what will be.

We send our love. We think of you often.

Your Bohouš

LETTER 42[239]

To his Family
[Paris] 22 October 1939[240]

My dear ones,

I know you've been waiting for news from me, but I don't want to write about much of anything. We came back home again. Outside it's already started to get cold. A lot has changed here – there are fewer people – in the evening the streets are dark. But otherwise, life is as it was – things are no more expensive than they were. I

[235] The cantata *Kytice* ('Bouquet of Flowers'), H260, composed in 1937.

[236] It was probably *Bergerettes*, H275, for violin, cello and piano which were performed on Saturday, 7 June 1939: the work had been completed on 20 February that year. But *Bergerettes* is only one of the eleven compositions for various combinations of three instruments Martinů composed before June 1939, and in view of the incomplete nature of the archives one cannot be certain.

[237] To avoid prison Stanislav Novák was forced by law in the Protectorate to separate from his Jewish wife (*née* Brandlová). She and her two daughters were later murdered in Auschwitz. When Novák discovered their probable fate, he died, a broken man, on 25 June 1945.

[238] *Cf.* note 232 on p. 79, above.

[239] Charlotte Martinů added a postscript.

[240] After the invasion of Poland by the German army on 1 September 1939, Britain declared war on Germany on 3 September and France followed suit on the same day. From then until January 1941, when Martinů left France, he maintained written contact with his family through neutral Switzerland. Correspondence, conducted partly in French, was delivered by Paul Sacher. In the heading of the letters, Martinů either didn't bother to write his address or wrote the names of various Swiss localities. He did not write directly to his family again before a postcard from Lisbon dated 12 January 1941, and postmarked 15 January.

might be going to have some job at the radio station and, if conditions get worse, we'll go back again[241] – or else we'll be invited somewhere. For now, I don't have any other obligations and might not be going to have any. I may be needed for other things, though, so I'll keep working. It's not easy to concentrate on composing, but a person has to force himself a little, and so I've begun to write a *Field Mass* for male chorus,[242] and I'll be done with it soon. I already told Talich, and I hope that I'll get copies of it there.

We think about you a lot – about what you're doing and whether you don't lack for a lot of things for a contented life, but you know we can only imagine what it must be like there – that it's more peaceful in the countryside. One can't help worrying. We think about you constantly and recall our little house – about what might have changed and how happy I would be to be able to come for a visit. I will send the *Mass* to a radio station in England, and it's going to be done here, too.[243] Otherwise, of course, all the programmes have changed and for now only the radio is working. But in Basel, there will be the premiere of the *Double Concerto*[244] and there'll be something in Geneva. Here and in London they're only just now planning the season, but I'll be represented there, too. I wanted to write to tell you that I got some news about the prize in Brno[245] and that even some members of the trusteeship themselves protested the decision on the basis of the fact that the whole thing was badly described to them. So, I'm curious what will come of it, although in these times who knows how anything will turn out. I have no news from Šafránek,[246] but his good friend was here and I spoke with him.[247] They're counting on me a lot, because he's convinced I have a good reputation abroad.

As for my health, it isn't bad, although we've both lost some weight, which isn't so strange – we all have! Otherwise we've been living quite normally – as if nothing had happened. It's worse with the publisher because now, of course, nothing will be published, and so it didn't work out with the publishing house in London,[248] but they nevertheless enlisted me for as soon as everything calms down. Dushkin will probably do the *Suite*[249] in America – he hasn't written either – and I have a

[241] To Vieux Moulin.

[242] The cantata *Field Mass*, H279, for solo baritone, male chorus and small orchestra.

[243] It was heard in Prague for the first time only after the War, in a performance by the baritone Theodor Šrubař and the Czech Philharmonic under Rafael Kubelík on 1 March 1946.

[244] *Concerto for Two String Orchestras, Piano and Timpani*, H271.

[245] The annual jubilee prize of the Smetana Foundation (the Board of Trustees of the Foundation was located in Brno). The judging committee was comprised of Antonín Balatka, Jaroslav Kvapil and František Pícha. Martinů was completely passed over. The prize of 10,000 crowns was shared by Boleslav Vomáčka and Osvald Chlubna.

[246] He was already in the USA.

[247] Undoubtedly Edvard Beneš, who travelled from London to Paris on 6 October 1939 for a few days of negotiations.

[248] Apparently he was counting on more reliable co-operation with Boosey & Hawkes. The company (already based in both London and New York) published Martinů's works especially in the second half of the 1940s and in the first half of the 1950s: for example, all six symphonies, the *Double Concerto* and the operas *Comedy on the Bridge*, *What Men Live By*, H336, and *The Marriage*.

[249] He did not perform the work until 1943.

great recommendation to Toscanini.[250] I probably lost the chance of Talich for the premiere of the *Ricercari* on 9th October. Unfortunately he couldn't be given the orchestral parts.

Is the radio sometimes playing something of mine?[251] Write to me by way of Basel. But the mail is moving slowly, so don't be upset if you don't hear from me for a long time and don't worry about us. If I were able to write more, I'd do it, mainly so you'd know that we're both well and that I continue to work and that in spite of all the news I'm in constant contact with my publishers and that we think about you and wonder what you're doing and that of course you probably think the same about us. For the time being we have to be content with letters even if it's possible to write only now and then. Say hello to all our friends for us. I get the news from them now and then, too. Don't worry about us at all. We hope that it'll all be over soon and that we'll see each other as soon as it becomes possible.

Love,
Your Bohouš

LETTER 43[252]

To his Family
Basel,[253] 10 February 1940

My dear ones,

I'm sure you've been waiting impatiently for a letter from me. Both of yours came – only the Christmas letter was lost. We, too, have been alarmed at what's been happening, and I don't want to write too often – if only we can know at least that you're well and that you know that we are, too. That's about all we can say and all we can hope for. You'll be happy to hear that yesterday was the premiere of the *Double concerto for strings*[254] here and that I had a big success. It was beautiful, and it was beautifully played. The rehearsals started on Monday. We're in the villa again like the year before last,[255] when I wrote the piece. It's quite nice here and we're probably going to stay until Monday. Everyone was enthusiastic and critics came from Geneva and even people from Berne. I can't describe it to you! It's going to be played in Berne and it will be broadcast from Basel. If I find out in time, I'll tell you the date or I'll ask Sacher to let you know. So, we got a breath of fresh air and some rest here. It's been a couple of beautiful days among good people. We're happy, too,

---

[250] Toscanini (1867–1957), then engaged in the USA, never conducted any of Martinů's works.

[251] After 15 March 1939 Martinů's music was performed in his own country only sporadically and soon it completely disappeared from the programmes. Of the few performances at the time, there might be mentioned that of 25 May 1940, when the *Intermezzo* (four pieces for violin and piano), H261, was heard in Polička. That may have been the last public performance of a Martinů work during the occupation.

[252] A letter from Charlotte Martinů was written on the other side.

[253] In this case, not a fictitious address: Martinů was in Switzerland at this time. During the 'phony war', before the occupation of France, he was still able to go there.

[254] In a performance by the Basel Chamber Orchestra under Paul Sacher, in Basel on 9 February 1940. It was the first in a series of premieres of Martinů's compositions that Sacher was to conduct.

[255] At Schönenberg, to which he returned after the War.

that things are all right with you and that your friends haven't forgotten about you.

Tell me in your next letter whether the money you have is available to you and whether you can withdraw whatever you want whenever you want or if you only receive it in small amounts. I say this because I don't know what you need and what you're able to buy.

The snow is already gone here, too, and winter will be over soon. It was quite cold this year, but maybe it's done with now. Mrs Leroux played the Piano Concerto with Orchestra[256] in New York, and I'm waiting for news of it.

I send my love, and I'm glad to have had good news of your health. I think of you a lot, even if I'm not able to write so often.

Love,
Your Bohouš

P.S. Do you know what became of Vanda Jakubíčková? Do you know where she is?[257]

LETTER 44[258]

To his Family
[Aix-en-Provence[259]] 17 October 1940

My dear ones,

We got your letter, and I'm glad that you heard my *Double Concerto*[260] on the radio. We listened to it, too, and I hope you understood what the music wanted to express. I'm doing a lot of work – they already asked me for a new composition[261] in America, and I've hardly begun it. Work is going well, but I think I'll lose a lot of time in the next few days, because Charlotte and I want to take a trip,[262] so there won't be much opportunity for work. We think about you a lot. We're well. It hasn't turned cold yet. I hope that Fanouš will come back soon, which would make everything happier at home. We have a lot more news from you than from Charlotte's parents – really none. Time is passing quickly and at work even more quickly. I'll probably send you a new address soon. The main thing is not to worry about us. We've made a lot of good friends who take care of us a little everywhere,[263] and if we're well and have almost everything we need and I'm able to work, everything will be all right. There

---

[256] The Second Piano Concerto.

[257] She had stayed in London and returned to Polička after the War.

[258] Written in French.

[259] Sent to Polička by way of Switzerland. After fleeing Paris before the arrival of the German army, they waited in Aix four months for an exit visa until their departure for Lisbon and thence for New York.

[260] On Radio Basel.

[261] *Sinfonietta Giocosa* for piano and small orchestra, H282: *cf.* note 112 on p. 54, above.

[262] Apparently to the French-Spanish border, where they sounded out the possibilty of leaving France illegally. They later made the journey legally.

[263] Especially Paul Sacher. In the Geneva music journal *Dissonances* in October 1940 an appeal was published asking for substantial support for Martinů, although his name, for understandable reasons, was not mentioned. In the end the Sachers paid the Martinůs' passage to the USA themselves.

*Paris, 1934: Martinů and
his wife with the painter
Jan Zrzavý (left) and writer
Vítězslav Nezval (right;
1900–58) – whose musician
father had studied with
Janáček*

really isn't any reason to worry – especially Mum. She should take good care of
herself and not overdo and try to look on the bright side of things.

Charlotte joins me in sending our love. We think of you all the time.

Your Bohouš

LETTER 45[264]
To his Family
[Aix-en-Provence] 8 December 1940

My dear ones,

Today we celebrated my fiftieth birthday! I'm sure that you were thinking about us
and that you would be happy to know how we are and that you would wish we were
at home. We also think of you constantly – of Mum. How is she? Is she still in the
hospital? I hope she'll be home for Christmas. We send you our good wishes for
Christmas and the New Year – that it will bring all of us a little happiness and, also,
what we all wish – that we'll soon be together. We're fine. I'm working a lot. I have
some commissions and a lot of friends who take an interest in my future, some of
whom I don't even know. All that gives me courage, and I'm certain now that good
days are coming. We must always hope so.

Did they play anything of mine on Prague Radio? We read that Kubelík died.[265]
Are they going to do *Špalíček* in Plzeň, as I heard?[266] I'm writing you again about the
money. Take of it as much as you need, especially for Christmas and for coal – don't
be sparing for my sake. Buy yourselves some nice things. We'll be far away,[267] but
we'll be with you in our thoughts. Mum should take it easy and not exert herself.

We send our love and good wishes.

We think of you often.
Bohouš

---

[264] Written in French. Charlotte Martinů added a long postscript.

[265] The violinist Jan Kubelík (father of the conductor-composer Rafael), on 5 December 1940, at the age
of 60.

[266] The performance did not take place.

[267] In the USA. It was the last letter from France before the journey to Lisbon and beyond.

LETTER 46[268]

To his Family

Lisbon, 14 March 1941[269]

My dear ones,

I know you've been patiently waiting for news from us. I didn't want to write before we left,[270] but I sent you three packages – coffee, chocolate, and soap. Did you get them already? And our postcards from Madrid and Lisbon? We've found friends everywhere and people who know me, which makes a person feel good. It's too bad that it was cold and that everything was under snow in Spain – we didn't see much of the country. It's beautiful here, but it's rained the whole time. We'll leave in a couple of days.[271] We were compelled to wait here a long time. Lots of people have drifted away, but now we have seats reserved and we're leaving. They're waiting for us there already. I got a telegram about a concert in February by the Society for Contemporary Music. Unfortunately, I wasn't able to come in time, but there will be other concerts – with Germaine [Leroux] and Ruda [Firkušný], who is already there. Sacher asked me for a violin concerto[272] and Dushkin is there with the *Suite Concertante*. Ansermet[273] gave the *Double Concerto* in Geneva. The reviews were excellent, and I'm sure that new works will be commissioned there, and I would like to continue working. All of us were very much shocked by the events, but now it will be better.[274] We've managed to get a rest. I was glad to meet Mr Psota here – the choreographer from Brno[275] concocted plans for us in America and he told me the news. Before we leave I'll send you some more chocolate and coffee. You surely must need it. I got news that they're giving *Comedy on the Bridge*[276] on the radio. I think I'll be able to write you now and you, too, only that the mail goes slowly nowadays. We must have patience, but the most important thing is that you know we're well, and I hope you're doing well, too. The winter must have been very hard for everyone this year.

---

[268] Charlotte Martinů added a lengthy postscript.

[269] The very same day, Martinů wrote another letter home with similar wording. He obviously wanted to be sure that at least one of them would arrive. Both did.

[270] For understandable reasons. He did not want to reveal to the authorities of the Protectorate, and especially the German authorities, the location of his residence at the time (it lasted more than two months). He acted appropriately, without being fully able at the time to know the risks involved in his situation: shortly before the occupation of Paris by the German forces in the summer of 1940, the Gestapo was searching for him in his last Paris apartment. Martinů discoved this fact only after the War. The regime of the Portuguese dictator António de Oliveira Salazar was well-disposed toward Nazi Germany.

[271] They sailed for New York on the *Exeter* on 21 March 1941.

[272] *Concerto da camera* for violin and string orchestra with piano and percussion, H285, composed in 1941 in the USA.

[273] Ernest Ansermet (1883–1969), outstanding Swiss conductor. In 1918 he founded the Orchestre de la Suisse Romande in Geneva, remaining its Music Director until 1967.

[274] Presumably the outbreak of war and the fall of France.

[275] Ivo Váňa Psota (1908–52), dancer and choreographer. During his engagement in Brno, he choreographed *Theatre behind the Gate,* among other works. During the War he achieved renown in North and South America.

[276] The news was incorrect.

Martinů's letter (45) of 12 December 1940 to his family – written in French because of censorship – from Aix-en-Provence, by way of Basel, with postscript by Charlotte Martinů

nous serrons encore les jours heureux, il faut toujours espérer. Est-ce qu'on a joué quelque chose à Prague à la Radio? Nous avons lu que Kubelik est mort. On m'a dit qu'on va donner Spalicek. Plein? Je vous écris de nouveau pour l'argent, prenez tous ce que vous avez besoin surtout pour Noël, et pour Carlson, ne faites pas des économies pour moi, achetez de bonnes choses nous serons bien loin mais dans notre pensée avec vous dans la petite maison et que maman se soigne bien et fait attention à elle de ne pas se fatiguer trop. Nous vous envoions nos meilleurs souvenirs et nos vœux, pensons à vous.

Chères Manny et Pedro.
Marienka.
Bohus avait le pressentiment que Manny était malade. J'espère que maintenant, elle est déjà à la maison mais que de soucis pour vous, chère Marienka, nous pensons sans cesse à vous, surtout en ces jours de fête, nous espérons bien qu'un jour, nous serons tous de nouveau réunis, j'ai de brèves nouvelles de ma famille, ils vont bien tous.

You can write to Šebánek[277] – Národní obrany 31/II, Praha-Bubeneč and let him know that I left and that in regard to the score of *Juliette*, I have to have it at my disposal. I'm going to need it there, but I don't want to take a risk with sending the manuscript. He will have to find a way to make a copy of the score and ask Talich for advice about who could pay for the copy. It's not urgent, because it always takes a long time with the theatre, but I would like him to begin with a copy because it will be a lot of work. I'll write to him, but you write to him, too, so they can get started with the copying – it always takes a long time. I'm sure that I'll succeed in placing the work in America, and I wouldn't want him to send the manuscript in these uncertain times.[278] Tell him, too, to give Talich and Stáňa our best regards. I'd be happy if he'd play the *Double Concerto* in Prague. It would be a sensation! You can also tell him that the Philharmonic or Talich could ask Sacher to *lend* them the score for a few days and to make do with the material. I think it's possible to send scores from Switzerland. I'm convinced that they'd really like it in Prague, and I very much wish they'd play it there now.[279] Write everything to Šebánek, and I'll write to him, too.

[277] Karel Šebánek (1903–80), a Prague music-publisher. He began as a bookseller, and worked with Mojmír Urbánek, then in the Hudební matice Umělecké besedy (a publishing company of the Czech Society of Artists), eventually becoming director of the music department of the publishing company Melantrich (which published musical scores between 1936 and 1949). After nationalisation, he served as director of the State Music Publishing House Orbis from 1949 to 1952. In 1956 he became director of the Central Music Archive of the Czech Music Fund. Already in the mid-1930s, he recognised the artistic merit and the potential commercial value of Martinů's work beyond the borders of the domestic market and attempted to make a contractual arrangement with the composer, especially in his position at Melantrich (Editions Melpa) and later in other places where he was employed. Thanks to him in particular, a series of compositions by Martinů was published in Czechoslovakia, although the repressive cultural policies of the Protectorate between 1939 and 1945 blocked his efforts to get Martinů's works published, and after 1949 their temporary repudiation hindered his efforts. He was able to resume the promotion of Martinů's music in modest terms after the mid-1950s at the Czech Music Fund. Šebánek's efforts (which never were allowed to result in actual business) bear witness to the borders of the discontinuity of Czech Martinů publishing activity and the ways in which his music was repudiated in Czechoslovakia. Martinů and Šebánek met in Prague in the 1930s and saw each other in particular at the end of that decade in Paris, where Šebánek was apprenticed to a number of music-publishing companies, among others Leduc, at that time the principal Paris publisher of Martinů's works. They met in Paris again after the end of the War. Relations between the composer and Šebánek represent one of the variants of the traditionally contradictory relations between an author and his or her publisher. In this case, the relationship did not suffer from the pressures of business, and it was less Šebánek's difficult character than restrictions imposed by circumstances that made it impossible for him to publish those works that were as yet unpublished and to export them worldwide, and also to exploit commercially those that were already published. Šebánek's lack of success, even though he was disposed to a wide, perhaps even worldwide, enterprise in editions of Martinů's work, tellingly documents how frustrating the possibilities of the Czech music-publishing industry were after February 1948. Thus, as *pars pro toto*, Šebánek led an unfulfilled but active life.

[278] He obtained the score from Prague only after the War, but nevertheless *Juliette* has not been performed in the United States to this day.

[279] The *Double Concerto* was not performed in Prague until 24 April 1947 (by the Czech Philharmonic Orchestra under Paul Sacher). Martinů obviously did not have an accurate perception of the cultural situation in the Protectorate, nor could he have been expected to.

*Paris, 1938: in front of Martinů is the publisher Karel Šebánek
and behind him the pianists Rudolf Firkušný and Josef Páleníček*

We think of you a lot in these sad and uncertain times, and there are many things I'd like to send you, but it's impossible. There was a big tornado here – perhaps you read about it in the newspapers. It's sad to be without news of you. Now I'll be able to write directly and to keep you informed regularly about what we're doing, but it will take a long time before the letters come.

What is Stáňa doing and my dear friends at home? – and Honzíček?[280] Say hello to them for us. I'm leaving space for Charlotte. We send our love and best wishes.

Bohouš

[280] No fewer than three Polička friends of Martinů had the name Jan (colloquially, Honza or Honzíček): Jílek, to whom he dedicated his 1920 piano piece *Foxtrot*, н126 *bis*; Novotný, for whom he wrote the piano piece *Black Bottom*, н165, during the summer vacation of 1927; and Janele, the brother of Vlasta Janelová, Polička teacher, a good singer and pianist, thanks to whom copies of a number of songs of Martinů from the 1910s have been preserved in Polička.

AMERICA
AND EXILE
1941–53

The nerve-wracking escape of Bohuslav and Charlotte Martinů from occupied Europe to the USA marked the sharpest change in the composer's life. He lost all income from performances of his works, which were forbidden in Nazi-occupied Europe. Having taken only four of his scores with him (*Juliette*, H253; the *Concerto grosso*, H263; the *Sinfonietta giocosa*; and the Piano Concerto No. 2), he had just a few months to establish himself as a composer and start earning money. It has occasionally been suggested[1] that his new working conditions had a major influence on the change in his musical style. But the first signs of this new style, which is oriented towards more prominent melody, less dissonant harmony, clearer structures and an affinity for symphonic music, had already appeared in the years immediately before his emigration; and the successful first performance of his *Concerto Grosso* in 1941 and the First Symphony, H289, in 1942, both in Boston, as well as the large number of professional orchestras in the United States played a crucial role in his inclination toward the symphony and symphonic music.

Notwithstanding his success with orchestral and chamber music, Martinů had to look for other sources of income and so he was happy to accept, for the first time in his life, various teaching positions – at the Mannes School of Music, music-courses at Tanglewood (the summer home of the Boston Symphony Orchestra), and later also at Princeton, at the Curtis Institute in Philadelphia and finally, after the War, at the American Academy in Rome.

Having lost his European publishers, Martinů signed a new contract with Boosey & Hawkes in New York. Starting from 1942 (and the Mazurka, H284), Boosey & Hawkes published some of his finest scores, including the *Double Concerto*, the *Toccata e due canzoni*, H311, and the entire series of six symphonies. The Second Symphony, H295, dedicated 'To my countrymen-workers in Cleveland', was premiered on 28 October 1943, the 25th Czechoslovak Independence Day. During the Second World War Martinů remained an official representative of Czechoslovakia (the government-in-exile under Edvard Beneš paid him a monthly stipend), which was suffering under the Nazi 'Protectorate' of Bohemia and Moravia, and he was seen by the American government as well as by audiences in general as the representative of an allied country. That view changed shortly after the end of the War. Although he was willing to return to his homeland with the return of peace, he first, in 1946, accepted a teaching position at the Summer Music School in Tanglewood. There, on 17 July 1946, he suffered a serious accident, requiring several weeks in hospital; he was dependent on medication for years

[1] For example, by Ernst Krenek in his article 'America's Influence on its Émigré Composers', *Perspectives of New Music*, Vol. 8, No. 2, Spring-Summer 1970, pp. 112–17.

thereafter. The communist putsch in Czechoslovakia in February 1948 then made a return home unthinkable, so that Martinů remained in the USA. But it was now a different country from the one he had experienced in the early 1940s. His origins, in what was now a communist country, automatically made Martinů suspect as a possible enemy, especially in the America of the McCarthy era.

Compounding his problems, at the same time all his works were banned from the concert hall in Czechoslovakia and he was treated in the communist press as a 'traitor' and 'renegade'. Nor was it simply his stay in the USA, where he received American citizenship in 1952, that made Martinů a non-person in Czech musical life: the so-called 'Zhdanov aesthetic' of 'socialist realism' was utterly opposed to the complexity of Martinů's scores. During the closing years of the Stalin era, under his Czechoslovak counterpart Klement Gottwald, from 1949 until 1955 there were almost no performances of Martinů's works in Czechoslovakia. Piling Ossa upon Pelion, the simultaneous rise of musical modernism, represented especially by the Darmstadt school, marginalised Martinů and seemed to make his music outdated. Hardly surprisingly, he felt a growing sense of alienation and disappointment, which can be discerned in his letters from the 1950s.

Aleš Březina

LETTER 47[2]

To his Family
[New York] 14 April 1941[3]

My dear ones,

I'm sure you've been waiting impatiently for news from us, so I hasten to write, even though I have a lot to do in these new surroundings. We got here all right, although it was quite rough at sea, and our friends were there waiting for us.[4] I was nicely received here – like a great composer. There were pictures, and The League of American Composers gave a reception in my honour. It was quite lovely, and I'm really surprised at the reputation I have here. On Sunday, my friends are giving another big reception for me. I've run into a lot of them from Paris and Prague here. One day I'll describe our voyage to you and the ship. You'll certainly find it interesting – and about what life is like here and about the city. The trip was very expensive. Imagine! We spent almost 6,000 French francs a day and that for a period of ten days, and Charlotte was sick and couldn't have any of the good things to eat. Our friends, whom you know, paid everything,[5] even our stay in Lisbon, and I got a request for another composition.[6] I have to tell you that it wasn't very good in the last days there, but after a few days here we completely recovered and I now feel quite well. My work should also go well now. They're giving the world premiere of the *Concerto Grosso*[7] in Boston on April 24th. Koussevitsky[8] is conducting and Boston has the best orchestra in America.[9] All the orchestras here are quite good, and they're in all the major cities.

I got your letter, and we were very glad to have some news from you. We hope that Mum is coming along well. We think about you constantly. In spring everything will be easier than it was this winter, which was hard everywhere. So be at ease as far as we're concerned – everything will go well and I'll be able to work again. They're waiting for a lot of things from me here, and I have enough courage to go on. Did you get the packages of coffee and chocolate that I sent from Lisbon? I gave

---

[2] Written in French.

[3] It was his first letter home from the USA.

[4] Miloš Šafránek and his wife Germaine Leroux, Samuel Dushkin and Consul Hejný.

[5] Paul and Maja Sacher.

[6] He most probably had in mind the *Concerto da camera* for Paul Sacher.

[7] *Concerto Grosso* for chamber orchestra, H263, composed in 1937. Its premiere in Boston did not take place until the following season, on 14 November 1941.

[8] Serge Koussevitsky (1874–1951), Musical Director of the Boston Symphony Orchestra.

[9] He was not exaggerating. The Boston Symphony was, under Koussevitsky's direction (from 1924), and later under Charles Munch (from 1948), the leading American symphony orchestra. It was the 'mother' orchestra of the 'American' Martinů of the time, for which he wrote a number of outstanding works. As early as 1927, the Boston Symphony Orchestra gave the first performance of *La Bagarre*, and then, in the 1940s and '50s, a series of other large works of Martinů, commissioned by Koussevitsky and then Munch.

PASSENGER'S RECEIPT AND COPY OF THE TRANSPORTATION CONTRACT	AMERICAN EXPORT LINES, Inc.	B

No. 51076

Passage Paid . $	700,-
Shore Excursions	
Port Tax . . .	39,30
Head Tax . . .	16,-
U. S. Tax . . .	
TOTAL . $	755,30

STOPOVERS: Stopovers may be arranged at any one or more ports of call enroute to port of final destination given below and within one year from date of sailing from original port of embarkation.

Date Issued **Mar 18th 1941**
At **Lisbon**
By **R/Mendonça**
Issuing Agent **Joh Beckmann**

THIS COUPON IS TO BE RETAINED BY PASSENGER FOR IDENTIFICATION PURPOSES, AND IS NOT VALID FOR PASSAGE.

COPY OF THE CONTRACT

In consideration of the sum of money stated above AMERICAN EXPORT LINES, Inc., hereinafter referred to as the Carrier, agrees to transport, subject to the terms of this contract, the passenger or passengers, male or female, named, hereinafter referred to as the Passenger, on the voyage and with the accommodations, as follows:

FROM **Lisbon** TO **New York** VIA   S.O.
S/S **EXETER** VOY. **70** SAILING **Mar 21st** HOUR **M.** RM. BERTH. BASIS In Room

FORWARD RESERVATIONS

FROM	DATE	TO	S/S	VOY.	ROOM	Berth	Basis
Voucher Müller Basel № 2 value $ 740							
Balance paid in Lisbon $ 15.30							

NAMES OF PASSENGERS		SEX	AGE	PASSENGER'S ADDRESS
Mr Bohuslav	MARTINU	M	A	
Mrs Charlotte	MARTINU	F	A	

ADULTS 2	CHILDREN.	INFANTS	SERVANTS	NAT. **French**	OCC.

(CONTINUED ON INSIDE OF COVER)

From Lisbon to New York, 21 March 1941: receipt for payment of fare on the S. S. Exeter

instructions for them to send you a couple of packages from time to time – I hope you'll get them. I hope, too, that I'll be able to write you more often so you'll always be informed of my work, and I also hope that things will be all right at home with Mum's health and with all of you. My address is the same: 120 West 57th Street. Write me the news of yourselves. I'll be glad when I know what you're doing. And don't be afraid to spend money!

> We both send a big hug.
> Your Bohouš

LETTER 48[10]

To his Family

[Edgartown, Martha's Vineyard, Mass.] 27 August 1941

My dear ones,

Your letter came today. We're always overjoyed when we get news from you. We think of you constantly, and I would like to write more often so you'd know about

---

[10] Charlotte Martinů added a postscript.

us, too.[11] We're still on the island,[12] and I've completed the violin concerto[13] for Sacher. I also got some good news from him in which he mentions that you wrote to him. The concert will be on the 23rd of January.[14] He also wants to conduct my piano concerto[15] on Radio Geneva. We have a lot of new friends here. Americans are fantastic people and everything is in such abundance here it's almost unbelievable. I wish I were able to send you something, but unfortunately that's not possible. They have everything you can imagine here – they are blessed by nature, and people are very kind. We were with the Šafráneks at their summer place and at the music festival in the Berkshires, where I spoke with Koussevitsky and with lots of artists. I have a good reputation here. They played my quartet and it was a great success. Emanuel Ondříček[16] invited us there. We'll stay until the 15th of September. I don't know our address in New York. We're going to look for an apartment, but you can write to the old address – Hotel St. Hubert, 120 West 57th Street, New York City, N.Y., U.S.A. We also got news from Charlotte's mum. They know we're here and they're all together, and that's all. Write to Šebánek and ask if he'd be so kind as to give my regards to Mrs Ludmila Brázdová at Spořilov 1176, Prague, and to ask how they are. I got his letter, but I don't want to write much directly.

You asked about the voyage. We had some severe storms when we thought the boat would capsize. You can't imagine what the ocean is like when it's let loose. It doesn't put one in an admiring mood! Charlotte was constantly ill and I was only so-so, so that when we arrived the earth was spinning and when I lay down on the bed everything began to sway. The ship wasn't all that big. There were also a few days of calm seas and that was very beautiful. The wind was always quite strong, especially on the top deck, and anyone who wasn't sick would do nothing but sleep all the time. But all that's far behind us. We're already getting used to things here, but it's very different from Europe, and I think we'll come back before we get completely accustomed to it. I wrote to Lisbon asking that they again send you some packages. It doesn't matter that it will cost you a few crowns, because at least you'll have a little coffee and chocolate for the winter. I hope they'll send it soon.

I'm not able to tell you everything that we're doing here and how it looks. It would be too long a letter and it might get lost. We think a lot about our homeland and about all of you with the news we hear and we both look forward to coming back to our forests. Do you know anything of Stáňa and Zrzavý – what they're doing? I hear that Stáňa got divorced from Fanynka.[17] English is quite difficult, but I'll get it. We communicate in French a lot, and there are a lot of our countrymen here. It's a strange feeling seeing everything at such a distance. It's a year from today that we left without a goal and not knowing where it would take us. But now we're doing

---

[11] Correspondence between the United States and the Protectorate was carried on without difficulty and with a rapidity which seems remarkable to this day. At the time, the war was in its second year.

[12] Martha's Vineyard is an island off the coast of Massachusetts. Edgartown, from where Martinů was writing, was used as the location for the film *Jaws* in 1975.

[13] *Concerto da camera.*

[14] 1942.

[15] Apparently the Second Piano Concerto.

[16] Emanuel Ondříček (1880–1958), violinist, brother of renowned violinist František Ondříček. From 1910 he worked in the USA, especially as a violin teacher in Boston and New York.

[17] *Cf.* note 237 on p. 80, above.

An undated clipping of Martinů with Rudolf Firkušný
in New York around 1943

well and, after all, I'll get the position at the conservatory and maybe quite soon.[18]
First I have to get through the winter, learn to speak English, and get to know a lot
of new people and have a lot of new experiences. I'll write more often now. The mail
goes a lot better by air. I think I got all your letters, and so I'll call this number 1. The
Bécourt[19] address is good. I hope they'll answer. I'm glad you're all well, especially
Mum. I hope most of all that she'll take it easy and let's hope we'll all be well when
we meet again.

We think about you all the time and about how you're doing. We send you our
love and good wishes. I'll write and let you know what they're planning for next
season and what they're going to play of mine.

Love,
Your Bohouš

---

[18] Martinů was employed as a teacher of composition at the Berkshire Music Center in 1942 and again in
1946. He also taught composition for several years at the Mannes School of Music in New York, and from
1948 to 1951 at Princeton University, to which he commuted from New York, as he did to the Curtis
Institute of Music in Philadelphia in 1955–56.

[19] The family of Charlotte Martinů's sister.

LETTER 49[20]
To his Family
[Jamaica, Long Island, New York] 21 November 1941[21]

My dear ones,

We're back from Boston and from my first big concert in America! I had a great success with applause, such as there hasn't been for a long time at the performance of a modernist work, they say.[22] Everyone was enthusiastic – even the orchestra and the conductor. The Boston Symphony is clearly the best orchestra in the world – really only select musicians! The conductor is Koussevitsky, who performed *La Bagarre* for the first time 7 years ago.[23] The reviews were excellent and the reception was beautiful! We were invited to stay in Cambridge near Boston at the home of a professor at the university and there were some receptions and a lot of picture-taking. In the end we were glad to be on the way home. Even on the train coming back some people I didn't know recognised me and congratulated me. There's a big article about it in the newspaper – it's a shame I can't send it. It's going to be played in New York in January. It was done twice in Boston and they're going to do it again in December. They've done a lot of publicity for me and that will help in the future.

I'd like to tell you everything in detail, but I'd rather write about some different things that are also important. I asked the people I know in Lisbon to send you coffee and chocolate, too. Did you get the packages? I'll send some more things this week so you'll have a Christmas present – it will surely come in time. Write and tell me if there's anything you need and what it is. It isn't possible to send everything – only some things. I'll write to Šeb[ánek] myself about the scores. Maybe he already wrote to you about the copy.[24] Write to Zrzavý and tell him that Diviš[25] has arrived here from Africa after protracted difficulties and is living in New York among other Czechs and is doing well here, except that he dwells on the old days – I don't see him much nowadays. We're living outside New York, and I think we'll stay here through the winter. New York is a very tiring city and you lose a lot of time here. I also have to tell you that I got a request from Boston for a big symphony and that I met with Mrs Coolidge. I couldn't have wished for a better beginning, and I hope that things will go well here. I would be happy if we didn't always have to wonder how you are and when we'll see you again – we're all going to have a lot to talk about. I hope you got my letter from here. We're with some very nice people and we're in a little house

[20] Charlotte Martinů added a postscript.

[21] This was his last letter to his family until 1945.

[22] The premiere of *Concerto Grosso* on 14 November 1941.

[23] For Martinů, a characteristic mistake. Koussevitsky had first conducted the work in 1927.

[24] That is, a copy of the score of *Juliette*.

[25] The peculiar and solitary painter Alén Diviš (1900–56), a friend of the composer from his Paris days, who lived a rather secluded life. His work, which defies comparison with the group aesthetics of the avant-garde of the period between the Wars, has been rightfully valued in his own country since the end of the 1980s, an appreciation long overdue.

Up to now it hasn't been possible to leave here in spite of all our efforts, but that will probably get straightened out now that the war in the Pacific is over. I also have some big premieres here this winter. It will be good if I'm there. I can't tell you how much we think of you and how much we look forward to coming home! What has become of Talich?[36] I wrote to Karel[37] and to Zrzavý and to Šebánek. I hope they all got the letters. I look forward to your letter a lot – I'll write you again soon. I have to leave space for Charlie. She wants to add something.

Lots of love,
Your Bohouš

LETTER 52

To Marie Pražanová

[South Orleans, Mass.] 29 September 1945

My dear friend,

How I wish that instead of sending you a letter I could give you a big hug to thank you for everything you did for my family during this terrible war! Mařenka wrote and told me how you took care of her and how without you they wouldn't have known what to expect. I really don't know how to thank you, but I hope that I'll soon be able to do it better than I can in this letter. I think we'll be back at the beginning of next year, finally at home again after these terrible years of a common suffering. But no longer will Mum be waiting for us at the station. What can we do? I look forward to seeing you, my family, and Polička. Even today I can see you waving goodbye the last time I left Polička,[38] so early in the morning and for what was to be such a long time! Who would have believed that between my going and coming such a tragedy would be played out and that it would be years before I'd see you all again? One more Christmas in foreign lands and then home again! I wish you and your family all the best and lots of good health! I thank you sincerely for everything, and I look forward to seeing you again.

Sincerely,
Your B. Martinů

[36] Talich was charged – without evidence – of collaboration with the Nazi Protectorate and with the occupying authorities. He was unlawfully imprisoned as, *sui generis*, the 'personal' prisoner of Zdeněk Nejedlý (*cf.* note 100 on p. 120, below) at Pankrác Prison in Prague from the end of May to the beginning of July 1945, not allowed to teach or engage in any other artistic activity and removed from his position at the National Theatre. He was permitted to resume his artistic work only in September 1946, but then and later with frequent interference. Martinů interested himself in the facts of the discrimination against Talich and took an unequivocal stand against it and gave him moral support. The 'Talich case' doubtlessly played a role in Martinů's aloofness from the post-War situation in Czechoslovakia and contributed to his scepticism about the future of political democracy, the rule of law, individual freedom and general culture in his homeland. The *coup d'état* in February 1948 confirmed his fears. It appears to be at the root of the real reasons for Martinů's refusal to return to his native land.

[37] Karel Novák (1902–68), younger brother of Stanislav Novák (who died on 20 July 1945). Karel was, like Stáňa, a violinist with the Czech Philharmonic. Martinů carried on a copious correspondence with him in 1946–49.

[38] At the end of July 1938.

The physicist and computer-scientist Dr Antonín Svoboda, Martinů, Rudolf Firkušný and Charlotte Martinů in Central Park, New York, 1945

LETTER 53
To his Family
[New York] 14 December 1945

My dear ones,

The Fourth Symphony had a huge success here! The concert was completely sold out and the orchestra played magnificently! The reviews were great![39] So, once again, another premiere. I'm still waiting for the Third Symphony – in January, I think.[40] Next Thursday I have the Sonata for Violin[41] here and on Friday we'll be in Washington for *Thunderbolt P-47*,[42] also for the first time. We'll be staying at the consulate. How was the thing in Polička?[43] It might be you've already written me about it. It's a shame we weren't able to be with you. Was Bartoš there?[44] What does Šebánek write? I think winter must be beginning there – it's already freezing here, but we have central heating, so we don't mind. But what about you? Have you managed to find a bit of coal or wood? Did any packages come? We hope that at least something has arrived so you'll have a little something better at Christmas. We'd be glad to get some news about the packages. Here anybody and everybody sends something and we're always waiting for acknowledgement that they arrived. It's already well over a month since we sent the first package, and since then we've been sending something every week, also to France. We hope that now they'll be able to send you something, too, and that as soon as the postal services get straightened out a bit you'll be able to live a calmer, more peaceful life with the help of the parcels. As long as we're here we'll keep on sending things. The main thing is that they get there properly. Were you able to make some kind of arrangement with the Intercontinental Agency? Or did they send it to you directly? Certainly they must have arrived by now.

I'm really glad that they take so much interest in me in Polička. Did we ever imagine it? You probably have our letters and so you already know that our plans have changed and how. Of course, Charlie misses her home a lot, but she admits that in this situation it's the best we can do – I think you also see that. I can never get

---

[39] The Fourth Symphony, H305, composed in 1945, in performance by the Philadelphia Orchestra, which played it for the first time on 30 November 1945 in Philadelphia, and later on tour in New York.

[40] The Third Symphony, H299, composed in 1944, was played for the first time by the Boston Symphony Orchestra on 12 November 1945. Martinů is thinking of the visit to New York by the Boston Symphony.

[41] The Violin Sonata No. 3, H303, written in 1944, had its premiere in New York on Tuesday (not Thursday), 18 December 1945.

[42] The orchestral scherzo *Thunderbolt P-47*, H309 (1945), composed for the National Symphony Orchestra in Washington. It had its premiere in Washington on 19 December 1945 (a Wednesday, not a Friday).

[43] The opening of the first permanent Martinů exhibition at the Polička Museum on 8 December 1945. Even before that, on 13 September 1945, the former Třebízský Square was renamed after Martinů. On that same day (13 September) Martinů was named an honorary citizen of Polička, and on 20 October made an honorary member of the choral society Kollár.

[44] The composer, musicologist and music-columnist František Bartoš (1905–73), who followed Martinů's career with interest and admiration, as did other members of the 'Mánes Group', on which *cf.* p. 17, above.

over the feeling that I can't rely on anybody very much and that the best thing will be – as always, for that matter – to rely on myself mostly, and I think nobody can reproach me after all the promises that have been made and all the experiences I've had.[45] We were really lucky that we got out of Europe just in time, but again it was not thanks to our representatives, who mainly saved themselves by getting out of Paris. Today it's as if nothing had happened – they're once again sitting comfortably in Prague or in legations around the world. If it hadn't been for Sacher and people who don't even know me except from my work, we would never have got out of France. I wrote about it in that article[46] and I make no secret about it. Charlotte and I were very pleased to hear about Talich's vindication, even though it took some time. But I was glad that it happened and that it was Kopecký who did it.[47] His speeches, which we have read here, made the most sense of any.

We sent a package with just soap (fragrant, because you can't send it together with food, so for a while you'll have good soap) and a few cigars and tobacco for Fanouš. He'll surely get them in time – if they're delivered at all. They say that from the First of January it will be possible to send 11 pounds, so we'll be able to send a substantial amount. It's still uncertain how things will finally be resolved and what the three great powers will decide and until they do, we won't know how everything will turn out. We're waiting for the elections at home but for some reason no one is saying much about it. I must in any case cling to the possibility of coming back here, because it will be necessary in order that I not lose what I've achieved here – and here the life is fast and people easily forget. It would be a shame if all the work I did went for nothing! It seems to me that at home a lot of people look on America disparagingly, but they're very badly informed and, unfortunately, that includes some of our people whom America took in and provided for. When they return they say bad things about it (for various reasons – maybe for opportunistic reasons), which certainly doesn't make a very good impression here and which damages our reputation. Our people are like that – they eat your food, they sleep in your house, and then they say unkind things about you. But Americans are straightforward. And they're pleasant, well educated, practical and self-confident – except that when someone makes too much of himself – which Czechs here are always doing – Americans don't fall for it.

Mr Buchta[48] is here from Polička at the consulate, and so is Miss Sommerová, a relative of ours.[49] The news of Venda[50] is really tragic because he was on the point of accomplishing all that he had longed to accomplish.

---

[45] He refers to the pre-War promises of a professorial position at the Conservatoire.

[46] In the article entitled simply '1938–1945', which first appeared in the monthly magazine *Tempo*, XVIII, 1946–47, Nos. 2–3, pp. 52–60 – not the music-magazine of the same name founded by Boosey & Hawkes in 1939 (and published by Cambridge University Press since 2002).

[47] Václav Kopecký (1897–1961), Minister of Information in the first post-war Czechoslovak government.

[48] Václav Buchta (1912–64), born in Polička, a skilled glazier and a restless traveller. He lived in London and Paris. In 1939 he went to the United States, where he worked as a common labourer. He fought on the western front as a volunteer in the American army. He later lived in Chicago.

[49] Most likely a relative of the Polička family of Karel Sommer (*cf.* note 29 on p. 40, above).

[50] The theatre historian and theorist Václav Sommer (*cf.* note 90 on p. 51, above), who died on 25 October 1945 at the age of 39.

We already have a large correspondence from France. Everybody we know is writing to us, saying how much they look forward to seeing us, but also that we shouldn't hurry to come back, and that things aren't as happy as they used to be and mainly that in Paris life is rather hard. We have better news from Vieux Moulin. They have some poultry and even a little pig, and they got a little coal, so they have fewer worries. Otherwise, everything is going to seed – clothes, shoes – everything is falling apart. All of Europe must be in a state that we can't even imagine. They do great things here to help, but all that's a drop in the bucket. Everywhere they need better communications and transportation. Until they get these, things won't get better.

I can't imagine how it is with you financially. If you need some money, tell me. I think it's possible to send something. We'll probably go to Canada next spring. Firkušný is playing my concerto[51] there and he constantly writes me from there that they'd like to get to know me personally. They also write to me from South America, but it's a terribly great distance. We couldn't have imagined how great the distances are here. I always thought that Boston and New York were next to each other, but it's 6 hours by express and that's really a short distance here – it's about four days to California. Of course, people mostly fly. We flew for the first time to Cleveland.[52] It's 2 hours, but by train it takes a whole day. Charlie didn't manage it very well, but it's pleasant and comfortable. I think that until everything here is put right again, which is already almost the case, it will be the easiest means of rapid transport – even to Europe. It will be fantastic how quickly it will be possible to travel for instance from Paris to New York. The standard of living here is so high that we can't even imagine it in Europe. And it's not only for the rich, but for little people, too, and for workers who, when they don't like something, really have the possibility to bring it before a public forum, and so no one can hide in some long, drawn-out paper process. Of course, it has its disadvantages, too, but on the whole you have to be impressed by it.

What's new in Polička? We still don't know what kinds of problems you had during the occupation. Were there any difficulties on account of me? Write and tell me now that we've put off our coming-back. I'd be pleased to know. I still have no news from Prague about the Conservatoire. I couldn't undertake anything now anyway because I gave my word here because Prague didn't work out. Don't try to do anything about it! I know they have lots of other concerns – it's just that we're both annoyed that you're looking forward to seeing us and that for now it keeps getting postponed and that we don't know how things will turn out. In any case I'd like to come home for a visit in spring. It's quite possible that they're going to need me in the propaganda service abroad, which I would regard as better than some other things. I have so many connections all over the world that I think I'd be more useful in such a position. Well, in any case that's all in the future. For now I still have work to do here. The main thing is that we're both in good health. It wasn't easy in the beginning adapting ourselves to life here. The climate is quite different and quite a lot more wearing than we were used to. And the weariness and the upset from all that's happened in the world doesn't do a person much good. But we've come through all that now and we can only hope the future will be better.

---

[51] Apparently the Second Piano Concerto.

[52] In October 1943, for the premiere of the Second Symphony on 26 October.

*The Martinůs photographed
in Darien, Connecticut, in 1943*

Say hello to all our friends for us – Honzíček, Rippl, and especially architect Šmíd and Mrs Pražanová. I'm anxious to know how the celebration was on the 8th of December.[53] We wish you a Merry Christmas and a Happy New Year, and I hope that everything will be better and that the packages that we'll be sending will in some way make things easier for you until things are again like they used to be. We hope, too, that even the postal service will get straightened out better and that it will be possible to send you a bigger quantity of things that you need.

Well, I wrote a whole novel today! We look forward to your letters. But only write when it's something important so you don't spend so much on postage. I sent you some thin, light paper and envelopes – it might be cheaper to mail. You know that we're always happy when a letter comes from home, but I think you need the money for lots of other things. The most important thing is that you not worry about my future! You know that there were and still are enough people in Prague who won't be glad to see me back, but that's not important. It's possible that everything will turn out quite differently than anyone imagined. For now, I have lots of new work and new plans. Time goes by more quickly now. At least we're able to write to each other now and to find out something about each other. These were hard times, when we didn't know how you were getting along and when you hadn't any word from us. But all that is behind us now and we must hope that everything will come right and that we'll find each other in good health.

We send you all our love. We'll be thinking of you at Christmas, about what you're doing, and we know you'll be thinking of us. Every Christmas Eve we were invited to our friends the Macháčeks. They're very nice people and quite unaffected. He's a photographer, an American, but he also wants to return home. It's always a lovely evening such as we'd have with our own families, only that several foreign languages are spoken out of consideration for Charlie, who speaks French one moment and Czech the next (the little that she learned from Mum before she died), and then English. We sing carols and have carp like at home.[54] The painter Diviš is here, too – we know him from Paris. Those first Christmases were, of course, quite sad, but the Macháčeks are such dear friends that we were able to forget about everything else. I'd better save something for my next letter!

We think about you all the time!
Charlie and Bohuš

---

[53] *Cf.* note 43 on p. 104, above.

[54] The traditional Czech Christmas meal, eaten at dinner on Christmas Eve, is fried carp and potato salad.

LETTER 54
To his Family
[New York] 24 December 1945

My dear ones,

Your letter came today – Christmas Eve. You know how happy it made us and how it saddened us to hear how things are in our country. We hope you've got the packages by now, so you'll have something, at least, for the holidays. You'll probably be getting things regularly now. It's already possible to send 11 pounds so at least we'll be able to put something into it – if only it gets delivered! We've already sent seven packages, and our friends sent you a little butter from Denmark. Something will probably also come from Sacher. If it comes, I expect it will make things a little easier for you. There's such bad news from all over Europe! You haven't told me whether you got the information about the package, which will come by Intercontinental, the dispatching courier service at Kotva in Prague.

I was overjoyed by the news from Polička! Popelka* wrote me, too, and also the choir.[55] I'll answer them soon. I look forward to getting Mum's memoirs.[56] As for Prague, don't worry your head about it. It isn't worth it. You know that Prague probably won't change its opinion of me. They're the very same people, anyway, who never liked me much and are now at the helm, so it's not to be wondered at that they might not like it if I come back. I know I have some good friends there, but also those who don't like me, so don't be surprised at my saying this – it's just like it was before. Ideals are for everyone, but a good position is only for some, and they don't forget to look out for themselves. I only ask you not to try to do anything on my behalf in Prague and don't try to urge anyone to anything. They could think they're doing me a favour, and I wouldn't like to see that. After all the news we've had here – I don't know how much of it is true – but from what I can see here, everybody is thinking mostly of himself, except that they talk as if it were for the good of the country when they get a good position, and they do everything to make their situations more secure, except for those few of us artists who see things in another way. I don't need any kindness from them. The whole world is open to me and everywhere they welcome me with open arms. It's only in Prague that there are some people who snub me, but it's all the same to me. I've known for a long time that all that talk about culture is just a lot of words and that everything is really about something else, so it no longer bothers me the way it used to.

I'll manage, too, and I'll think carefully before I do anything. All that's more or less of little interest to me. It's a shame to waste the paper writing about it! I'd rather write to you about something else. Sacher has also advised me to wait here until things calm down in Europe. He invited us to stay with them for a couple of weeks over the holiday. All our friends in France are sorry that we postponed our

---

[55] The Polička choral society Kollár.

[56] At the suggestion of František Popelka, Karolína Martinů wrote a brief recollection of the composer's childhood and youth. It was first published privately in 1946 as *Vzpomínky matky a sestry Bohuslava Martinů* ('Memoirs of Bohuslav Martinů's Mother and Sister') and later, in 1979, released in an edition by the Town Museum of Polička; it has since been included in a number of collections published elsewhere.

departure. They're looking forward to seeing us, but they also approve of the fact that it's doing us good here, and that we have an opportunity to live a peaceful life and to do our work. Šebánek wrote from London. He says the appointment was delayed only for administrative reasons.[57] Of course, we sent him a package, too, and also Mrs Pražanová and the Šmíds. We won't send any clothes or material, at least for the time being, but later we will. A lot of things might disappear from the packages just now.

I have to say, too, that Charlie is a big success here with her appearance and the way she presents herself. They like her everywhere because she's so unaffected, and they think highly of her. Of course, she also misses her home and her mum a lot, but she's more or less getting over it. She'll add a few lines of her own. She's always on the go – she doesn't stop all day long.

We wish you all the best and hope that you've started to get the packages and that they'll at least make life a little easier for you.

Much love
Your Bohouš

LETTER 55
To František Popelka
New York, 26 December 1945

My dear friend,

I thank you with all my heart for your kind regards from home and for your good wishes on my birthday! You know how much I enjoy every reminder of home. I thank you, too, for your interest and your willingness to do what you're doing for me in Polička, and I look forward to all of us getting together again in better times – let's hope it will be soon! My sister already wrote me a number of times about the effort you're making and the work you're doing in my hometown and, believe me, it makes me very happy. It's a great consolation for me. I look forward to reading Mum's reminiscences[58] – I hadn't known about it. Thanks for doing that. I'm curious, too, about my own memoirs.[59] I don't remember what I wrote about any more.

My sister wrote to me about your exhibition in Polička and about all the things you're constantly doing for me in the way of public relations. I hope I'll soon be able to thank you personally for everything at home. I'm already eagerly looking forward to coming back and to seeing all my friends and acquaintances. You know that I

---

[57] Administrative reasons: Šebánek, as Martinů from time to time complained in his letters home, sometimes expressed himself in an oracular manner. The reality was simple: in 1945 Martinů could have been named only a Master Class professor at the Prague Conservatoire, because the institute of higher education, the Academy of Music, did not yet exist. It was founded in 1946 and began its activities on 23 January 1947.

[58] *Cf.* note 56 on p. 108, opposite.

[59] Martinů had written his memoirs in 1934 or 1935 at the urging of his Polička friend Jan Jílek for the Polička periodical *Jitřenka*, although they were not printed at that time. They first appeared in a private publication by František Popelka in Polička in 1945, and later in an edition published by the Town Museum and Bohuslav Martinů Centre in Polička in 1979.

haven't forgotten about Polička, either. Of course, Mum will no longer be there to meet me at the station.

I think of all of you a lot – about how once again you're going to have a difficult winter. Maybe things will get straightened out soon. We all hope so much that it will be so. My wife and I send you our best regards and our best wishes for the New Year, and we hope we'll see each other soon.

With sincere regards,
Your B. Martinů

LETTER 56
To his Family
New York, 28 February 1946

My dear ones,

Your letter of February 15th came today, and we were happy to know that you had received the packages and that they'll be of some help. Let's hope that the others will come, too, including the one with soap (we don't want to send the fragrant soap together with the food), and that they'll arrive sooner and with more regularity. You know we'd have sent more, but we can only send those things that will survive the journey. Also, a lot of good things aren't on the market – the kinds of things they had in the army. They're still gathering those for the UNRRA parcels.[60] It often left a bitter taste in our mouths when we thought of you and of everyone in Europe and of what you'd have given to have it. Here and now it's a little – not much – worse – but from the start we saw how much went bad and was thrown out – which would have fed a lot of people. Here people didn't experience any such misery. It's true that we had ration cards here, too, and there were times we didn't have something we needed, but it was never long before it appeared in the shops again. So we really had it good, but at nearly every meal we thought of what you'd have given for it and of how much it would have helped you. We were really nervous when the packages took such a long time to get there – I'd like to know who caused them to be held up for so long! Things got sent to France right away and from there to you took half a year. Maybe they had other things to think about – maybe communications were in bad repair.

I'm going to have a lot to tell you about this country. It's very interesting, and we really don't know much of it. All of it is a little different than they had told us. It's not easy to get used to it. We have a completely different style of life, which is foreign to them, and I can't say that I've grown accustomed to theirs, and Charlie has even less. But I must say that we have been received as if we had lived here all our lives. It really is a huge country, and I've only seen a small part of it, in spite of the fact that we've travelled a lot. Distances are very big, and each region has its own characteristics. There's still a lot of something that I would call 'pioneer-like'. Everyone knows how hard people here had to struggle with nature and with other

[60] United Nations Relief and Rehabilitation Administration, international organisation providing food and medicine to countries suffering in the aftermath of the War. It was in operation until 1947.

people before some of them became millionaires. And not everyone is in such good circumstances. But everyone has the possibility of achieving something if given the chance, only that they have to be able to do something and not just talk, because you don't get very far with that here. They have an abundance of everything, of course, and the standard of living is quite high. There's some confusion now because people won't put up with it, and the situation is getting more complicated now, but I think it'll soon come right. You can see from what we're sending you that things have got better – everything comes prepared – but there are still a lot of things that can't be sent. I'm glad I was able to see with my own eyes that life here is quite different from what you read. There's a great personal freedom here and much is done for the benefit of all. Of course, to us many things seem too uniform and mechanical, but that simplifies life to a great extent. Of course, what we miss is just that we were used to a different lifestyle – one not so intense, fast-paced and exhausting.

Mařenka Pražanová wrote, and her letter made me very happy. How gratifying it is to know that you're all thinking of us and looking forward to seeing us again.

There's powdered milk in the package and dried eggs. You have to experiment to find out how much to use. We don't use it – we get everything fresh. I don't know whether we sent tomatoes – also in powdered form – or powdered bacon – next time! Sometimes things like that don't arrive – also cans of various kinds of vegetables – they last longer. We'll write. Tell me what you might need most of all – coffee, rice, cocoa, chocolate – we'll go on sending it. And if you need things like spices, pepper, paprika, salt and so on, let me know. I bought a different kind of tobacco – something more ordinary – I don't know much about it. I'll make a point of bringing some clothes for Fanouš with us. The quality isn't very good here. Everything used to come from England and from our country. It's the same with silk and such things. I'll try to bring as much with us as I can. The trouble is only that we'll fly from Paris and you can't take many things with you. What size clothes and shoes do you take?

About the money from Melantrich[61] it's all right or 'O.K.' as they say here. Don't worry about it. I'll take care of it.

Charlie sends her love.

Love,

Your Bohouš

LETTER 57
To his Family
[New York] 25 March 1946

My dear ones,

I have a little time today, and I'd like to go back to my last letter and straighten matters out.

It's a difficult question for all of us because my definitive return home must probably be postponed. You see what kind of interest they take in me in Prague

---

[61] Martinů saw to it that Melantrich would send his royalties (or advances, as the case might be) to his family in Polička.

so long as I let myself be conspicuous and as long as it doesn't cost them anything. But otherwise, as you also see, you can't count on them. It's almost a year since the liberation, and so far no one in official circles has asked about me. Of course, I'm not going to chase after them. I think that something will be found in Prague for Fanouš with the help of Šebánek,[62] and that would be one less thing to worry about. But it's more difficult with Mařenka.[63] I don't think she'd like being in Prague now. According to the news from UNRRA, which was just announced here, it seems that the situation in Europe is even worse than had been thought, and improvements won't come easily nor in the foreseeable future. You can find things more easily in the countryside, and you can find people who will help more than in Prague, where I guess there's a sizable black market and everything is scarce and hard to come by. It might be better, anyway, if you could just endure these hard times in Polička. There are probably going to be difficulties with all the reforms, because the main thing is work and production, and it doesn't seem that they're on the right road. Less politics and more work would be more to the point because, although the owner might change, the work has to be done the same as before and now even better. There's going to be a fierce competition in everything if we don't protect our exports as we did before in order to acquire income from abroad, and that won't do us any good. It seems we're not worrying about it much, and that we'll count on Russia, which alone will have a huge production capability probably quite soon and alone will sell abroad. And as for buying things we urgently need, we need money and nowadays a lot of money before everything gets mixed up in politics. The world market will long ago have come into other hands, and they're not going to raise our standard of living.

That's why if it were possible to find someone so you wouldn't be alone at home (it might be possible to arrange that through Prague), that would be one solution until the time when conditions are more settled and I can think about coming back to Prague definitely which, as it seems, won't be for two years, because I wouldn't have a pleasant position there now in spite of the enthusiasm of the audiences. I don't want to argue about it or discuss it any further. You see what they're doing with Talich[64] and that's another person who did a lot of good work. Now he's dependent on people who simply don't like him and do the worst they can to him. He won't even conduct at the festival, although if today the Philharmonic is at such a level, it's thanks to him. I'll write it to them, too. I think that I, too, gave enough of myself and that I also sacrificed a lot, and yet everyone snubs me and, as for the help they gave me, you know yourself how little interest they took in me all those years, so I don't feel much indebted to them. As for my duty to my country, I hope no one will deny that I have fulfilled it as have few others who are now comfortably ensconced there and give the orders. If they hadn't interfered with my plans all those years, I think I would now be able to manage my own affairs as I always did!

Do you have any idea what you might best envisage for yourself? I don't think it would be a good idea to change positions now. You're accustomed to it and there's no place like home, especially now when everyone has so many other worries

---

[62] He wrote to Šebánek about this matter on 1 April 1946.

[63] Martinů's sister and brother had apparently given some thought to living in Prague with Bohuslav and Charlotte.

[64] *Cf.* note 36 on p. 102, above.

and will continue to have them for a long time to come. Perhaps you could take a vacation somewhere. As for winter, you unfortunately don't have much choice. It's the same everywhere for you. You can't go south like they can in France. Even in Prague things aren't much happier, according to the letters I receive.

Your letter of March 19th just came. I also received some very nice reviews of the *Field Mass*.[65] I still don't know anything about *Lidice*.[66] Sacher will come perhaps as early as next season. Just now they have a lot of work on the festival. We still don't know anything about the papers. They're making a lot of difficulties with regard to the situation, which quite suddenly got complicated again. We're worried about it and have lots of work filling out papers and documents and time passes quickly. Write and let us know what your financial situation is.

Charlie sends her love. She'll write next time.

All this dragging things out is getting on her nerves too. No one knows how things will be resolved. We just have to wait and see.

We're glad the packages are arriving – we'll go on sending them. Send me Honzíček's address[67] – I'd like to send him something, too. I'd been going to ask for it for a long time, but I always forgot.

I'll write again soon.

Love,
Your Charlie and Bohouš

LETTER 58

To his Family
[New York] 9 September 1946

My dear ones,

I got your letter of May 9th with the four-leaf clover – I hope it will bring me luck! I'm answering at once so you'll know the news. I'm back in New York again and I hope that everything will be all right. I wrote to Charlie asking her to come back, because going to Europe is out of the question now.[68] I've got to get better and it's going to be about three or four months until I'm in good shape again.[69] For the moment things are all right, except that walking is still hard for me. Everything will be all right with time. I still don't know how my right ear is going to be. I'm afraid everything isn't what it should be. The doctor said I can congratulate myself that it's not worse than it is. The injury was very serious. I fell from the terrace. It was the

---

[65] The premiere was in Prague on 1 March 1946, given by the Czech Philharmonic Orchestra under Rafael Kubelík.

[66] Martinů's *Memorial to Lidice* was performed in Prague on 14 March 1946, with the Czech Philharmonic under Rafael Kubelík.

[67] *Cf.* note 280 on p. 89, above.

[68] On 25 July 1946, while he was teaching in the composition workshop at the Berkshire Music Center, Martinů suffered a serious head injury after falling from a balcony, and was hospitalised in Great Barrington. Charlotte Martinů was at the time visiting her family in France. He had been intending to travel back to Europe after completing his work at the Berkshire Music Center.

[69] It took considerably longer: the effects of the injury were felt for years afterwards.

school's carelessness.[70] The terrace wasn't enclosed in one place and it looked to me as if there were a staircase there, but in fact there wasn't anything, but you couldn't tell that in the dark of night. I had a fractured skull and a concussion, I suppose, and my ribs are damaged, but not broken. It was the most serious with my head. That's the reason I was in the hospital so long, and the doctor said I could easily have been completely paralysed. I'd rather not write about it. I'm out of danger now, but it's going to be a while before I recover completely. I'm sure you can imagine how I suffered. I've made some good friends here who took care of me the whole time and are still looking after me now.[71] I'll tell you about that later, too. It was as if my Lord God sent someone in Charlie's place to take care of me. I almost think it was better that Charlie wasn't here. She'd have fallen ill and wouldn't have been able to help me at all.

So don't worry about me. I'll be all right again if I'll just be patient. I'm sorry my coming-back has again been put off. I'd certainly like to see you all again, but what can we do? Fate is more powerful than we are. We have to be patient.

I'm glad you got the package. Again, it will help for a time. I ordered another one like it for you, because I haven't been able to send anything for a long time. I'm waiting for news from Charlie – I hope she'll be able to get a plane back. She's been looking forward to my coming, but she understands that it wouldn't be a good idea for me to undertake such a journey. I'm just now getting to all the unanswered correspondence. I'm going to have a lot to do.

Much love,
Your Bohouš

LETTER 59
To his Family
New York, 19 December 1946

My dear ones,

I think it's been a while since I've written. I have a lot of work and I get tired easily. Charlie is back at work. I also had some money problems. Doctors are quite expensive and for now I have to pay everything myself. I'm going to file suit, but for the time being I have to pay the bills and, wouldn't you know, Prague just stopped the social security that they'd been sending me! Of course, everyone there offered to help, and if they had done everything they promised, it would have been great! Everybody made promises, but nothing came of them until Dr Clementis[72] arrived

---

[70] The Berkshire Music Center in Tanglewood, where the Boston Symphony Orchestra was in residence, regularly organised summer music courses (including a course in composition) beginning in 1940 and concurrent with the Berkshire Music Festival, regularly held from as early as 1934 (in Tanglewood from 1937). In 1946 the composition course was moved to nearby Great Barrington, where Martinů also lived.

[71] Rosalie (Roe) Barstow, to whom he dedicated the String Quartet No. 6, H312, composed in 1946. The long-term love-affair between her and Martinů is much less well known than his short relationship with Vítězslava Kaprálová before the War. Halbreich mentions it (*op. cit.* p. 40) and Rybka (*op. cit.*, pp. 163 *et seq.*) discusses it at length.

[72] Dr Vlado Clementis (1902–52), state secretary in the Ministry of Foreign Affairs at that time and, after the death of Jan Masaryk, Foreign Minister until March 1950. In 1951 he was accused of 'Slovak bourgeois nationalism', put in jail in the 'Slánský' show trial in late 1952–early 1953 (the result of a split in the Czechoslovak Communist Party) and finally executed on 3 December 1952.

Martinů with students and fellow staff members at the Berkshire Music Center,
Tanglewood, in summer 1946, shortly before his fall

and quickly took the matter into his own hands – it was settled in two days and better than I had ever expected, so I have the greatest respect for him. He also promised me that whenever and whatever I might need I had always only to turn to him directly and at once. And my health is better now, too, but I'm going to heal only very slowly, or at least it seems so to me. I can walk down the street alone, but I still don't risk walking very much or very far. So, at least for now everything is in order.

Charlie had a very bad trip – nearly twelve days on a ship. She was sick almost the whole way. I heard from Prague, but it's still not very clear what the Academy of Music really is.[73] The pay seems very good. For the time being there's nothing to be done, because I still can't leave. Charles Munch is here.[74] He's going to conduct in New York in January. He visits us all the time. I was glad to see him again after so many years. He's been a good friend. Šebánek is back in Prague. He already wrote saying he has a cottage for me somewhere in the Šumava[75] for the holidays. Šafránek also wrote that he's going to go to see you. We both wish you a Merry Christmas and a Happy New Year! We wish you all the best and hope that we'll finally soon meet again at home and that everyone will be in good health. It's already been long drawn out and I'd be glad after all these years to see you and somehow to make life a little more comfortable for us. I certainly hope it will be next year! The most important thing is that I get my health back soon. Give my regards and my best wishes for Christmas to everyone. I have to get to my correspondence now. I have a great lot of letters waiting to be written. I kept putting it off, but now I've got to get to it.

We think of you often.

Love,
Your Charlotte and Bohouš

P.S. We hope Marka is better!

[73] Martinů was appointed 'interim instructor' of composition by the Ministry of Education at the Academy of Music in November 1946, together with Pavel Bořkovec, Jaroslav Řídký and František Pícha (the news appeared in *Tempo*, No. XIX, 1946–47, Nos. 2–3, p. 91).

[74] In 1946 Munch enjoyed considerable success as guest conductor of a number of North American orchestras, including the Boston Symphony, of which he was Music Director, after Koussevitsky, from 1949 until 1962. His co-operation with Martinů in the 1950s was as fruitful as Martinů's relations with Koussevitsky had been in the 1940s, producing commissions and world premieres of Symphony No. 6 (*Fantaisies symphoniques*), H343, and *The Parables*, H367.

[75] Known as the Bohemian Forest in English (and *Böhmerwald* in German), the Šumava is the mountain range that runs along the border between the Czech Republic and Germany and Austria.

LETTER 60[76]
To his sister Marie
[New York] 24 February 1947

Dear Mařenka,

I wrote a letter home and meanwhile a letter came from Maruška[77] and from you, so I'm writing again directly to you – and they can forward the other one to her.[78] I asked them to send me some documents that I need for the appointment.[79] I hope Fanouš will take care of it. I'm glad you're also finally getting a little rest. Your nerves will get themselves in order and you'll see things entirely differently and have different thoughts. I'm still not all right, and I sometimes get awfully tired. It drags on and I can't see an end in sight. True, it's much better than before Christmas when I couldn't even go outdoors alone, but the pains in my head and my ears make it impossible to work, because my nerves are on edge. They constantly write to me from Prague as if I were already there, but for now we'll probably take some time before I go. It's possible that I'll at least send Charlie to the festival, so she can look around for a place to live[80] and so she can think different thoughts, because just now it's not much fun being with me. It's going to be difficult to find an apartment. They can't make any decision until they know when I'm definitely coming back. They can't hold it for me, at least according to what they write, which is probably true, as I understand it. They offered me an apartment somewhere in Vinohrady[81] – two rooms and a kitchen. They don't know of anything else for the moment. All the same, I can't ask them to keep it for me because I don't have any idea when I'd be able to start teaching. Then, too, I'd rather have something that's not right in the middle of the city. I won't have so much to do in town, so I'd rather live somewhere at a little distance from all the hubbub and from all the intrigues, too, which don't interest me. I don't like getting involved in those things, as many people seem to imagine, and so I'd rather be far away from it all. Also, it seems to me too small. I'm surely going to have some private pupils and I'm also going to need quiet for my own work and not always to be living on top of one another as we have up to now. Well, they are all questions that will get resolved when I know definitely when I'll be able to return.

The premiere in Basel[82] must have been wonderful! I got the reviews today. They're full of praise and Sacher was enormously excited about it and so was the

[76] Charlotte Martinů added a postscript.

[77] Marie Pražanová.

[78] From Polička to Žamberk, where Marie Martinů was being treated in the respiratory sanatorium.

[79] The document Martinů required to be tenured as professor of composition at the Academy of Music in Prague.

[80] She went to Prague in May 1947, at the time of the 'Prague Spring' music festival, and explored the possibility of buying a small villa on the outskirts of the city. She also visited her sister-in-law in Žamberk.

[81] A district in central Prague.

[82] That of the *Toccata e due canzoni* for small orchestra, H311, composed in 1946 at the request of Paul Sacher, who gave the premiere, with the Basel Chamber Orchestra on 21 January 1947.

orchestra. My Fifth Symphony[83] is going to be played at the festival, and I think Munch is also going to do something.[84] Once more, I won't be there. It's as if I were under a spell that prevented my coming home. Again and again it gets put off. The solitude is depressing, but there's nothing to be done about it.

I'll write to Maruška. It was nice of her to take you there. Just where is Žamberk?[85] I've got plenty of correspondence. Most or all of it I neglected because of the illness, so now I've slowly got to get caught up. It's still hard for me. I can't let my head be bent over for long, and that's a problem for me. So, enjoy it there and get a good rest. It's going to do you good. I'll leave room for Charlie. She wants to add a couple of lines.

Lots of love,
Your Bohouš

LETTER 61
To his sister Marie
[Keene Valley, N.Y.] 10 July 1947

Dear Mařka,

You must be back in Polička by now.[86] I wrote to the doctor in Žamberk at once. Maybe you were still there when he got the letter. What's the news at home? Is Fanouš there or in Prague? I'm in the mountains[87] with Rybka.[88] Maybe you remember him – he was in Polička at the Tills. It's beautiful here! The air is like it is at home, and it's doing me a world of good. I feel better with each passing day. Charlie writes me often. There were three weddings there, so she was quite busy. Apparently thing aren't so good with her mum.[89] About our plans, we still don't know anything definite. Everything depends on how quickly I recover enough to be able to make the journey. I wouldn't like to have to come back to move our things, and I don't know if it wouldn't be more sensible to stay here through the winter. I

---

[83] H310, composed in 1946 and dedicated to the Czech Philharmonic Orchestra. The first performance took place on 28 May 1947 during the Prague Spring festival, with the Czech Philharmonic conducted by Rafael Kubelík. As Martinů was too ill to attend, he was represented by Charlotte.

[84] Munch conducted the Czech Philharmonic on 16 and 17 May as part of Prague Spring, but nothing by Martinů was performed this time.

[85] Žamberk is in the Pardubice region in eastern Bohemia. It seems odd that Martinů would not know, but there is no suggestion of irony in his tone.

[86] From the sanatorium in Žamberk.

[87] The Adirondack Mountains in New York State.

[88] Frank (František) Rybka (1895–1970), Czech-American organist and cellist, a native of Moravia, a loyal and close friend of Martinů during his years in America. He studied organ and composition with Janáček. He took up residence in the USA shortly before the First World War and was quite successful there. He apparently had been acquainted with Martinů as a young man in Polička, to which he used to go, being an admirer of the daughter of Karel Till, a Polička businessman and president of the local Sokol (cf. also p. 156, below). In the 1950s Rybka used to spend his holidays in Europe, often travelling with Martinů. In 1957 he visited the composer's brother and sister in Polička. Cf. F. James Rybka, *op. cit.*, pp. 232–33, 241 and 251–52.

[89] Charlotte's mother was Amicia Quennehen, *née* Raimbaut (1866–1948).

still wouldn't be able to teach, and the winter is always harsh at home. I'll talk with Charlie about whether she thinks I'd continue to recover here as quickly as I have up till now. A couple of weeks and I should be all right – of course I'm going to have to take care of myself. My address is now: B.M., Keene Valley, N.Y. (U.S.A.). So, as soon as you get settled, write and tell me the news and how it is for you there. It seems like everything is mixed up in politics again. I'm doing quite well here for the time being. If we were there, we'd be at Zbiroh Castle[90] for the first time. We're invited there, and they say it's quite beautiful. Šafránek wrote me and said he liked Polička a lot.

I send my love. I think of you often.

Your Bohouš

LETTER 62
To his Family
[New York] 25 November 1947

My dear ones,

I think I owe you a letter and that you've been waiting for it. Again I had a couple of very bad days. The dizziness keeps coming back and I have to put everything else aside. It's better, though, than it was. It's associated with the changes in the weather. I'm probably going to feel it for a long time. Apart from that, nothing in particular has happened here, but we read all kinds of news from our country. True, it's somewhat slanted, but I can sense that everything isn't as it should be. It does seem that there won't be peace in the world for a long time so that people might live and work in calm. There's nothing we can do about it. We just have to accept what comes our way. I'm only annoyed that I still can't work. My head hurts constantly. True, it's nothing serious – the doctor prepared me for it – but it's unpleasant. Well, I've just got to get through this, too.

The conductor Munch is here with us,[91] as he visits us quite often. And Ansermet[92] is coming – probably next month. No one writes from Prague, so I don't know what they're doing there. Jirák[93] is in America now, and I spoke with him about that matter that had seemed so intriguing, but there was hardly anything to it. I read a very nice article in *Tempo*,[94] which praised Mr Popelka for his work. I'm glad someone noticed it. I guess he enjoyed reading it. It's possible that now some people will be envious of him. I can't find his address. Write and let me know what it is. I'll send him a letter, too, and maybe a package with some tobacco. We also sent you something – I hope it will come all right. You don't still have to pay duty, do you?

---

[90] Zbiroh Castle is a complex of buildings set in woodlands just to the west of Prague, dating back to the twelfth century and much extended over the years. During the Second World War it was used as a headquarters for the SS; in private ownership since 2004, it is now a luxury hotel.

[91] Munch was guest-conducting in the USA at this time.

[92] *Cf.* note 273 on p. 85, above.

[93] *Cf.* note 155 on p. 63, above.

[94] Ota Fric, 'Rozjímání na svatojakubské věži v Poličce', *Tempo*, XX, 1947–48, No. 1, p. 22.

Winter hasn't set in yet. We still go out in an overcoat.[95] Prices are going up here, too – everything is expensive now. In short, everything is getting more and more tangled up, and I don't think much good will come of it. I'm glad you found a bit of coal. As for the other things, I'll send them. As long as I'm here, I'm sure you'll get by. And, in any case, it's not going to last forever. I got news from Vienna that Sacher played the *Double Concerto* there. And in South America they're playing my work a lot now. I'm having a great success. They like it a lot. I'm going to have some premieres – at big concerts in January. Things are going well except that I get tired easily. I still can't go to big social gatherings where there's a lot of noise. Write me and tell me what's new. I hope everything is all right. When is Mařka going to the sanatorium?

Lots of love.
Write soon.
Bohouš

LETTER 63
To his brother František
[New York, 25 December 1947]

Dear Fanouš,

Thanks for your letter and your good wishes! They came just at the holiday, which we celebrated at home, though it wasn't much to speak of – here in this Babylon! You don't even know that it's a holiday except that the room is heated and that for the whole winter, and that you can buy what you want, albeit for a lot of money. Prices are going up a lot here, too. So we had carp, and Firkušný came for supper. Then we went to the city for a while. Christmas here is celebrated like we celebrate New Year's Eve. It was quite jolly, as I suppose it wasn't at home. It seems like the whole world has somehow gone crazy. Everybody wants to do something for future generations, but for the present generation they haven't much regard. I was touched by your letter. It gave me the impression that I did the right thing by not hurrying home so quickly, but it's probably the same all over the world, just that here there's always enough to spare, even if things are expensive and people would rather worry about the next presidential election – which will be next year. Otherwise, the information seems much distorted on both sides. It's a fact that all over Europe people don't have enough two years after the war and that it doesn't seem things will get better soon. So in the meantime we've just got to muddle through. I don't think we can expect things to get better in our own lifetime. I really hope that future generations will have it better, but I'm even in doubt of that, though that's their worry. Of course, I can't complain. My health is much better even though I'm still not completely over it, but it does seem it's getting better. At least I can work a little now, so that everything is beginning to look a little different. I hope I'll be home for spring. Of course, it's impossible to predict today. A lot of unexpected things could happen before spring – but I'm certainly counting on coming back. I'll send

---

[95] Perhaps more correctly 'without an overcoat'.

you some packages from CARE.[96] They say there are a lot of things in them that you might need. Our thoughts at Christmas were of how we're scattered here and there around the world and are unable to get together. I send my love to you and to Jindřiška and wish you both all the best – at least the best that we can hope for in today's world – for the New Year.

Love,
Your Bohouš

LETTER 64[97]
To his Family
[New York] 21 June 1948

My dear ones,

We got your letter. You might be surprised to know we're flying to Paris tomorrow morning. That Swiss conductor referred me to an excellent specialist here in injuries like the one I have. So we decided to do it, and we're leaving tomorrow. I have to be back in the United States in the middle of September. I had an offer of a position as professor at Princeton,[98] which is one of the best universities in America. It pays well, and it will give me a big lift. And in New York I'm going to have one morning a week at the Mannes School,[99] which is also a very good school. I'm sorry that I don't think I'm going to have time to come home, and I know you'll be sorry, too. I looked forward to it so much, but I think the treatment will take some time. I might have to go to Switzerland. I still don't know, and neither do I know if I'd ever get out again if I did come home for a visit! I have all kinds of news of conditions in our country, and of people who are getting out if they can, which, of course, doesn't speak very well of those conditions. I think you understand me. We won't change the world, and we won't even have much to say about the changes that do occur. And you know that I certainly won't get to the Conservatoire so long as someone who persecuted Talich holds sway.[100]

I wanted to let you know this and to give you a new address, which will be c/o Charles Quennehen, 62 rue Pierre Charron, Paris 8. Don't say much about it – a lot of people are going to want to use it against me – but you must be aware that I'm not dependent upon them and neither am I much concerned about them. People in

[96]Cooperative for American Relief Everywhere (CARE), a charitable institution founded in 1945 in the USA.

[97] Charlotte Martinů added a postscript.

[98] Martinů taught composition there until 1951.

[99] The Mannes School of Music, founded in 1916 by violinist David Mannes, had an excellent reputation. Martinů taught composition there in 1947–48 and again in 1955.

[100] Martinů refers to Zdeněk Nejedlý (1878–1962), the radical left-wing musicologist and critic who became the first Minister of Culture and Education after the Communists established the Czechoslovak Socialist Republic in 1948, remaining in the post until 1953. It allowed him to institutionalise the political prejudices he had imported into his musicological writings, which promoted Smetana at the expense of Dvořák. Nejedlý used his powers quite ruthlessly to impose his own view of Czech musical history: disagreement could mean arrest and imprisonment.

*Martinů, New York, 1950, with fellow
Czech émigrés Frank Rybka (centre) and the
composer-conductor Karel Boleslav Jirák*

positions of authority understand that I still have some work in front of me, which for sure does not mean coming home but to go on working, and in order to do that I have to get myself in as good health as I was before. I'm sorry, of course, that I'll go on not seeing you – although we'll be quite close. We just have to reconcile ourselves to it.

I sent a fanfare for the rally. The Sokol asked me for it. They're going to play it at the opening of the rally.[101] I haven't received so much as a word from Prague. I wasn't sure if if they were counting on me,[102] so I accepted the position at Princeton. It's a great honour – Einstein[103] is also there and a lot of other very famous professors.

We sent one more CARE package. I think you'll get it in time. We understand that we shouldn't send cigarettes anymore. The package for you and Mr Popelka might still arrive. I think we sent them in March. Sometimes it takes three months to get there. I don't think anyone pilfered it. I think you've gotten everything up till now.

About Karel Novák[104] and Šafránek, I haven't had any news at all from them even though I wrote them several letters which, it seems, they didn't receive. I really don't want to write much because, it seems, letters from America can cause unpleasantness.

I got a copy of *Jitřenka*, and I'll write an article for them from Paris.[105] That's all the news I have. Write to us in Paris and let us know how you're doing and how things are taking shape. If you need me to send anything, just let me know, and when I get back[106] I'll take care of it.

Charlie and I send our love. We think of you often.

Bohouš

---

[101] It was not played at the 1948 rally, but it has been preserved and is H320 in Halbreich's catalogue.

[102] In regard to his professorship at the Academy of Music in Prague.

[103] Martinů was interested in the Theory of Relativity of Albert Einstein (1879–1955) and in modern physics long before his coming to Princeton. Martinů dedicated *Five Madrigal Stanzas* for violin and piano, H297, composed in 1943, to Einstein, an accomplished amateur violinist. Einstein accepted the dedication and played the composition.

[104] *Cf.* note 37 on p. 102, above.

[105] He eventually wrote it only after his return to the USA from Europe: it was dated 11 March 1948. It was in the form of a letter (*cf.* LETTER 67, pp. 124–25, below) which first appeared in the Polička periodical *Jitřenka*.

[106] That is, to the USA.

POSTCARD 6
To Václav Josef Rippl
[Sent, possibly from Schönenberg, around 21 August 1948]

Congratulations and best regards on your 90th birthday! And greetings to all of you there!

Hello to Vašek[107] and Láďa![108]

B. Martinů and Charlotte Martinů

LETTER 65
To his Family
Basel, 29 August 1948

My dear ones,

It's a long time since I've written, and I know you've been worrying. I wanted to be alone for a while. Charlie and I are staying with Sacher for a couple of days, and I'm seeing a well-known doctor he knows in Zurich. It's not that I'm doing badly, but that I want to take advantage of this opportunity – they tell me he's an expert in this kind of injury. So don't worry about me! Now about another matter – Mr Šebánek and I missed each other in Paris, and I only got his letters now, and now it's already too late to go back – I have a lot of things left to do in Paris, and I have to fly from there on the 23rd of September. Classes begin at the beginning of September,[109] but they more or less gave me a vacation until the 24th. I wrote to him, and I hope that he'll be able to come to Paris before my departure and that we'll be able to talk everything over. It's nice that they want to see me in Prague, but I'd like to see some guarantees regarding my departure and, as a matter of fact, an invitation from the Minister himself. Šebánek is a private person – and he's my friend and my publisher – but that's all. He alone can't promise to guarantee my departure.[110] I haven't received any letter from the Ministry – only from Šebánek. It's not that I don't believe him, but that with all good intentions, his concern is only with making money for his publishing house. It's not that I don't have confidence in him. You know how much I'd like to return to my own country, and I doubt that they would want to put me off if I decided not to stay, but I wanted to use my stay here to restore my health. It's for that reason that I completely cut myself off from the world. I didn't even see many people in Paris. I wanted peace and quiet, and so I arranged things that way. For that matter, they know in Prague what my goal is, so it isn't necessary to try to persuade them of anything. I'll return – when I have more official assurance! I'm going to talk with Hoffmeister, who is now the ambassador in

---

[107] That is, Václav Rippl.

[108] The engineer Vladimír Rippl, Václav's older brother.

[109] In Princeton.

[110] Martinů at the time still held Czechoslovak citizenship.

Paris,[111] and also with our ambassador in Bern.[112] He's married to Berta Masaryková. And Anička Masaryková[113] is going to Bern next week. I hope we'll still be here. I telephoned there to ask them to let me know when they're coming. So don't worry about a lost opportunity. Another and a better way will be found. In any case, I'll see Šebánek, and I'll find out in more detail what the problem is. Sometimes he gets overly enthusiastic, but of course it's always with the best of intentions. Needless to say, I'm sorry that I wasn't able to see you, but I think we can all look forward to that happening sooner than we might think. *Again* I got a letter from the Ministry of Education asking if I would accept a position at the Academy, even though I have in fact already been named to the position![114] So you figure it out! I think we'll stay here another week so, if you answer this letter right away, you can send it to me in care of Mr Sacher, Schönenberg, Pratteln, Basel, Suisse.

I think of you a lot, and I send you my love.

Your Bohouš

LETTER 66
To the magazine *Jitřenka*
[New York] 11 March 1948

Dear friends!

I should really say 'Dear *Jitřenka*!' I recall the time of my youth, when we joked about our local magazine, giving it all sorts of funny names other than '*Jitřenka*,' which told us about the daily life of our town and its surroundings. To tell the truth, we didn't really read it – we only subscribed to it!

And now suddenly one morning when I got the mail, there among a lot of letters from various countries with various kinds of stamps, I unexpectedly found in my hand a simple envelope with a postmark from Polička. It was a recent edition of *Jitřenka*, which was beginning a new life in new circumstances after a long hiatus filled with tragedy and unhappiness for the whole world. I can't tell you how surprised I was and what happiness it gave me, both that *Jitřenka* was again being published and that you remembered me and sent me this greeting from home! I assure you that I'll read it more closely than *The New York Times*! It's a kind of link between you and me. I'll find out what you're doing and what's happening at home. I'll follow your plans – all that has been done and all that you have in mind for the future. Everything that happens there – even if only the building of a road – interests me greatly. I am drawn to your work, even though in an entirely different way and in an entirely different setting.

I see a lot of new names there – names I don't know or those I knew as a boy –

---

[111] The writer and painter Adolf Hoffmeister (1902–73) served as ambassador of the Czechoslovak Socialist Republic to France from 1948 to 1951.

[112] Dr Jaromír Lang, ambassador in Bern in 1948–49.

[113] The pianist and editor Herberta Masaryková and her sister, the art historian Anna Masaryková. *Cf.* also note 141 on p. 59, above.

[114] *Cf.* note 73 on p. 115, above.

who now go on creating something that is supposed to serve not only us, but all of mankind and should be for the good of all. I read about your interest in cultural life there – in concerts and theatre. Our dear old theatre! How often I've thought of how I used to walk down from the tower on a cruel winter evening to a rehearsal with my dad. Those were precious evenings! And of how we began to build a new, unusually large theatre – what criticism there was – what conflicting opinions! But for all that, it was finally completed. With both theatres my thoughts are indissolubly linked with thoughts of beloved František Martinů,[115] to whom you deservedly paid tribute in the last issue of *Jitřenka* for his devoted and untiring work in that endeavour and for the joy and energy that he gave to our theatrical life.

And I find other names in *Jitřenka* that take me back long ago to the days of my youth. As a boy, I used to go almost every day to Lázně just before daybreak in all kinds of weather and in all seasons. Up on the hilltop I invariably met Mr Rippl, running up the hill with more élan and energy than me. All day something would seem to be missing if I hadn't seen him. Perhaps, if I had stayed at home, I'd now have had such a beautiful life as he had at his age. Fate, however, carried me far from all of you, and I had to give up the walks to Lázně and to all the beauties associated with it, but my memories of that precious little piece of earth are always with me. And now I return all at once in the pages of *Jitřenka,* which calls forth these memories again.

Many changes have taken place, and much of what I once knew is gone forever. My mum departed, and I wasn't even able to go with her on her last journey. I didn't even know she had already long rested in the cemetery, to which I had gone with her to dad's grave. I learned of it all only much later, when correspondence with all of you at home was finally resumed.

Many of my friends and acquaintances are gone, making room on the earth for a new generation. And all these young people who come after us carry on new work and live lives that are bound up with my own, even over the great distance that separates us. I wish you success in all your endeavours! I thank you for *Jitřenka* and send you and all my friends and acquaintances there my affectionate regards and most sincere good wishes from New York.

B. Martinů

LETTER 67
To František Popelka
[New York, sometime in May 1949]

Dear Mr Popelka,

I thank you for your letter. I am greatly honoured and pleased by your suggestion that the music school in Polička should bear my name. It is with pleasure that I

---

[115] František Martinů (1873–1946), no relation, an official in the regional health-insurance system, for many years a dedicated amateur actor in the theatre company Tyl, of which he was director for a number of years.

accept your proposal![116] I ask only that you leave off the title 'maestro'. Let it be called simply the B. Martinů Music School. I'm so glad that we finally have such a school in Polička, and I see by your letter that it is in good hands.[117] Please accept my sincere wishes for all success in the future and in generations to come.[118]

With many thanks for your continued interest and with best wishes for success and prosperity in your work.

Sincerely yours,
B. Martinů

LETTER 68[119]
To his Family
[Paris] 21 June 1949

My dear ones,

We got your letter. I haven't written in a long time – I've had a lot of work. We've decided quite suddenly to come to Europe for a visit! I know how glad you'd be to see us, but I don't think we'll get home this time, and I don't think that my presence would decide anything special in regard to financial matters, anyway. I'm the only artist in our country who hasn't been paid – not even from my own money! Nothing can be done with the National Bank. There has been no word in spite of the promises of the people at the Ministry, as you know,[120] and for that matter it seems that sentiment has turned against me, which still hasn't caused any problem for my works, which are played and even enjoyed. That some young persons play politics because it serves their purposes is understandable. Let them say what they want! It won't change me and it won't change my music!

I thanked Mr Popelka and gave him an answer before we left.[121] I've already had a

[116] The Music Institute of the Town of Polička (the first name of the Polička Music School) began its activities on 3 September 1948. With Martinů's agreement, the school used the name Bohuslav Martinů Music Institute for years or, in a variant, Music School Bohuslav Martinů. The school was later forbidden, for political reasons, to use the composer's name and was allowed to do so again only in June 1988.

[117] Its first director was Jaromír Chalupský; *cf.* p. 212, below..

[118] He again wrote to the teachers and students of the Polička Music School in a letter of January 1951, which is included in this collection: *cf.* LETTER 75, p. 134, below.

[119] A letter from Charlotte Martinů was written on the reverse.

[120] Martinů was still a member of the Prague OSA (Authors' and Composers' Union), which collected royalties from performances of his works in his own country and abroad. But the National Bank refused, in spite of income from performances of his works in the west, to pay him at least part of those royalties in dollars, not even in inflated French francs, and thus threatened his ability to earn a living. On the authority of the composer's instructions, it later at least made payments arising from royalties to his brother and sister – in Czech crowns, of course. Similarly, his earnings from his Prague publishers were frozen in Czechoslovakia. Martinů therefore withdrew from OSA and gave his new and, for the most part, most frequently performed compositions to foreign publishers, for whom the publication of his works was a highly profitable source of income, as it was for ASCAP (American Society of Composers, Authors and Publishers), the most important organisation representing the rights of its members both in and outside the USA. Martinů became a member in 1952.

[121] That is, left the USA for Europe.

letter from him, and it made me very happy. If people everywhere worked with such enthusiasm as he, perhaps everything would turn out differently! So you're going to have to be patient a while longer. It may be that we'll see each other sooner than we'd thought. Things look more promising now – as if somehow everything will be put in order. I don't hear much now from my friend[122] who wanted to live at the Vieux Moulin – he doesn't answer my letters. Maybe he has a reason. Write again to Moravská Ostrava Theatre or ask Prague Radio where *Comedy on the Bridge*[123] was performed so they can send you the royalties or at least let you know who they paid them to. There will also be some royalties for *Špaliček*.[124] They might be going to Melantrich. I'll write soon, and for now I send my love to all.

Your Bohouš

LETTER 69
To his Family
[Évian-les-Bains] 13 August 1949

My dear ones,

You've probably been waiting impatiently for a letter from me, but I haven't had a chance to write. Everything is in such a state of confusion and we're constantly travelling, so I haven't had time for anything. There are such a lot of tourists from America here that it's impossible to find a quiet spot. Every place is full to overflowing and travelling is unpleasant. It's as expensive here as it is in New York! You can get whatever you want but for a pretty penny. Charlie went on ahead to the Riviera. I had things to do in Paris. The heat everywhere is unbearable. I hope you got a good rest up on the hill at Mařenka's.[125] I'm so close to you that I could be home in three hours by plane. You know how happy I'd be to see you, but I don't think I'll get there. I was told it would be better to stay away for the time being. As for the money, I'm making an effort to get it, but I can't promise much. As I already wrote to you, I can't give absolute authority to anyone. You just don't know nowadays what might happen two weeks from now. For that matter, Šebánek already has a certain authority in that he owes me the money! It's in the contract! What annoys me the most is that I can't give him any more compositions for publication,[126] in spite of the fact that I'd be happy to see them published in Prague, and he's obviously angry because of it. He hardly ever writes – only once every two months – and so I don't know what to think. But surely if he's not able to pay me then there's no advantage for me, and the consolation – that my money is with him – isn't worth much, because I can't buy anything with it! That's how it is.

---

[122] Karel Šebánek.

[123] Staged for the first time in Ostrava on 9 January 1948, and in Brno on 27 November 1948.

[124] At the National Theatre on 2 April 1949.

[125] At the weekend house of Marie Pražanová at Lucký vrch near Polička.

[126] For reasons that are understandable: in addition to his earnings from teaching, he was entirely dependent upon fees he received for the publication of his works or, as the case may have been, upon occasional one-time payments from those foreign interpreters who commissioned works with exclusive rights to first performance.

We'll be back in Paris at the end of August, so write to the old address – c/o Charles Quennehen, 62 rue Pierre Charron. One just doesn't feel much like writing these days – everything seems as if it's going from bad to worse, and no one knows what awaits us – things don't look very promising. We'll be going back to New York at the end of September if there aren't any strikes – nowadays you have to count on that possibility. Write and let me know if you need anything and what it is, and if you're receiving the royalties. I don't know who has the money from performances of *Špalíček*. Everything is in such a muddle – but it's certain that someone is getting it – maybe Melantrich, although for the theatrical performances I should be paid directly. In short, I don't know anything and I can't find anything out, and if I found something out I wouldn't get anything anyway!

Otherwise, I feel fine. We were in the mountains where the air is good to breathe – and it's free! We think about you a lot, especially now that I'm so near.

My love to all,
Your Bohouš

P.S. Did Popelka get my answer in regard to the music school?

LETTER 70
To František Popelka
[New York, sometime in October] 1949

My dear friend,

It's been a long time since anything gave me so much pleasure as your article in *Jitřenka*,[127] which I found among my correspondence when I got back to New York. It took me back to the adventurous life we shared – back to that time long ago in the tower. I returned with you to our dear Polička, which as a boy I gazed out on for years – from the tall Polička tower to which, although I would seem to have been isolated there, I was tied with the strongest ties – more than it seemed at first. So much has happened since that beginning. You describe it so well and you write in a style that touches me deeply, because you put it so simply – in words that go straight to the heart and which testify to real friendship, to love, and – to something else that you write about – our Vysočina[128] – something eternally true – something we can count on with certainty. This is the well-known secret I took with me when I went abroad – faith in Man – unbroken faith – and there is no bigger reward for the artist than when he sees his ideals confirmed and especially in that form – simple and direct – as you described it. I thank you and I wish you all the best!

B. Martinů

---

[127] *Jitřenka*, Vol. LXIV, Nos. 13–14 (1 July 1949), pp. 133 *et seq.*, and No. 15 (1 August 1949), pp. 147 *et seq.*, under the title 'Bohuslav Martinů (Přednáška k I. večeru Poličského hudebního máje)' ('Bohuslav Martinů (Lecture for the First Evening of the Polička Musical May)').

[128] The Vysočina is the highland region that straddles south-eastern Bohemia and Moravia.

LETTER 71[129]

To his Family
[New York] Christmas 1949

My dear ones,

Again a Christmas filled only with memories. I hope that it was at least a good one for you. Ours was quiet. It's like spring here – it's not been cold at all. Of course, we had carp like at home in the old days, and we thought of you – of how you might be spending the holidays. Who knows what the new year will bring us. One doesn't even want to send New Year's wishes, because it's worse every year, but still let's hope that this year 1950 will at least bring us something cheerful. Especially, I would wish you – and myself too – that we could finally be with each other again. It's been a long, long time that we've only looked forward to it.

I was awarded – as I read in the newspaper – the Academy Prize[130] for my Third Symphony[131] – the work that was panned so rudely in *Rudé právo*.[132] All the same, I won't get anything out of it. I constantly make efforts to get the money and, as it seems, Šebánek is quite optimistic, but I don't much believe it anymore. As I may have told you, I was allowed a sum of money from the National Bank before the holidays, and the consulate in Paris told me when I was there that it was already on the way, but it's always on the way and up to now I haven't received anything and, according to the assurances of those who have experience, I won't get anything in the end – and I'm beginning to believe it! I think it will finally work out that I'll accept membership in the local authors' union[133] and that they'll recover the money – at least what the OSA has of it.

Kubelík was here.[134] He came to dinner. He's making quite a career for himself here, and he has something of mine on every programme. Ansermet is also here from Switzerland. He's doing my *Concerto Grosso* on the radio. All the while I have something on a concert programme, mostly chamber works. It's also going well at the university.

We don't know if Mařka is already in Žamberk. I hope so, for her sake. It

---

[129] Charlotte Martinů added a postscript.

[130] The first so-called anniversary award of the Czechoslovak Academy of Arts and Sciences was presented on 13 December 1949, in the amount of more than 10,000 crowns, of which Martinů never saw a penny. With the consent of the composer, the prize was paid to his sister Marie in Polička but not until the following year.

[131] Composed in 1944, first performed in Prague on 13 October 1949.

[132] *Rudé právo* ('Red Law', the official newspaper of the Czechoslovak Communist Party) did not review the Third Symphony. Martinů undoubtedly had in mind the crude attack on the work by Bohumil Karásek, one of the Prague exponents of the aesthetics of Zhdanov in 'Third Symphony' of B. Martinů in Prague', *Práce*, 21 October 1949, p. 5.

[133] That is, membership in The American Society of Composers, Authors and Publishers (ASCAP).

[134] Rafael Kubelík (1914–96), conductor and composer, son of violinist Jan Kubelík, musical director and conductor of the Czech Philharmonic from 1941 to 1948 and, after emigrating to the West in 1948, director of a number of outstanding international orchestras and opera companies. He was a frequent interpreter of Martinů's work. The composer dedicated to him *The Frescoes of Piero della Francesca*, H352, composed in 1955.

seemed to me, according to your last letter, that it still hadn't been decided, or else I misunderstood.

Write and tell us how you spent Christmas and what the news is. Mr Popelka wrote and thanked me and told me about plans for my 60th birthday.[135] They're already starting to celebrate it, but I'm not looking forward to it. I'd rather I had fewer years to celebrate – forty-five would be nice. But, there's nothing we can do – we simply grow old. Venda Rippl wrote me, too. The old man is holding on. Stop in and see him, and give my regards to everyone. I'll write after the holidays.

I read that everyone there is going to school to be re-educated for the New World, where future generations will be the happiest on earth. We probably won't be here then, so the teaching will hardly help us.

I'll leave some room for Charlie. I wish you all the best. I really don't know what that might mean these days except at least that you might be together and live at home and in peace. Whatever you're going to need, tell me and I'll send it. You don't have to be shy. You know I have money there, and I wrote you and explained why I haven't been sending you anything. It doesn't mean that I'm saving it for myself. Thank God I'm earning more than I can spend! Nevertheless, I'm not pinching pennies, so whenever you need something, just tell me.

My love to all,
Your Bohouš

P.S. Your letter of December 20th came today. Send me your address!

LETTER 72[136]
To his sister Marie
[New York] 12 February 1950

Dear Mařenka,

I hope Fanouš sent you my last letter, which I mailed to Polička. I got your letter, but I had a lot of work just then, so that it took me some time to respond. I hope you're still at the sanatorium. I just sent some cigarettes, but I didn't know how many were allowed. The regulations are changed every day, both here and there, and I didn't want you to have to pay duty, so I didn't send you many. It isn't worth it – such a little package – the postage costs more than its contents! I suppose you've already got them and given them to people. I also see in the newspaper that there are new regulations there about sending letters – that each one has to be authorised at the post office – and so maybe it will be even more difficult for you to send letters. I think they'll be censored. Well, whatever we write to each other they can read at their leisure! I sent a new CARE package to Polička so you'd have something in reserve in case you need it. It's possible, too, that that will be stopped and that it

---

[135] The Communist authorities allowed only modest celebration of Martinů's 60th birthday in Polička the following year, with a single unpublicised concert on 19 November 1950, under the auspices of the music school. Apart from this event in Polička, the birthday does not seem to have been celebrated anywhere in Czechoslovakia.

[136] Postcript by Charlotte Martinů.

won't be possible to send much. Fanouš wrote and told me that the little boy is there with him[137] and that he's a lot of fun to be with. I hope you've been getting a good rest and that they'll let you stay there longer although, of course, there are so many people there. I think a lot of people just want to relax and recover after all the hardships they've been through. I think Fanouš is quite satisfied with the way he spends his time. I think about you often – about how you're getting on there. I'm sure it's not easy. We don't know anything about it here. We live like stay-at-homes – I won't elaborate on it.

I had a few concerts this month, and so I've been very busy. They were all quite successful and put me – seriously – in the category of the best composers. Also there's a great demand for my things in Europe. Of course, it's complicated everywhere now with mailing something abroad and with getting mail from abroad, mainly because I'm not getting money for performances from anywhere. The money stays there and I'd have to go and spend it there. It's like it is at home – I doubt I'll ever see the money. So for an artist it's like it was before. Someone is doing well with the money, but not the one who did all the work!

We're having such a mild winter that it's unpleasant. We still haven't seen any snow, and the weather changes every day. It rains – it's cold – and then half an hour later it's like summer. It's as crazy as everything else in this world, so we've just got to be satisfied with what we've got, as they say. I got a request from Sacher again. He's going to celebrate my next birthday – my 60th – in December.[138] Ansermet from Switzerland also has some concerts here. He did my *Concerto Grosso*, which had a great success in Europe last year. They played it nearly everywhere – in Vienna, at a festival in Lucerne, in Amsterdam, and in London – only Paris left me out. They didn't play anything there until this season, but I read that they're preparing something for next year. Everyone looks out for himself there. As they say – out of sight, out of mind. At home, as I see, a lot is being played. I received a prize from the Czech Academy[139] which, of course, is only an honour, because I'll probably never have the prize in my hand. Otherwise, everything is like it was. Time flies – winter is almost over again and we can think about the vacation. I'll leave some space for Charlie. Write soon and tell me your news.

Lots of love,
Bohouš

---

[137] Jaroslav Hynek (b. 1944), whose mother was raised by the childless Jindřiška Martinů.

[138] Undoubtedly the request in response to which Martinů composed, in 1949, his *Sinfonia Concertante* for violin, cello, oboe, bassoon, orchestra and piano, H322. Sacher premiered the work on 8 December 1950.

[139] For the Third Symphony; *cf.* note 131 on p. 128, above.

Martinů's brother, František, around 1950

LETTER 73
To the family of Václav Rippl
New York, 12 April 1950

My dear friends,

I can't tell you how the news of the death of our dear Vašík affected me.[140] It saddened me so much that it's difficult to write about it. I know I can't cheer you up. I know what sorrow you have in your hearts at such an unexpected and eternal leave-taking. Over the great distance that separates us, I am sincerely with you in your sorrow. How happy I'd be if there were anything I could say to console you, but I know that whatever words I might write would be empty. They would be empty for me, too. I only know that again one of my friends has left and that I'll never see him again. And I had always so much looked forward to coming back and had thought that my first trip would be to the bookstore and that I'd suddenly surprise him. Fate didn't permit it to us. It seemed to me, not long ago, as if I were in Polička and we met by accident on the corner near the Hotel Holý. Vašík wasn't at all surprised to see me, and I of course saw him as I had known him in those days long ago when we played chess together. It was a lovely dream. Please accept my sincere sympathy and my regards. True – I'm far away from you – but I'm with you in your sorrow.

Sincerely,
Your B. Martinů

LETTER 74
To the family of Ladislav Pražan
New York, 17 December 1950

My dear friends,

I thank you most heartily for your letter and for your good wishes on my 60th birthday. Your words, so full of friendship and remembrance, touched me deeply. It pleased me, too, because every such expression leaves a deep impression on our souls. I thank you many times and many times again. I often think about our countryside around our town. You know that I have not forgotten it and never shall. I'm sure than even the tower itself must from time to time ask what has become of me. I wandered off and couldn't find the way back. But I lost none of my love for our part of the country and for all of you, and even though a great distance and countless experiences divide us, I'm still with you in spirit and in my memories with the hope that I'll see you once again in order that I might once again recall those happy days when I was starting out in life – when I didn't know yet what the world was like and what awaited me – and what awaited us all. And I know, too, that despite all the changes going on in the world around us, one thing hasn't changed – and that's you, my dear friends. I thank you very much.

As for the fact that I've turned sixty, I must say that it isn't all that bad, and that

---

[140] Rippl died on 21 March 1950.

I'm even doing quite well, and I don't mean considering my age but also for the fact that I don't have time to think about it. My time is constantly taken up with work. I'm doing something which, even though I'm alone, will perhaps one day also be counted an asset of our people. Fate set me on this journey, and I understood the responsibility it put upon me. And so, even when I'm sixty I'll do what I'm able to do and I'll do it as well as I can. I send you my warmest greetings and my best wishes for a joyous Christmas, a happy New Year, and lots of good health!

Your
B. Martinů

In Vermont, 1950

LETTER 75[141]
To the Music School, Polička
New York, January 1951

My dear friends – all of you who know me and all of you who don't know me,

I have in front of me the annual report from the music school in Polička and your letter on the occasion of my sixtieth birthday, for which I sincerely thank you. It all takes me back to a time long ago. Half a century has passed since I was in much the same situation as are all your students – a young student full of hopes and dreams and plans for the life that lay ahead of him. Polička was probably more or less the same then as now. I don't think it's changed much. You still have the same Lázně there where you can go for a walk and think your thoughts and still the same promenade around the pond and many other lovely places. Of course, life has changed a lot. You've got a lot of new aspirations for the future of mankind and for a better life and better conditions, and one of the proofs is in your new music school.

You know something of my life in Polička and of my beginnings. Nevertheless, I'd like to make one thing clear: please, don't take as your model the example of Maestro Martinů, who made a place for himself in the world, but rather the example of the young boy Martinů, who lived in the same neighbourhood of Polička, which hasn't changed, who took walks around the pond with his head full of plans and hopes for his future life, who never dreamed that life would take him to far-off foreign countries, and who timidly came to understand that one day it would be he who would assume responsibility for the legacy of Smetana, who would represent his nation in the whole world, and who never dreamed what spiritual strengths would be needed in the struggle – how hard it would be to traverse the way from our dear little town to the great cities of Europe and of the whole world, where parochial interests are not what's most important, but rather the value of what is created – its strength, which comes from the integrity of the composer's artistic convictions. This is the legacy of Smetana, as I understand it. This student Martinů didn't have the good fortune to proceed from the beginning in systematic thinking and training as your pupils have the possibility now. From the beginning, I had to search everything out for myself. Maybe that was a good thing, but it took a lot of time.

I must here also very emphatically include my own experience, which in a certain way is connected to your new school. As you know, my first violin teacher was Josef Černovský,[142] an amateur. In my recollection, no one could have taken his place even though he did not hold teaching credentials – he had no diploma or anything of the kind. It was a time when we accepted whomever we could get. But he had a great love of music and art, which even he wasn't entirely aware of, and he was the first to show me the way, although it was up to me to follow in that way. I want to give you one example that is indelibly imprinted in my memory, even though so many years have gone by since then. One day we were playing a quartet in which there was a

---

[141] This letter was included in the publication *Dva dopisy do Poličky* ('Two Letters to Polička'), published by the Town Museum/Bohuslav Martinů Memorial, Polička, 1984.

[142] Josef Černovský (1862–1939), tailor, graduate of various Austrian Army bands, and a versatile instrumentalist. The young Martinů became his pupil around 1907.

solo for violin, which it fell on me to play. It was Offenbach. I played it quite well. Even I was surprised at the result. And when it was over, and I turned to Černovský, I saw something in his eyes that I'll never forget. And now, after so many years, I see it clearly in my memory. It was a look full of both love and pride. Černovský was a modest man who didn't let his feelings show, but at that moment we were both happy. It was that human contact that can be so encouraging and which encourages so much hope. He was proud that his pupil was able to play impeccably something so difficult, and that it was the result of his work. He suddenly felt a responsibility that he took on when he began to teach me, even though it was really his job on the side. Here we see what paths lead us to the fulfilment of our dreams. But we still don't know how much strength will be needed to make the journey of life. I would like you to tell your pupils not what I achieved, but how I achieved it. Tell them that at that time I, too, was a young boy – a student, like they are, and that nothing is impossible if we really want it and if we have the patience to achieve it. Don't condemn the pupil who doesn't immediately show ability. A young person has lots of problems and puzzlements that often show themselves only later and that require time before they can be resolved. One thing that your pupils must realise, of course, is that you are here to save them that time – that they needn't search all alone – that they have a steady hand to guide them from the outset. The teacher must also be aware that there are many things, especially in music, which the pupil must discover on his own.

Don't think badly of me because I tell you these things. Because the school carries my name, I feel responsible for it in part and would like everyone to share in my own experiences. Who knows what might happen. It's possible that some of the young pupils who are now under your guidance will one day take on what I took on as a young student. Of course, you live in different circumstances – you have new ideals for the future of humanity – from which I don't exclude myself and which are always connected to art as art is always connected with the person of the artist, which unites in one person the ideals of all people, which isn't an easy job and demands a complete person and most of all a person-to-person relationship. I'm very happy that all you young people, whom I don't know and who don't know me, have such a possibility to learn what music is and what it does, and to use it for the benefit of all – not only for our town and not only for those around us – but for all people of good will in all the world. As we know from the events of history, although the circumstances of peoples throughout the world are varied and are ever-changing, good art is eternal and is founded on circumstances that are timeless.

Your
B. Martinů

LETTER 76
To his sister Marie
[New York, April 1951]

Dear Marie!

I'm writing to you at the sanatorium, and I hope you'll forward the letter to home. I got your letter and I hope that you'll get a good rest. We all need a lot of rest. I, too, am looking forward to my vacation. For whatever reason this year's concert season tired me terribly. I was constantly on the go, and now I, too, would like nothing better than to get away somewhere in order to forget all that's going on in the world and to breathe a little fresh air. In certain ways I miss my home a lot – our hills – but it doesn't look like I'll see it very soon. The news I have from home isn't good. Everywhere they're ignoring me now – as if I had never written any Czech music, even though here I continue to be appreciated as a Czech composer. It's an unpleasant feeling when someone has pursued something all his life and often to his loss, and in the end someone reproaches him for not being Czech enough![143] I don't have a lot of time to think about all that, but all the same it's unfair somehow. Of course, times are different now, but it won't change my work much, because it's always been Czech and always it's been bound up with my homeland, so we just have to live with it and wait to see what history will make of it. For now I don't see that there would be so many Czech composers to take my place. They're mere dabblers who are trying to stay afloat – not for the sake of their work but so they'll look good – and keep their places at the trough.[144] But it has always been that way in the world, so it's nothing new. It's just that the true value of a work can't be judged in this way but is always and only determined over time. There are still a lot of people there who appreciate my music – who know what they like and what they don't like and can't be led astray in their judgement. It isn't for nothing that for so many years we've had the Czech Philharmonic and the National Theatre, which was created by the nation for ITSELF![145]

There are various bits of news I could tell you about myself. *Comedy on the Bridge* will be given here in May,[146] and if I could get the material for *Juliette*[147] I'd have it produced here immediately. Firkušný played my new piano concerto[148] in Europe –

---

[143] What Martinů euphemistically calls 'an unpleasant feeling' was entirely justified: attacks on his music and on the composer himself by Prague followers of the aesthetics of Zhdanov, led by Zdeněk Nejedlý, came to a head soon after.

[144] Surely an unfair judgement – but an understandable reaction to attempts to exclude Martinů from the context of Czech musical culture. In reality, the composer made discriminating judgements. For example, he valued the music of Václav Trojan (1907–83), and he knew that in Czechoslovakia there were composers who did not seek official favour.

[145] Above the curtain of the National Theatre in Prague is the legend 'Národ sobě' – 'From the Nation to itself'; i.e., the Theatre was created by the Czech nation as a statement of pride in national achievement.

[146] Performed at Hunter College by the Opera Workshop of the Mannes School of Music in New York on 28 May 1951. The work received the New York Music Critics' Circle Award as the best opera performed for the first time in New York City in 1951.

[147] I.e., the parts and conducting scores.

[148] Piano Concerto No. 3.

in London – the one which was broadcast from here to Europe, and he's also going to play it in Paris with Munch. A lot of things are being played on the radio here. I now have quite a few recordings and every week there's something on the airwaves and there'll be new recordings for next season.

It's going to be spring, but for whatever reason it's slow in coming. It's still cold and rainy, and that's not very cheerful. I'm still commuting to Princeton, but I don't know how it'll be for next year. All the young men are joining the army[149] and the university might be empty. At the Mannes School at least there'll be some girls studying composition and also I'll have some private lessons. I still haven't got around to answering the letters I received on my birthday. I'm terribly lazy about writing, as you have perhaps also noticed, but I'll get to it soon.

Mr Sacher played the *Sinfonietta*[150] outside Basel and in London and Italy. I haven't had any news from him in a long time, and in fact I have very little news from Europe. People I know in France don't write at all. I think no one is in much of a mood for writing. That old composition *The Kitchen Revue*[151] was very nicely recorded on disc in Paris and the Concerto for Quartet and Orchestra in Vienna. Both pieces were brilliantly played. It's a shame you can't hear them. They're on that new kind of record called 'long playing'. The whole composition can be played without changing records, so if I sent it you wouldn't be able to play it, because you need the new kind of record player.

I don't have any plans yet for the holiday. I'll decide what we're going to do when we get there. I need to get a lot of rest this year.

So now I've told you all the news I can remember. There's more, but again I'll save it for next time. I wish that spring would return as soon as possible for you. Somehow we do our best when the sun is shining!

Give my love to everyone, and Charlotte's too. She'll write more in my next letter.

Love,
Your Bohouš

LETTER 77[152]

To his Family
[New York] 29 [to 30] May 1951

My dear ones,

I think Mařka is already home, so I'm writing to you. I got your letter. I already heard about the attack on me.[153] Well, someone has to earn a living! It's just that he's got it easier than I have, because I have to do something that's of some value.

---

[149] Because of the Korean War.

[150] Martinů had in mind, rather, the *Sinfonia Concertante* for violin, violoncello, oboe, bassoon, orchestra and piano which Sacher conducted in December 1950.

[151] Suite from the ballet *La Revue de cuisine*.

[152] Charlotte Martinů added a postscript.

[153] It is difficult to say which of the Prague attacks of the time Martinů was thinking of. It might have been one of the 'invectives' not published in the press.

Yesterday we had the premiere of *Comedy on the Bridge*[154] staged and with an English text, and it was a huge success. It was beautifully done, so it's obvious that maybe even old Klicpera[155] can be bought! They're doing it again today, and I'm looking forward to it. There's really a big difference between hearing it on the radio and seeing it played on the stage. It's a pity that the plan to invite the Olomouc theatre, which produced the work,[156] to Polička wasn't realised. Now it'll probably never happen, although it seems to me that the work is precisely what the guardians of culture are talking about so much nowadays – very Czech, very human, and quite simple and informal, and it seems to me it would have something to say to people. Here it was a complete triumph. But, as Dad used to say, you can never please everyone.

Next month, Firkušný is playing the new piano concerto[157] in Paris with Charles Munch. They also did the cello concerto[158] in Vienna. Sacher has the new work, which he's playing on a European tour.[159]

I'm not surprised that the weather is bad. It's not very good here, either. It's not very good anywhere nowadays. Let's hope that at least the weather will change for the better and that we'll see the sun again. That always helps everyone a little in trying to forget their troubles. I'm sorry about Fanouš's hearing problem, but I'm glad he's bearing it courageously, since there's not much else he can do. I hope, too, that Mařka has recovered somewhat at the sanatorium and that she's finally able to spend a few nice days in the garden.

I had to interrupt my writing of this letter – I'll finish it today – Wednesday. Yesterday *Comedy* had a huge success and it's moving to another theatre. About the *Juliette* scores, I got news from the National Theatre that they were saved to be sent to the Ministry of Information in December. So it seems to me that Šebánek isn't taking care of it at all. It's really a pity, because there's great interest in it here, and several years have already been lost.

I'll probably be in New York until the middle of June. Charlie is flying to France tomorrow, and I have to stay here. I don't yet know how long it will be or where I'll go or what I'll do, so write to me here. I got a card from young Rippl[160] saying he got married, which was a surprise to me because I always imagined him as a boy still. We don't notice that we're all getting older. We don't have time to think about it, and that's a good thing.

Write and tell me who the Minister of Information and Culture is now

---

[154] First staging outside Czechoslovakia of an opera originally commissioned for Czech Radio, Prague.

[155] Václav Kliment Klicpera (1792–1859) was a Czech playwright and author. Martinů wrote his own libretto based on Klicpera's play of the same title of 1828.

[156] Not Olomouc, but Ostrava, and soon afterward it was produced by Brno Opera (both in 1948).

[157] The Third Piano Concerto.

[158] It is not clear whether this reference is to the First Cello Concerto or to the Second, H304, composed in 1944–45.

[159] The *Sinfonia Concertante*, H322.

[160] That is, Václav Karel Rippl, son of the Václav Rippl, about whose death Martinů writes in LETTER 73 (*cf.* p. 132, above).

(Kopecký?).[161] I think it'd be best if I wrote him directly. I got a nice letter from him a couple of years ago.

I send you all my love. I'll leave room for Charlie. She wants to say something. I wish you all lots of sunshine and a good rest this summer.

Bohouš

LETTER 78
To his Family
[New York] 22 June 1951

My dear ones,

I got a letter from Mařka telling me she's about to come back from the sanatorium, so I'm writing to you at home. About the poem you sent me[162] – I don't think I can do anything with it now. I'm really so busy I don't have time for it and I don't even know if it would seem to be approriate just now. It might be more aggravation than pleasure. The poem is lovely, but I don't think I'll do anything with it now. I'm sure you know how things are turning out for me now at home. I'd rather we put it off until later. I'm getting ready to leave. It's already getting quite hot in New York. Charlie is in France already, and I think I'll buy one of those auto campers with someone else[163] that we can travel around in. We'll go out West, a part of the country I still don't know, so for the time being I'm not going to start anything new. You might have seen this kind of camper in films sometimes. It's like a bus. It has a kitchen and a fridge and a place for sleeping. In brief, it's like a small apartment. It's comfortable and you can stop wherever you want. You don't have to look for a hotel – you live in it! And pleasantly! You just connect it to the car and pull it along. So I think we'll take a look at the West, where there are still Indians. It's a long way away, of course, and in Czechoslovakia people don't have any idea how big America is. We might go to California, which is about like going from Paris to Moscow – maybe even farther – but we've got time, so we don't have to hurry. I'd like to get to know that part of the country. They say it's fantastic in Colorado and in Arizona – and also that famous park in Yellowstone. There are still bears there and other 'critters' – and geysers with boiling water. I'll see lots of new things and it'll be a good change from the Babylon of New York. I think we'll leave next week,[164] but write to me here. The mail will follow me – I don't know where I'll be. I'll write you from wherever we are, but send your letters to the address here in New York.

As for our friend,[165] I know it's not easy sometimes, but I think he really didn't

---

[161] Václav Kopecký (1897–1961), a hardcore Stalinist, was minister of information from 1945 to 1953 and Minister of Culture from 1953 to 1954. He was a tireless promoter of 'socialist realism' in arts. At the time of this letter Zdeněk Nejedlý, one of Martinů's staunchest opponents, was Minister of Culture and Education.

[162] Apparently a poem by Jaroslav Daněk (1916–82), who served as dean in Polička from 1946 to 1949. In 1954, Martinů based his *Hymn to St James*, H347, on this text.

[163] With Frank Rybka.

[164] They didn't make the trip, but the Martinůs and the Rybkas did spend their holiday together.

[165] Karel Šebánek.

worry about it much. Just now I needed something in a hurry, which wouldn't have been lot of trouble for him, but I didn't get any answer at all. Maybe you can help me. It's about a play by Gogol that's called *The Marriage* or *The Wooing*[166] – I can't find it in translation here and I need it badly. It's sure to have been published by Otto in Prague, and it's possible that they have it in the theatre library.[167] If they could let me borrow it, I'd be very happy. Just now I don't know whether you're able to send anything at all, but if you could, send it by airmail. I don't think you need permission since it's a play. I don't think Gogol is forbidden. You could try. I wrote to Prague, but I haven't had an answer, and I need it as soon as possible. They're sure to have it at the theatre.

Apart from that, nothing much is happening here. I probably won't be at Princeton next year, because all the young people are going into the army, so there won't be anybody in the music department. I'm working on some new theatre pieces, and there's some interest in them on Broadway, which means that if anything turned out for me there, I wouldn't have to do anything anymore and not even earn my living by teaching!

You may have read that Koussevitsky died.[168] He was already quite old, but still full of energy. It's too bad. He did a lot for music and for me, too – here especially. I hope life will be easier for you this summer, and that you'll be able to spend some time in the garden. I'd like to send you something again, but it's a lot harder now than it was before. Maybe you've still got some things on hand. Write soon and tell me all the news! And if you can find the Gogol and send it to me, I'll be happy.

I send you my love. Give my regards to all my friends, especially the Šmíds and the Pražans.

Love,
Your Bohouš

LETTER 79[169]

To his Family

[New York,] 23 December 1951

My dear ones,

Thanks for your letter and for your good wishes! Another year has gone by and soon it will be Christmas. And each year we'll console ourselves in thinking we'll see each other next year, and then we'll put it off until the following year, which is about all we can do – merely to think about what each other might be doing and how they might be celebrating the holiday. Enjoy it as much as you can! You'll be in our thoughts, you know that! Both of us wish you all the best in the New Year and good health most of all. If a person has his health, he can cope with whatever comes

---

[166] For work on the libretto for the comic opera *The Marriage*, composed in 1952 on commission from the television company NBC.

[167] In the library of the Polička amateur theatre group Tyl.

[168] On 4 June 1951.

[169] Postscript by Charlotte Martinů.

along. Perhaps we'll never see those days again – somehow, things just don't seem to be working out.

The main thing I'd like to ask you to do right now is to write to our friend[170] and to ask him to try to get the request to OSA taken care of as soon as possible – to pay you as soon as they can – perhaps as a gift for the New Year. A lot depends on it – better that you should already have it in hand because all kinds of things could happen so that they wouldn't pay you at all. Write and tell me what you think the chances are of getting it soon. I can't tell you everything – only that I'm going to have to apply for a new passport in the near future,[171] and that that might also tie up all my money there. I also have to change the union that handles my copyrights and get one here[172] that will look after my interests – otherwise all my earnings will go to Prague and I'm earning a lot in royalties in Europe and I also need it for myself – everything is quite expensive now – so let me know. I'm enclosing a photograph. I had to trim it a bit so it would fit in the envelope. I'll let you know my plans later. I've got a lot of work to do and some new possibilities and life here is lived at such a pace that I sometimes don't think to write. Give my regards to Mr Popelka from Tyršova Street and thank him for his good wishes. I don't want to write to him myself,[173] so do this for me, won't you? And say hello to all my friends. I wish them all the best, too!

Love,
Your Bohouš

Let Šebánek know that I asked the National Theatre for the materials they borrowed for *The Miracles of Mary*. Tell him to let me know how far along the copying of the manuscript is.

LETTER 80

To his Family
[Cassis] 15 June 1952

My dear ones,

Your letter arrived, but I'm surprised you haven't received ours from Paris – it must have gone astray somewhere. The postal service isn't very well organised here. At least you got the letter from Cassis.[174] The owner of the villa where we lived is coming back soon, so again we'll have to look for something else. It was really beautiful here, but the season is beginning, and in a few days it's going to be full to overflowing. I have some business to settle concerning the publication in Italy, so

---

[170] Šebánek.

[171] That is, become a US citizen (from 1952).

[172] ASCAP.

[173] A frequent reference in letters to his family which have to do with other friends and acquaintances, characteristic of the atmosphere in the early 1950s.

[174] Westernmost resort on the French Riviera. Charlotte Martinů had already stayed there in the summer of 1951.

I'll go there for a couple of weeks. Charlie is going back to Pierrefonds,[175] so write to her there. I'll give you their address, although I'll probably be travelling a lot and so, for the time being, won't have a permanent address. The news of Vlaďa's death[176] hurt a lot. All my friends are slowly taking their leave, and I'll never see them again. It's a strange century we live in. It would have been easy to go home, but instead of that we've forever been wandering about here. I got a good rest here and feel all in one piece again. I was awfully tired. We sent you a postcard so you could see how beautiful it is here. Now, of course, the hot weather is setting in again, but it'll be like that everywhere now. I hope you'll have good weather there, so you can work in the garden – everything is more bearable when we can be with living, growing things. I hope that things will improve for Fanouš, too. I'm very sorry about his eyes. I think you wrote that he's going to Pardubice for another examination.

I've been almost completely cut off from the world here. I don't even read the newspapers, and that's good for me. There's so much uneasiness everywhere in the world that a person finally feels uneasy himself – here I had forgotten that. We go strawberry-picking. We have cherries and almonds in the garden. And for fish and lobster we go down to the village. So, we lack for nothing, and we almost never have to put on our best.

I wish you all the best! I hope you'll be able to get everything straightened out over the summer. I'll write and let you know where I'll be. We might go to see Sacher in Switzerland later on. For the time being we have no other plans. I don't know how long I'll stay in Italy – travelling is terribly expensive. Charlie will write to you from Pierrefonds.

Lots of love,
Bohouš

LETTER 81
To his Family
[New York] 25 December 1952

Mařka and my dear ones,

So, once again, a Christmas Eve is behind us. We spent it at home and thought how different everything would be if we could be together and not be scattered all over the earth. Who knows when we'll meet again. We had supper at home, but instead of carp we had potato dumplings, which are a delicacy for both of us, and then we went to see Charlie Chaplin's latest film *Limelight* and afterward we stood at a bar and drank the Manhattan cocktail (vermouth and whisky mixed) to our health. Then we went home and had some French goose liver with a glass of white wine and listened on the radio to carols being sung in church, and then it was time to go to bed. This morning New York is just like a village – everybody is either still asleep or they've gone to the country.

---

[175] Town near Vieux Moulin, where her sister lived with her family.

[176] The engineeer Vladimír Rippl (1891–1952), who died on 31 May in Polička. He was the older brother of the composer's friend Václav Karel Rippl.

Your letter arrived, and we're glad that you managed to get to Žamberk again, where you'll be able to get a good rest. Fanouš wrote, too – that is to say, Jindřiška wrote – he dictated the letter. We were very sorry to hear about all that has happened to him – that he can't do anything – neither read nor write. But maybe they'll find some possibility in Pardubice that can help him. Don't worry about me! You know I wouldn't neglect something like my eyes. Of course, writing those little notes doesn't improve the eyes, but it was only fatigue. I had some work that had to be done in a hurry, so I overdid it a little. It was probably also because at that time of year it was dark almost the whole day, so I had to work by electric light. But everything is fine now. I still go to the doctor for an examination every three weeks. So don't worry! I feel well, only that I still haven't been able to get rid of the rheumatism in my leg. It prickles constantly, but they say you just have to be patient and it will go away by itself. So I'm being patient. And, anyway, it doesn't bother me particularly, and in the summer I'll sweat it out again at the seaside somewhere. I'm glad they let you have the money, although I was under the impression that I had more than that there. Otherwise, no one writes to me and I don't write to anyone. I don't know what good it would do. I don't know how our friend[177] is getting on or where they sent him or, for that matter, who has his position now. I'll write the information for Mr Šafránek later. I don't remember much of what I wrote as a young boy – it was a long time ago. I see that Bohouš Šlerka[178] has already departed this life. Lots of my friends didn't live to see Christmas this year.

It's quiet here today, like we never knew it in New York. It's really rare. The newspapers and the radio brought good news from the Far East today, with a suggestion that the two most powerful men in the world today meet and talk about world peace. That would be the best Christmas present for everyone. It's what millions of people are longing for. What did you do on Christmas Eve? I suppose nothing special was to be done and you could only think about past times and hope that somewhere something will get better and that one Christmas we'll all be together again at home like in the old days, which is what we all look forward to. As it is, we have everything here that we could wish for, and I'm doing well here, except that it's not my home, and I constantly long to go back – to be with you once more and to again see the countryside where I spent the days of my youth.

But for the time being nothing is going to change much, and I must be glad that at least I have it as good as I have it. I always have enough to do,[179] and now with the new opera after Gogol I'll have a lot of work. It's supposed to be produced on television here as soon as February,[180] so it's going to be a busy month. It isn't cold here at all. Yesterday we went to buy some presents and it was so warm I went without an overcoat. Only in the evening it's always a little cold and damp, and I feel it in my leg. We have no hope of snow, although you can't be sure of anything here – everything can change overnight. New York was quite beautiful this year. They put

---

[177] Šebánek.

[178] Polička-native Bohuslav Šlerka (1893–1952), a friend of the young Martinů. He studied at the teachers' training college in Polička, but worked away from the town after the First World War.

[179] Apparently co-operation on the musical rehearsals of the television production of *The Marriage*, which had already been completed on 30 November 1952.

[180] It was broadcast on NBC on 7 February 1953.

up trees with Christmas lights on all the avenues and on the squares everywhere, and in the parks, and it was lovely to take a walk in the evening in their blue light.

I'm addressing this to Mařka out of habit. Send her this, won't you,[181] so she'll know how we are. I'll write to her after the New Year, and Charlie will add a few lines. Today she's housecleaning. We're expecting company, so she doesn't have much time. I hope that in spite of everything you had a nice, albeit sad Christmas Eve. I'm sorry I can't send you some things you might need.

Again I wish you all the best in the New Year. We can only hope it will bring us something good, even though we've hoped for that for so many years without much result. The most important thing is that our health not desert us.

I send you both my love and all my good wishes! Send this to Mařka. I'm sure she likes it in Žamberk. She'll have had a good rest after the winter.

Lots of love,
Your Bohouš

LETTER 82[182]

To his sister Marie
[New York] 4 April 1953

Dear Mařka,

I'm writing you today to let them know at home that our time here is growing short. We leave again on the fifth of May. We'll spend May in Paris and then I go to Brussels for two weeks to judge some new works.[183] I don't have any plans beyond that, but I might go to Italy again – I still have to make up my mind.

I suppose it's spring there by now. Somehow the weather here can't make up its mind if it should be nice or not. It's still rather cool. I've been hard at work so as to get a headstart on it so that I'll have some free time in Europe again. We got your letter. I'm sorry about Fanouš. You were probably still hoping he'd get better. There's nothing to be done about it. He's just got to live with it. I'm sure it must be very tedious for him. I'm still having to go to the doctor about my ears – the result of the injury – so I'm not too happy about that either. I'll look around in Europe. There are some fantastic specialists there.

It's been a little quieter now with the concerts although I still have two evenings – one trio and something with flute. *The Marriage* is already being printed[184] and when it's done there's a request, I think, that the premiere of the opera be in Europe.[185] If by chance you hear from [Jan] Novák, thank him for sending me a copy of my opera.[186]

---

[181] To the respiratory sanatorium in Žamberk.

[182] Charlotte Martinů added a lengthy postscript.

[183] As one of the jurors of the first Queen Elisabeth Competitition to be devoted to composition.

[184] By Boosey & Hawkes.

[185] At the Hamburg State Opera.

[186] Brno composer Jan Novák (1921–84), Martinů's private student in New York in 1947–48 – his second and last Czech student after Vítězslava Kaprálová. Martinů remained in contact with him by letter until his death. The reference is probably to a copy of the score of *Theatre behind the Gate* or *The Miracles of Mary*.

It must have been a lot of work for him. Tell him it wouldn't be a bad idea if in his spare moments he would adapt one of my symphonies for two pianos.[187] There's no hurry, of course, but it's just that it might come in handy some day. Maybe he could get my publisher in London interested in publishing it. I don't want to write him myself, so I hope you'll do it for me. I also wrote to Orbis.[188] I'm requesting that they release the things of mine that they've published, because they're of utterly no use to me this way. I won't get the copies of the scores printed in Czechoslovakia and, as for the opera, no one wants to get into legal disputes,[189] so there they lie. I don't know who's at Orbis now, but I hope the person will at least answer me. I don't have any news from our friend,[190] and I don't want to write him myself – you know why. Perhaps he'd acknowledge it, but it does seem strange to me all the same that he never answered and told me what he's doing now and if he has a different job or anything about himself. Some other people asked about him. I'll send you word about new compositions for Mr Š[afránek] which you can pass on to him.[191] There's no hurry. I still have such a strange hope that I'll finally be able to go home. It's going to be a while yet, but I think we'll live to see the day. It would be wonderful! It seems like things are settling down in the world a bit and that everybody is more hopeful that the superpowers will come to some kind of agreement and that the world will change for the better. I met Mrs Ježková[192] here. Do you remember Jára Ježek,[193] who was with the Osvobozené divadlo? The poor guy died here in New York a few years ago. She told me he's very much respected at home. We were saddened at the thought of his passing away without knowing how appreciative of him people were. Voskovec,

---

[187] Novák did not take up this particular challenge, although his own worklist contains a set of *Variations on a Theme of Martinů* (1949) for two pianos (orchestrated in 1959), the theme being from the *Field Mass*.

[188] The 'National Music Publishing House' Orbis, active from 1949 and successor, after nationalisation, to all Czechoslovak music-publishers up to that time, although at the time – as a music-publisher – it no longer existed. On 1 January 1953 it was incorporated in the State Publishing House of Literature, Music and Art (SNKLHU, later Odeon), which came into existence at that time. SNKLHU took over Orbis just as, before that, Orbis had taken over the music department of Melantrich and other nationalised music-publishers. Martinů was obviously unaware of these changes.

[189] Martinů doubtless tried to obtain the orchestral and vocal scores of *Juliette* so that Boosey & Hawkes might offer the work for performance. Later, the new Czech theatre publishing agency DILIA published the orchestral and vocal scores. Melantrich had published a piano reduction as early as 1947.

[190] Karel Šebánek. He didn't answer for a simple reason: after the liquidation of Orbis, of which he was the director, he did not go on to SNKLHU. For a period of time he found himself clearly outside the world of music-publishing.

[191] For the monograph on Martinů on which Šafránek was working.

[192] Frances Ježková (1900–86), widow of the composer and pianist Jaroslav Ježek and a good friend of Martinů. He dedicated his chamber cantata *Legend of the Smoke from Potato Fires*, H360 (1956), to her.

[193] Martinů had known Ježek (1906–42) since their first meeting in Paris in 1928, and Ježek visited him in Polička on a vacation trip in the 1930s. Ježek composed songs and dances for the revues of the avant-garde Osvobozené divadlo (Liberated Theatre) in Prague from 1927, a year after it was founded, until 1938, when it was closed down because of its political outspokenness. Ježek left Czechoslovakia – where he had established himself as a highly original jazz composer – for New York in 1938 after the Nazi occupation. Never having enjoyed robust health, he died of chronic kidney disease on 1 January 1942, two days after marrying Frances Bečáková.

Some of the members of the jury of the first Queen Elizabeth of Belgium composition
competition: from the left, Léon Jongen, Martinů, Frank Martin, Nadia Boulanger,
Marcel Cuvelier (chairman), Gian Francesco Malipiero, Camargo Guarnieri,
Victor Legley and Jean Van Straeten (secretary of the jury)

from the same theatre, is here, too. Just now he's playing on Broadway,[194] and that's a big success. I see him sometimes. The writer Hostovský[195] is here, too, and he drops in sometimes – but you know that no one has much time here. The cost of living is high, and distances are so great that to go and see someone is almost always a trip and sometimes a long one.

I've been working on a new symphony[196] for Charles Munch, who recently conducted my First Symphony here. He wants to do it in Paris. I also got some letters from Holland. They've fallen completely in love with me there. A choir there[197] sang my *Field Mass* and they were so excited about it that they've been writing constantly ever since, inviting me to come and telling me they'll prepare a big ovation. You know I'm not much for ovations,[198] but their letters are so sincere they can't help but make me happy. So we might go to see them. They want me to let them know when we are in Belgium. They want me to write something for them. It's a male chorus – something like our Prague Teachers' Chorus, and they come to rehearsals from all over Holland. They just had a disaster there – they were inundated by the sea! I'll write something for them[199] – they can donate the earnings to the victims. It must have been absolutely tragic. I'm not going to want to do much work now. When we have sunny days I'm going to want to go out. We have a big park across the street with a zoo. I'll go for walks there and it will be soon.

---

[194] The dramatist, actor and playwright, Jiří Voskovec (1905–81) was, with Jan Werich, one of the founders of the Liberated Theatre in Prague. Based in New York from 1951, he appeared in many films, the best-known of which was *Twelve Angry Men* (1957); he played one of the jurors, an immigrant watchmaker.

[195] The novelist Egon Hostovský (1908–73). During and after the War (during which he lost most of his family in the Holocaust), he served in the Czechoslovak Embassy in the USA and then for a short time in Denmark and Norway. In 1949, having returned to Czechoslovakia, he emigrated to the USA.

[196] Symphony No. 6, *Fantaisies symphoniques*, composed in 1951–53.

[197] The amateur but excellent men's chorus Die Haghe Sanghers, devoted interpreters of cantatas and other choral works of Martinů.

[198] Rybka (*op. cit.*, pp. 244, 259, 260 and 295) cites several instances of Martinů's apparent stage-fright as further evidence of the presence of Asperger's Syndrome.

[199] He composed the short cantata *Mount of Three Lights* (*Hora tří světel*), H349.

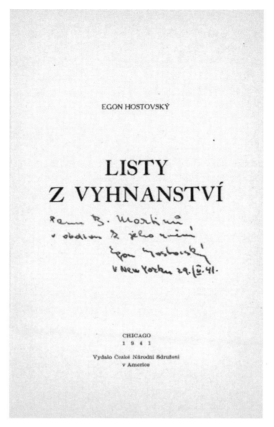

The Czech writer Egon Hostovský, mentioned in LETTER 82, *had likewise fled
from Paris to New York via Portugal in 1941. This inscription to Martinů
on his collection of poems Sheets of Exile reads:
'To Mr B. Martinů, in admiration of his art'.*

Now I've told you all my news. Let us pray that the powers that be will come to an
agreement so that I might come home for a visit. I hope you're doing well and that
you're getting a good rest. Give my regards to any of your acquaintances who might
be there[200] and to everyone at home!

Lots of love,
Your Bohouš

---

[200] At the respiratory sanatorium in Žamberk.

Part IV

RETURN TO EUROPE 1953–59

In 1952 Martinů received American citizenship but nonetheless immediately started to think about returning to Europe – but definitely not to his native Czechoslovakia, which at that time was at the height of its Stalinist personality-cult, represented by the president, Klement Gottwald. It was rather the two countries he had visited as a young man – France and Italy – that tempted him to settle. The first of two Guggenheim fellowships allowed him to move to Nice for an entire year and compose there his comic opera *Mirandolina*, based on Goldoni's play *La Locandiera*. With the exception of only a few months, he spent the rest of his life in France, Italy (where he taught composition at the American Academy in Rome) and finally, upon the invitation of Paul and Maja Sacher, in Switzerland. The seven last years of his life were filled with continuous work on some of his major works, such as the Symphony No. 6, (*Fantaisies symphoniques*), the operas *Ariane* and *The Greek Passion*, concertos for oboe and viola, the oratorio *The Epic of Gilgamesh* and the small chamber cantata *The Opening of the Springs*, which opened the concert stages of Czechoslovakia to him and became the work of his that his native land loved most.

The last months of Martinů's life were overshadowed by cancer. He was nevertheless able to compose, up to the very end, hauntingly beautiful works in a number of genres, from pieces for solo piano, via symphonic music to his final opera *The Greek Passion*.

Buried originally at the private estate of Paul Sacher at Schönenberg near Basel, twenty years later he was transported to his birthplace, Polička – with another twenty years to wait before his native country became free and democratic. Today Martinů is one of the most widely performed composers in Czechoslovakia and his international reputation is secure.

Aleš Březina

LETTER 83
To his Family
[Paris] 16 May 1953

My dear ones,

We're back in Europe, but this is the first chance I've had to write. There were a lot of things we had to take care of first and lots of friends to see, as you can imagine. It's been quite cold and only today did we finally see the sun. We had a good trip. It was uneventful except that there was a storm when we left New York and the rain came down in buckets. But as soon as we had taken off we climbed above the clouds and it was gorgeous. After a good supper, we slept the whole night and didn't wake up until we touched down in France.

It's quite expensive here, but again we'll go to Belgium and after that maybe somewhere in the south. As you probably know already, we've decided to spend the whole year here, so we'll look for a place to stay the winter. We still don't know just what we'll do. Maybe we'll be in Paris or maybe we'll go to Italy or Spain for the winter[1] and who knows if the situation in Czechoslovakia might not change somehow so that we would be able to come for a visit. It probably wouldn't be in winter, though. Nobody knows what will happen, but it seems that things are getting better. We're quite happy here. It's like our second home, you know, and there isn't the rush everywhere like there is in the States. I'll write more later – we're still not settled. I just wanted to let you know that we had a good journey and that we're both well. I have my work with me, so I'll write[2] and only get a real rest in the summer.

I send you lots of love. We're no longer quite so far away and, if the Lord permits, we'll finally see each other again. I hope you're having good weather, too. It makes everything more bearable.

Be well!
Your Bohouš

You can write to us at rue Pierre Charron, Paris 8ᵉ.

---

[1] After Brussels and a stop in The Hague on their way back to Paris, they left for Brittany in July, spent August at Vieux Moulin and at the beginning of September settled down in Nice; *cf.* note 192 on p. 70, in Josef Šíma's Villa Point Clair, where they had already lived from November 1937 until January 1938.

[2] He was completing the Sixth Symphony (*Fantaisies symphoniques*).

LETTER 84[3]
To his Family
[Nice] 7 September 1953

My dear ones,

I hope you've already received my last letter from Nice and that you know why you haven't had any news from me in so long.[4] We've already been here another week and it's been lovely. The weather has been gorgeous, and it looks like it's going to last until winter is upon us. We're going to furnish the place. I'm looking for a piano. In the morning I do a little work in the garden. There are gardens all around, so we're surrounded by greenery. Our trunk hasn't come yet, but we're expecting it any day now. Mrs Ježková wrote to say she got your letters and that she's glad the package arrived.[5] Write and tell me what it's permitted to send now so you won't have to pay more than it costs to buy. It isn't possible to send much. It's not allowed to send canned goods.

I'll have more time now, so I'll get together the list of new works for Mr Šafránek. I don't know whether I told you that the theatre in Wiesbaden is very interested in producing *Juliette*,[6] and it seems things will begin to go forward on it if I can just get it back from Orbis.

It seems strange to me that our friend[7] doesn't reply at all. Haven't you heard anything? As I see it, you don't have much news of what's going on in the world, though it wouldn't be much use anyway. It had seemed that the leaders would come to some kind of solution to the predicament the world is in and which no one likes, but now it seems it's going to drag on for years because neither side wants to give in to the other. Actually, I haven't read the papers much, either – it isn't worth the trouble! Everywhere there's the same discontentedness. At least they're not talking about a third world war anymore! Of course, people are right when they go on strike because they want to live, too. If you saw the showing off, the way some people dress, the gala affairs here and elsewhere, you'd know it could cause a person to think twice about such things.

I think about you often. I think it's crazy that I can't come to see you even though I'm constantly going here and there and always so close to you. Charlie is going to add something to the letter today. She's got a lot of work here getting the place in order, but she still goes out of her way and always thinks of something else she can do – it's just her nature.

Much love
Your Bohouš

LETTER 85

---

[3] Charlotte Martinů wrote a letter of her own on the reverse.

[4] It was the result of a strike by French post and railway workers.

[5] Apparently a parcel of food sent to Polička, which Frances Ježková had prepared.

[6] The Hessen State Opera in Wiesbaden produced *Juliette* on 25 January 1959, only the second staging of the work since its premiere in Prague in 1938.

[7] Šebánek.

To his Family
[Nice] 3 November 1953

My dear ones,

We got both your letters. I'm curious why my last letter took so long to get there. Maybe someone read it – though there was nothing in it. I'm just now writing to the bank requesting that they release the money that was somehow depleted.[8] I don't understand how it was 'tied up' and 'not tied up', although the man you spoke with in Prague[9] assured me (while he was still writing) that there's nothing in the account anymore and that you received everything in Polička. So I don't know. In any case, go and see about it. I hope they'll give you the money if they don't need a receipt from a lawyer and so on again. As far as my friend wanting to save something for you goes, I'm in agreement, but not at the cost of my not being able to do what I want to with my compositions. No one is performing them there, either, so there's nothing to be saved.

We were happy to hear that you went to see Zrzavý![10] We think about him and speak of him often. Someone is always making up a story and spreading it around that he's deathly ill. About me, too, they say I came to Europe in hopes of getting a visa to Czechoslovakia.[11] People don't have anything better to talk about! I'm also glad you talked with Karel Novák.[12] I'd like to write to him but I wouldn't want it to somehow create a problem for him. I won't write to anybody – only to home. As for the cantata,[13] I'm going to think about it and try to find time for it. Just now I'm busy with the opera,[14] of course, and I devote all my time to it. It's not easy– you know how the orchestra is. I can't write too much for it if they're going to be able to play it – and the chorus, too, for that matter.[15] But I'm thinking about it and I'll find time

---

[8] That is, 'depleted' by the currency reform of 30 May 1953.

[9] Šebánek.

[10] *Cf.* note 77 on p. 49, above.

[11] Martinů became a US citizen in 1952. He would not have been able to get a visa at this time even if he had wanted to – in a letter to his family of 5 December 1953 (not included in this collection), he writes: 'as things are, I wouldn't be able to come, because it is written in my passport that I am "forbidden to travel to the Czechoslovak Socialist Republic" because of that matter with the American journalist who was in prison there'. Martinů's reference is probably to a chain of events that took place in 1950. Two employees of the American Embassy in Prague in 1950, Lubomír Eisner and Dagmar Kačerovská, both interpreters, were arrested and later accused of spying; on 18 April 1950 they were given long sentences: Eisner to eighteen years in prison and Kačerovská to fifteen. The next day Joseph C. Kolarek, the press attaché of the Embassy, was accused of 'transmitting untrue, imaginary and slanderous news' and distributing it, supposedly for broadcast to Czechoslovakia by Voice of America. He was expelled and had to leave Czechoslovakia within four days. On 23 April the Ministry of Foreign Affairs gave the US Ambassador, Ellis O. Briggs, two weeks to reduce his staff by two-thirds. It signalled the beginning of an anti-American campaign and was one of the reasons for the Iron Curtain policy at the beginning of the Cold War.

[12] *Cf.* note 37 on p. 102, above.

[13] The *Hymn to St James*.

[14] *Mirandolina*, H346, composed in 1953–54.

[15] Here Martinů returns to the idea of composing a 'Hymnus' to a text by Jaroslav Daněk, dean of Polička, and to the possibilities of presenting the work in the choir loft of the Church of St James in Polička.

so you can have a premiere if it will be allowed while I'm on the index.[16]

I hope it's nothing serious about Mařka and that she'll remain in the hospital for as long as they're willing to keep her. At least she'll be warm! It suddenly turned quite cold here, too. It came from Italy. There were heavy rains there and flooding and we got the dregs of it. But the forecast is already promising good weather again, so we won't prepare for winter yet. Let me know when you find out something from the bank, and if there's anything else that needs to be done, write and tell me. But I think that now it's already somewhat set that they'll send it to you in Polička, so there won't be any problem with it.

There was a big Czech concert in New York on October 28th. They say it was quite an occasion. Kubelík conducted. Apart from that I don't have much news from New York, except that Frank Rybka is loyal to me. He constantly thinks about Miss Till,[17] and sometimes Mrs Ježková writes and tells me some gossip and some tales from the Czech quarter of New York. But you don't know her, so it wouldn't interest you. A couple of artists whom I knew well were killed. I'm sure you read about it or heard it on the radio – Jacques Thibaud, a world-class violinist, and W. Kapell – Polish-American – young and very talented – both in an airplane crash.[18]

We don't know anyone here yet. We don't go anywhere. I met only a writer[19] – an Italiano – from Sicily, who lived across from us on the rue de Vanves in Paris. We talked about old times and about how things have turned out. The consul who lived here, a Czech and a good musician, is in America now.[20] It's a shame. He had a huge villa here with a fantastic garden full of tall palm trees and cactuses. Now there's a new apartment building there. It's quiet in town again. There's no longer the fair like there was in the holidays. Only the motorbikes that everyone complains about make an awful racket. In the afternoon I always go for a walk on the Promenade des anglais by the sea to the flower market. I wish you could see it – it's really beautiful! And I wander in old Nice in the narrow streets, where a person would be afraid to go in the evening. But it's lively here in the daytime – especially the Italians – debating and arguing and shouting. You'd think something terrible had happened, but it's just the way they are. They don't like to stay in the house – they prefer the street. They're just like they are in the Italian section of New York – always on the front steps! Sundays we go to the mountains for a bit. It's not far, and in the afternoon it's perfectly quiet there. You can already see some snow on the mountaintops. To put it briefly – winter is inevitable. We think about how difficult it will be for you in the winter. At least the next generation won't have to place orders for coal – a little box of atoms will suffice! But I guess we'll have to get along without it. Who knows if people will be happier that way. The way things look, they probably won't be.

That's all I have to relate. Charlie will write next time. Today she's busy with

---

[16] The premiere took place in the choir loft of the Church of Saint James in Polička on 31 July 1955.

[17] *Cf.* note 88 on p. 117, above.

[18] Thibaud (born in 1880) died on 1 September 1953 when the plane in which he was travelling crashed on its approach to Nice airport; William Kapell (born in 1922) died 58 days later, on 29 October, when the plane in which he was returning from a tour of Australia hit Kings Mountain, south of San Francisco.

[19] Antonio Aniante (the pseudonym of Antonio Rapisardia (1900–83)), with whom Martinů discussed the correctness of the Italian pronunciation during the preparation of the Italian libretto of *Mirandolina*.

[20] His identity has not yet been established.

the laundry but, then, she's always occupied with something. The garden is already cleaned up and looking beautiful. We still have to burn the dry leaves – every day we rake together another pile.

We think about you all the time and we send you our love.

Your B. and C.

I'm enclosing an autograph for the Dean.[21]

LETTER 86
To his Family
[Nice] 16 January 1954

My dear ones,

We waited a long time for each other's letter. I thought you'd never write. But the strike is to blame – and the fact that the trains weren't running. There was a heavy snowfall everywhere. I suppose it's all white there, too, except for some things that are black. We think about you in the winter – how hard it must be for you and how you have to use the coal sparingly. There are reports of the same kind of weather everywhere – avalanches in Austria, snow and freezing temperatures in Italy. In New York they had some 30 centimetres of snow overnight – so everything ground to a halt there, too. Only here it's never been below zero, not even at night. And it's beautiful in the daytime – people sit outside at cafés on the waterfront. So I must admit we chose well. We both caught a cold as soon as we got here, because we weren't prepared for the sudden change of climate, but we're well now.

I wrote to you at Christmas – you've surely had that letter by now. We were home on New Year's Eve, too, and in fact we celebrated all night and on New Year's Day we opened a bottle of champagne. We didn't go to Marseilles – it wasn't a particularly nice day. We received a lot of lovely cards wishing us well. So here we are in the New Year already, and it really seems that things are getting better and that we'll come to some kind of understanding, which is something all people of whatever religious or political belief are in need of. On both sides, the ones in charge have changed their opinions and it suggests that there are finally some more pleasant surprises in store for us this year. We frequently listen to the radio. They're playing my music almost everywhere. It's a shame you can't hear something. Perhaps, as it seems, we'll see a change. There's been no invitation from Prague, but I got a letter from Paris with an invitation to a festival from some society for cultural relations.[22]

Some well-known artists play here from time to time. Pierre Fournier,[23] the cellist from Paris was here. He played my concerto[24] in Hamburg and in Switzerland.

---

[21] Jaroslav Daněk, author of the text of the *Hymn to St James*.

[22] The State Society for Foreign Cultural Relations, which was incorporated into the Ministry of Culture in September 1953.

[23] Fournier (1906–86) had in his repertoire several of Martinů's works for cello. He was a frequent guest artist at the Prague Spring Festival.

[24] The First Cello Concerto, the second and third versions of which were dedicated to him.

They played on the radio here the little symphony[25] I wrote for the orchestra in Los Angeles, California, and played it well. I got an invitation from Belgium again, inviting me to that festival, but I had to cancel, because I'm hard at work again. I'm writing a new comedy based on a Goldoni text in Italian – a full-length work[26] – so I'm quite busy. I'm glad I took that new transparent composition paper with me – it's easier to make copies of. They don't have any here. They played my Quartet[27] in New York. We're sending you a clipping with a photo in which I have a big nose – I don't know where they found it!

Your news of our friend[28] made me happy. I sent another letter to Orbis. My lawyer wrote to them that although they produced a good edition, it's of no use, especially abroad, and so I'm withdrawing my permission. They still haven't answered. Honzík N[ovák] sent me some songs with a dedication, and I sent him a ticket. I don't want to send letters because I don't want to cause any trouble for him. Give him my regards and my friend, too. If it should be possible I wish he'd write. I have a lot of news from New York. The building we lived in has been torn down and they're putting up a glass palace. We got out just in time – I'd have had to move again.

Now and then I get a highly welcome cheque in dollars from the musician's union that I'm a member of.[29] So it's obvious that I'm on the programmes a lot. It's not like OSA, from which I was getting 200 crowns a year. Things are rather cheap here if one lives and eats at home. They have nice things here, too. When you write to Šafránek, tell him that our old friend, who took such good care of us, passed away. His name was Vathier.[30] He also writes about him in the biography. I'll write back to the Society for Cultural Relations and tell them that I doubt I can accept their invitation considering the fact that my works are prohibited. I'll see what will happen.

That's all my news for now. Charlie will write next time.

We send you both our love. Let's hope that something will change for the better this year.

Love,
Your Bohouš

---

[25] The *Sinfonietta La Jolla*, H328, written in 1950 at the request of the Musical Arts Society of La Jolla, the music society in the town of La Jolla, California.

[26] *Mirandolina*.

[27] Which of Martinů's seven string quartets or two quartets with piano this might have been is difficult to say.

[28] Šebánek.

[29] ASCAP.

[30] More correctly Vautier (alias *père* Gogo), a rather special variant of the Parisian *clochard* with whom Martinů became friends in the rue de Vanves and who rescued the manuscript scores, correspondence and furniture from the composer's apartment in the rue des Marroniers just before the arrival of the Gestapo, after Martinů's hasty departure from Paris in the summer of 1940.

LETTER 87[31]
To his Family
[Nice] 31 March 1954

My dear ones,

I'm answering your letter right away and enclosing the list of compositions. Send it to Mil[oš Šafránek]. I was happy to get Talich's letter and especially to hear that he's back.[32] Needless to say, I've had enough of this roaming the earth, and I could still do a big piece of work together with him – I'd be happier coming back. But he himself surely knows we can't be choosy and that we've all had bitter experiences and that we all deserve some sweetness. I, too, have had my ups and downs. I got a letter from Prague about *Juliette,* and I think we'll reach an agreement. Orbis hasn't answered. We're happy about Germaine Leroux's success. She hasn't had it easy, either, and she deserves it. She's got courage!

Honzík Novák wrote and said I'm already beginning to appear on some programmes.[33] He's really a good fellow. Do you know what he asked for? – that I give him my telephone number so he could hear my voice again! Isn't that nice of him? But unfortunately, I don't have a phone (actually it's fortunate). It was the first thing I did away with. I had enough of it in New York. I don't think it would do him any good anyway, and nowadays a person never knows. Conversations are surely being monitored. I'd rather write to him and explain. There's been no news from our friend.[34] I hope he'll soon find the kind of position he deserves. I think about the *Mass*[35] and hope I'll find time for it. I don't have much, because the opera[36] has to be finished soon. Otherwise it'll have to be put off for another year. They played *The Marriage* in Hamburg for the first time. I got a programme and a photograph. It seems they did it very well. I'm waiting for the reviews, but they[37] wrote from London that it was quite successful.

It's spring here, but the weather is very changeable. People say it's because of the testing of atomic bombs on those faraway islands,[38] which might be so. The flowers in the garden are already in bloom, and we're still burning the last of the leaves. I'm hard at work. I lost a lot of time with the Dostoyevsky piece[39] and with looking for

[31] Charlotte Martinů added a postscript.

[32] At the Czech Philharmonic after his engagement in Bratislava from 1949 to 1952.

[33] In Brno, where the 'third period' of Martinů's music in Czechoslovak concert life began – the 'second' being the short non-Communist period between 1945 and 1948. (The Nazis had banned his works from concert programmes during the occupation.)

[34] Šebánek.

[35] The cantata *Hymn to St James.*

[36] *Mirandolina.*

[37] Presumably someone at Boosey & Hawkes, publisher of *The Marriage.*

[38] On 1 March 1954 the United States exploded its biggest-ever thermonuclear hydrogen bomb, code-named 'Castle Bravo', on Bikini Atoll in the Marshall Islands, one of no fewer than 23 nuclear devices exploded there between 1946 and 1958. 'Castle Bravo' caused widespread radioactive contamination over the Pacific Ocean.

[39] He was considering composing an opera based on Dostoyevsky's novel *The Possessed (The Devils).*

the libretto, and now I've got to finish it. But it's quiet here and no one bothers us, so I'm able to get a lot of work done. Of course, an opera like that is a lot of work – a lot of writing.

We'll save some stamps for you and I'll send them with the letter. Charlie wants to add something, so I'll leave room for her.

I send you all my love,
Bohouš

LETTER 88

To his Family
[Nice] 18 July 1954

My dear ones,

I finished the *Hymn*[40] today, and I'll send it immediately. I'll have a copy made so you can have it for yourselves. I won't send the original manuscript until you have received the copies, in case they go astray, so I could have a new copy made. Of course, you have to add on the title page now *who wrote the text*.[41] There isn't much time and I don't know what the orchestra is like there now, but the piece can be performed as it's written – just organ and one aria with cello alone. But it can be played by two or three cellos if they have them. They'll surely find somebody who could fill out the orchestra.[42] It's only necessary for a few bars at the beginning (there's a slight suggestion of it in the score) and then as accompaniment in the final chorus. It won't be hard to arrange. On the whole it'll be simple to arrange so there won't be any difficulties in performance. And if there should be, the organist can correct it – for example if the soprano part in the chorus is too high – although I don't think it is. Arranging the orchestral part shouldn't be difficult. Of course, he knows the orchestra better than I, and he has it right there. A small ensemble would be quite enough – mainly strings, horns and a few woodwind instruments. Everything else is in the organ part. Just explain it to the organist. They will have to write out the parts themselves.

I'm glad I found time to write it. Let me know on what occasion it will be performed.[43] At least you'll have that to look forward to. Give one copy to the dean.

---

[40] The *Hymn to St James*.

[41] Jaroslav Daněk, dean of Polička.

[42] For the Polička premiere, Jaroslav Maděra (1923–81) completed the score with a view to local possibilities and directed the work. He was a graduate of the organ department of the Brno Conservatoire where he studied with, among others, Josef Blatný, František Michálek and Václav Kaprál. After his graduation in 1946, he taught in Polička (from which he absented himself only for two years of military service) until the end of 1961, mainly as organist and director of the choir at Saint James'. At the Polička Music School he taught piano from the time of its founding in 1948 (he successfully completed the state examination in piano in 1953) and was its director from 1954 to 1961. At the same time, he taught at the Science and Technology Gymnasium, directed the choral group Kollár and the local orchestra. From 1962 he was engaged in Moravská Třebová as director of the music school. In 1974 he was removed from his position but was later reappointed and once again removed by decision of the Svitavy regional bureaucracy. Just as previously in Polička, he markedly influenced the musical life of Moravská Třebová, among other things as conductor of the local chamber orchestra and as director of the choral group Smetana.

[43] 31 July 1955, first Sunday after St James' (the Elder) Day (25 July).

I think he wrote the text, but I can't remember his name now – write it on the title page. The piece has a choral part and solo parts for soprano and alto as well as solo parts for bass and for narrator who recites an epistle from the Bible.[44] If there are any questions, write me and I'll check them in the score here. You'll get it in about four days. Let me know if it arrives all right.

Much love.
Your Bohouš

P.S. I'm enclosing the text you sent me[45] so in case my handwriting is illegible it can still be checked, and I'm also sending *Locandiera* in the French translation.[46]

The organ part is written as it would be for piano, so it will have to be corrected and added to as well as adding the pedal indications and so on. Where the score is marked allegro, all octaves should be played.

LETTER 89

To his Family
[Nice] 11 November 1954

My dear ones,

I attended to some 40 letters today. While gazing out at the sea, a whole heap of them piled up, and so today I got them off my hands. My head is still reeling, but if I make a start I'll manage to write you a letter, which will finish my work for today. The piano is here already and is in good condition, in spite of the fact that it's been fifteen years since I last played it.[47] So now I have to get down to work, but I have so much to do that I don't know what to do first and so I'm not doing anything. I got used to loafing here – studying the sea and the clouds. I have to compose *Gilgamesh* for Mr Sacher, the cantata for Holland,[48] and just now they wrote from Philadelphia about the Quintet for Wind Instruments and Orchestra[49] and also from Australia that they'd like a concerto for oboe and orchestra.[50] So I don't know what to do first, and I'm losing time trying to decide and in the meantime I'm not doing anything except putting my correspondence in order.

I had a sudden surprise about my taxes. They found that I had somehow failed to report everything I had earned, and they're right. They went back to 1952, when I also cheated them, and now they've charged me almost a thousand dollars. That's the way it is in these capitalist countries, and because in the States those people don't find it funny, they just wait and keep adding interest! So, with a heavy heart, I sent them a cheque today, and you can be sure their ears are ringing! Of course

---

[44] Matthew 26: 37 and 38.

[45] The original text of the *Hymn* in Daněk's manuscript.

[46] A French publication of Goldoni's *Locandiera* – *The Innkeeper's Wife* – *Mirandolina*.

[47] An upright piano, which Martinů bought in Paris in 1932. It is now in the Bohuslav Martinů Centre in Polička, as is the piano he used in Polička before 1920.

[48] The great oratorio *The Epic of Gilgamesh*, H351, composed in 1954–55, and the cantata *Mount of Three Lights*, written shortly after the date of this letter.

[49] He did not compose this work.

[50] The Concerto for Oboe and Small Orchestra, H353, written in for the oboist Jiří Tancibudek, engaged in Melbourne.

you have to admit that they need a lot of money for elections and for atomic bombs with which they'll destroy the whole world one day and that will be the end of taxes! But as long as the world exists, people have to pay them. So I got my money back because I didn't pay anything this year, but next year I'll cheat them again, so we're caught between the devil and the deep blue sea. But they're very nice about it – they come to your home and explain everything and then they simply send the bill! So my purse is a little lighter now, and I know I'm just going to have to raise the prices for some people again.

Mrs Ježková wrote and told me that two guys from Australia came on account of their eyes, but that no one was able to help them.[51] She's going to keep looking. Our friend[52] wrote and everything is in order. I told him that as a reward for his labours we'd make an agreement with Diviš and persuade him to get married and that for each new child he'd get an allowance from the state, and that the more of them she has, the more benefits he'll get. Diviš says, though, that he gave up the idea of marriage long ago because his life is already behind him. I wrote and told him all these things.

My *Czech Dances*[53] and *Field Mass* were announced in Japan. I think it's because Germaine [Leroux] played my concerto[54] there, so they're interested in having more things. I thanked Germaine for her beautiful performance in Paris and she wrote back and we both recalled old times when we were all together in Paris.

Well, now I've sapped all my energy in writing, so I'll end here and send you all my love,

Your Bohouš

LETTER 90
To his Family
[Nice] 5 December 1954

My dear ones,

My birthday is now before me.[55] We'll celebrate next week, but it doesn't interest me at all. It's been a lot of years! And when I think that those rascals from Prague who studied in Paris – Páleníček[56] and the others – already called me the tottering old composer 15 years ago! Well, what can we do? At least a fellow deserves a little

---

[51] They probably asked for her help because her late husband, the composer Jaroslav Ježek, had very poor eyesight. *Cf.* notes 192 and 193 on p. 145, above.

[52] Šebánek.

[53] Probably *Three Czech Dances* for solo piano, H154, composed in 1926, or *Three Czech Dances* for two pianos, H324, written in 1949.

[54] Leroux had the Second Piano Concerto in her repertoire.

[55] His 64th.

[56] The pianist, composer and piano teacher Josef Páleníček (1914–91) studied in Paris from 1936 to 1938, especially piano with Alfred Cortot and composition with Albert Roussel, sometime teacher of Martinů. Páleníček used to visit the composer during his tours abroad, on the last occasion shortly before Martinů´s death. Páleníček was a devoted interpreter of Martinů's works, not only of his music for solo piano but also his chamber works (especially the sonatas for cello) and the Piano Concertos Nos. 3 and 4 (*Incantation*). In 1989 he was elected chairman of the Czech Bohuslav Martinů Society, a position he held until his death.

respect! They won't dare to be cheeky to their elders – not always anyway! When I think about how much I've been through in this life! But I don't think about that much. Only sometimes – when I'm in a fit of temper! I'll celebrate my birthday anyway – as is fitting and proper.

Charlie is going to send you a long letter. She had a cold and so she found time to write. Apart from that she's always thinking up new things to do. We got used to winter with our central heating in New York, and now again we have to get used to things as they are when we have to heat ourselves, although the winters here aren't even worth mentioning – it's only foggy. When I recall our winters at home and how our teeth chattered, I can't help but wish that you could have ours. The sun came back again today, and we still have roses on the terrace.

I just wrote to Honzík [Novák] so he won't be jealous that I ask someone else when I need something. Šeb[ánek] wrote to say they gave him some kind of financial support. Just now I'm working on the sonata for piano for Rudolf Serkin[57] – I promised it to him years ago. Don't let them do anything with my old compositions like *Butterfly*[58] and the like in Prague! What did Šebánek want it for? Better he should take a look at *Half-Time*.[59] I think the Czech Philharmonic has the score.

I send my love. I know you'll be thinking of us.

Bohouš

LETTER 91
To his Family
[Nice] 21 January 1955

My dear ones,

The performances of *Fantaisies*[60] in Boston and New York were a huge success as you'll see from the reviews I'm sending. It's a long time since anyone got unanimous rave reviews like these! I'm only sending the ones from New York because I have a copy of them, but the Boston critics were enthusiastic, too, and the critics from the other newspapers, so they'll surely make you happy. Miloš [Šafránek] can translate them for you or maybe you can find someone else who knows English. I would also like you to copy the article from *The New York Times* by Olin Downes[61] in which he writes about the Moravian influence and send it to Zouhar[62] – it would be worth

---

[57] Rudolf Serkin (1903–91), renowned Bohemian-born American pianist. Martinů, who had become acquainted with him in Paris in the 1930s, completed the Sonata a few days after the date of this letter.

[58] The ballet *The Butterfly that Stamped*, H153, composed in 1926.

[59] Martinů's creative career can be divided into two parts, the division being represented by the orchestral composition *Half-Time*, H142, composed in 1924; at the time of this letter, it was still unpublished.

[60] The Sixth Symphony, *Fantaisies symphoniques*.

[61] Olin Downes (1886–1955), highly influential music critic of *The New York Times* from 1924 to 1955.

[62] Dr Zdeněk Zouhar (1927–2011), professor of composition at the Janáček Academy of Music and Arts in Brno, chair of the Department of Composition and Conducting, chairman of the Czech Bohuslav Martinů Society, was employed at the time in the music department of Brno University Library and as director of the choral group OPUS (an acronym from Obec přátel umění sborového: 'Society of Friends of Choral Music'). He inaugurated an extensive series of concerts of Martinů's music in the library for several years, beginning in 1954. He conducted OPUS in the first public performances of, among other works, the cycle *Petrklíč* ('Primrose'), H348, composed in 1954 for OPUS, and the cantata *Otvírání*

The Martinůs with Sylvia and Benno Rabinof, first interpreters
of the Concerto for Violin, Piano and Orchestra, about 1955–56

publishing – and also where he writes that I'm an American citizen now but that my roots are in my own country. Now you'll have something to enjoy and to occupy yourselves with, although I know you've got lots of other things to do. Give them to Miloš when you finish with them. He might need them, and in case he gives them to the newspapers, they'll see that in America they respect people even if they are of a different nationality. It's a shame I didn't hear it myself, but I hope that, because it had such a great success, Munch will do it in Paris, so I'd be able to listen to it here. In fact all the critics asked that it be repeated. I was just waiting for the results in order to be able to tell you that the result was 20-0 – twenty for me! Apart from that there's nothing of particular interest. The weather still can't make up its mind what it wants to do. Zouhar wrote and asked for another composition, but at the moment I'm working on *Gilgamesh* and I have some other things planned. So enjoy! I was happy for the success.

Love,
Your Bohouš

---

studánek ('The Opening of the Springs'), H354, written in 1955. He was in correspondence with Martinů from 1949 and arranged and edited the first Martinů Festschrift to appear during the composer's lifetime (*Bohuslav Martinů. Sborník vzpomínek a studií*, Krajské nakladatelství, Brno, 1957). He continued to promote Martinů's work even after the composer's death, especially in the period of his engagement at Radio Brno in the 1960s.

LETTER 92[63]

To his Family

[Nice] 25 March 1955

My dear ones,

The package came today, and we were very pleased by what we found! But the picture[64] made me sad. It was as if I were suddenly at home. So many memories came back – the snow-covered roofs – the tower – and my childhood! Suddenly it was as if it were all present. But it's far, far away, and I wander around the world but cannot go to that little corner of the earth that I long for. So, in a word, it touched me very deeply, and I thank you along with Charlie, who was so happy with the beautiful tablecloth, although we don't know when we'll be able to use it in this spread-out life. Well, I mustn't complain. Fate had something else in store for me, and I think it was a blessing. It left me to scrape through all kinds of difficult situations when all of us were about to give up hope. And it let me experience all kinds of things that I wouldn't otherwise have experienced. Nevertheless, it makes me sad when I see our tower and the bare trees and know that there's nothing I'd like better than to be able to come home.

Again, many thanks for the tablecloth – it's going to be a big hit! You know that Charlie will save it – maybe until the day we sit down together somewhere somewhat permanently – perhaps it will be at home, which is what we all wish for. The years went by, and although the tower is still the same and the cottages at *Na valech*[65] are the same, we've changed a lot. And what of it? *C'est la vie!* The package arrived within a few days and we only had to pay a little for it. Charlie will tell you the rest of the news – the happiness it gave her – and what a sensation it will be on the table!

I have the picture on the table in front of me. It makes me feel closer to you. Many thanks!

Your
Bohouš

LETTER 93

To Miloslav Bureš

[Nice] 4 July 1955

Dear Mr Bureš:

Thank you for your kind letter. Your poem about 'The Spring'[66] touched me deeply, not only because you love the Vysočina, but also because it's beautiful. It called forth many memories – and precious ones. Of course I'll set it to music! One doesn't

---

[63] A letter from Charlotte Martinů was written on the reverse.

[64] Postcard with a photograph of the tower of St James Church in Polička.

[65] One of the streets Martinů used to walk on a daily basis during his years in Polička.

[66] Bureš originally called his poem 'Song of the Spring Rubínka'. He later renamed it to accord with Martinů's cantata *The Opening of the Springs*. Bureš originally contemplated offering his poem to the composer Václav Trojan (*cf.* note 144 on p. 136, above) for setting, but at the urging of František Popelka he sent it to Martinů instead.

come across such a beautiful text every day! Let me make a suggestion – the people in Brno want to honour me next year – we could do the world premiere in Polička! What do you think of the idea? They're still eager to get a new work from me, and they want to give a performance in Polička. They have a good women's chorus[67] – so it could easily be made possible. I like this idea! This way at least it would give me a chance to come home for a while. I'll try to use the whole poem just as it is.[68] I'll send you a photo soon. I thank you, too, for 'The Bride'.[69] I don't know whether I already thanked you in those stressful times. I'm looking forward to the work. It's a long time since I worked with a Czech text, although this is the only language that speaks directly to my heart. If you go to Polička, stop and see our family!

I send you my best regards,
B. Martinů

LETTER 94
To his Family
[St Moritz] 13 August 1955

My dear ones,

I hope you've got all my postcards. I didn't have time to write a letter until we got to the mountains today. I drove through part of Italy, through towns where I'd been with Stáňa [Novák] and the Czech Philharmonic,[70] and now I'm in the mountains at an altitude of 1,800 metres. The sun is warmer here than in Nice. I'll go back to Vieux Moulin soon – Charlie is looking forward to it. I'll go to Zurich first and then straight to Paris. I missed Rybka when he was in Milan. He most likely went to the sea. I'll probably see him in Paris when he comes back. I hope I'll find a letter from you at Vieux Moulin. I'll get there around Thursday, and then I'll write more. On the road one has neither the mind nor the time for it. There are lots of people everywhere and everyone is in a hurry, so I'll be glad to get back to Vieux Moulin. I hope you're having some sunshine there, too, and that you're enjoying working in the garden.

Much love,
Your Bohouš

[67] Zdeněk Zouhar's choral group OPUS.

[68] In the event he eliminated a number of verses, most notably the seventh, and the final song.

[69] A collection of lyric poetry by Bureš, published in Brno (it bears no date of publication). In it Bureš inscribed this dedication: 'Dedicated to my dear friend, composer Mr Boh. Martinů, given in remembrance of Polička by Miloslav Bureš, Polička, February 1930'.

[70] The Czech Philharmonic had toured Italy in April and May 1922, when Martinů was still playing in the second violins.

LETTER 95[71]
To his Family
[New York] 15 December 1955

My dear ones,

I'm writing to Fanouš today to wish him all the best and lots of good health and that his 75 years won't weigh too heavily upon him and, of course, that it will be granted to us that we all might be together once again at home, which will perhaps come to be. Tell him all this and that, of course, Charlie joins me in these wishes and that we both think of him a lot as we do of all of you.

The letter sent to 28th Street found me today, and I thank you again for all your good wishes and hope that at least that one wish will come true one day. Old age won't wait for us, and I'll probably be an old geezer before we see each other again. I've received so many letters from home in recent days that I won't be able to answer them all – from Brno and from Prague – very nice letters and good wishes – it seems that everyone really expects me to come back. I have some correspondence here, too, and I can't get to it either. I'm writing a sonata for viola and piano,[72] and time flies here, and I haven't got much done. We also have to go and see people and so on. We've been here three months and I haven't got a lot done. I haven't even written any letters. I'll get to it at Christmas, but even then there won't be much time, because we'll be moving to the new apartment and it's going to be a while again before we get everything arranged and get adjusted. For now, write to me at 108 East 60th Street, New York, N.Y.

I'm surprised you make no mention of whether or not the medicines for Mrs Stehnová[73] got there. I sent them by airmail a good two weeks ago, and I wrote you at once to say they'd been sent and that you could claim them in Pardubice, as you suggested, and I never heard any more about it. I assume it arrived. It was sent by registered airmail, so it couldn't have got lost. Of course, the mail takes a long time nowadays because everything is slowed down and held up by all those Christmas cards, of which there must be thousands, and letters from you take over a week. I haven't heard any news of the concert in Polička,[74] but the music school sent their congratulations and Brno likewise. I had a letter from Šebánek, but I haven't answered him yet, either. I heard they did *The Springs* in Prague as a preview.[75] They say it was very well received. I still haven't got an answer from London about

---

[71] Charlotte Martinů contributed a lengthy postscript.

[72] H355, dedicated to Lillian Fuchs. It was first performed in New York, by Fuchs and Arthur Balsam, on 12 March 1956.

[73] A resident of Polička, Matylda Stehnová (1899–1961) was well-acquainted with Martinů from her youth.

[74] A concert for Martinů's 65th birthday, 8 December 1955, organised by the Parent-Teacher Association of the B. Martinů School of Music. František Smetana and Ladislav Simon played the Second and Third Cello Sonatas, H286 and H340. It was not permitted to put up posters advertising the concert.

[75] At the club of the Composers' Union on 7 December 1955.

making the film.[76] Charlie and I wish you a happy Christmas, and you know what we would all wish you for the New Year!

Much love,
Bohouš and Charlie

LETTER 96
To the Local Office of the National Council in Polička
Attention Josef Hlavsa, Chairman
New York, March 1956[77]

My dear friends,

I most heartily thank you all for your kind letter with its congratulations to Bureš and me for our *The Opening of the Springs*. It gave me great pleasure that the work had its premiere in our hometown[78] and that it was received with such enthusiasm. I'm only sorry that I wasn't able to be with you, but perhaps one day even this will be possible. I'm going to make a point from now on of working with our poet and of dedicating another work to Polička, the town, and to all of you.

With best regards and sincere thanks.

Your
B. Martinů

LETTER 97
To his Family
[New York] 4 March 1956

My dear ones,

Your letter finally arrived – it really takes a long time nowadays. I suppose they must just lie waiting somewhere. You've probably received my letter by now, because they always seem to cross. So again I'm writing in answer to yours of 19 February. I didn't hear from Dr Berkovec,[79] and that *Bouquet* from the [Czech] Music Fund[80] didn't arrive either. Karel Novák wrote to me about the performance of *Fantaisies Symphoniques* and Miloš Šafránek wrote to me that he spoke with Munch in Paris and he wants to do it in Prague, and that he'll probably take the Boston Symphony

---

[76] A film based on *The Opening of the Springs*. The film-makers' request for agreement by the publishing company Boosey & Hawkes turned out to be unnecessary because the cantata, H354, was eventually published by the Prague State Music Publishing House (1st edn., 1956). *Cf.* also LETTER 98 on p. 172, below.

[77] Postmarked 22 March 1956.

[78] On 7 January 1956.

[79] The musicologist and composer Jiří Berkovec (1922–2008). Dr Berkovec was clear that he never wrote to Martinů, and so the information from Polička must have been erroneous.

[80] In 1956 the Czech Music Fund published the orchestral and vocal scores of the cantata *Bouquet of Flowers* (composed in 1937) as hire material.

there this summer.[81] We'll send congratulations to Zrzavý[82] – I think he's 65 too. I think Mařka is taking all that business about the diplomas too seriously – it's only paper! I think everything is in the package, and I found a new package, mostly programmes, and I'll send them to you too. There are letters there, too, from Bruno Walter, from Lindbergh,[83] and so on. But don't worry yourselves about it. I'm only sending it so it can all be kept together – here it just creates a pile of stuff.

A letter came today from Zouhar. He sent a photo from Polička with a big picture of me in the stage.[84] He has a lot of new plans. I see that he's doing his best to ensure that I could now only write for Brno in order to keep them occupied.[85] Šebánek also wrote – nothing special today – that Jan [Novák] had a premiere in Prague and that his wife is rehearsing my Piano Concerto No. 3.[86] Zouhar wants to perform – that is, he's asking me – whether it would be a good idea to do the little opera after Tolstoy in concert[87] – that they like it a lot. That could happen. Maybe they'll start rehearsing it. They'd certainly do it in our town. He says they'll go there again in the spring. I'm sending the autographed programme. We hope the winter has already let up for you a bit and that it will be warmer now. A card also came from the Janeles[88] in Prague. They and Kollár sent congratulations. Charles Munch tells me he's doing *Fantaisies* again in Boston next week and that we should come. He's going to do it in Paris in June and maybe also in Prague on the programme of the tour by the Boston Symphony to Europe in the summer. (I already wrote you about it.) Kubelík will conduct the first performance of *The Frescoes of Piero della Francesca* in August at the festival in Salzburg,[89] and we'll probably have to go there, too.[90] Miloš Šafránek also wrote. He's still in Paris and I guess is working on that book about me. He'll surely write to you. He must have a lot to do. On Monday I have the premiere here of the Sonata for Viola and Piano. It's a new work. In addition to that I'm already at work on an opera,[91] and I'll send you the book[92] from France. We'll be

---

[81] The Boston Symphony Orchestra did give a concert in Prague, on 11 September 1956, but did not perform the Sixth Symphony.

[82] *Cf.* note 77 on p. 49, above.

[83] Bruno Walter (1876–1962), one of the world's leading conductors of the first half of the twentieth century. Charles Lindbergh (1902–74), American pilot. After his non-stop flight from New York to Paris in 1927, Martinů dedicated his symphonic work *La Bagarre* ('Tumult') to him. Walter's letters and Lindbergh's letter of thanks are preserved in the Martinů Centre in Polička.

[84] A photograph of the stage of Tyl House in Polička with the choir OPUS (*cf.* note 67 on p. 166, above) after the premiere of *The Opening of the Springs* on 7 January 1956.

[85] This ironic comment suggests Zdeněk Zouhar's 'new plans' for OPUS involved Martinů rather more deeply than he had expected.

[86] Eliška Nováková, *née* Hanousková (b. 1928), played in a piano duo with her husband, the composer and pianist Jan Novák, Martinů's former student in New York City. *Cf.* note 186 on p. 145, above.

[87] One-act opera *What Men Live By*, composed in 1951–52, after Tolstoy, originally written for television. Zouhar conducted a concert version of the opera in 1956.

[88] From the Polička resident Fráňa Janele, who with his wife spent several months in Prague at that time.

[89] Premiered in Salzburg on 26 August 1956.

[90] They did not go.

[91] *The Greek Passion*, H372, composed in 1954–59.

[92] French publication of Kazantzakis' *Christ Recrucified* (1948), the source of the composer's libretto for *The Greek Passion*. Martinů worked with an English edition of the novel to produce a libretto in English. *Cf.* also note 139 on p. 181, below.

The Martinůs with the Rybka family in Jamaica, New York State, 1956.
From left to right: Mary Carolyn Rybka, Doris Rybka, Charlotte Martinů (standing),
Martinů, his friend Frank Rybka, Mary Carolyn's fiancé Ed Bishop (standing)
and James Rybka

there in a couple of weeks.[93] I'll start work in Rome in October.[94] What we'll do after we get there we don't know. I'm waiting for Firkušný so we can go to Washington to find out what they would think about a visit to Prague. I've got to be very careful I don't get mixed up in anything – things are very delicate here just now, as you probably know. That's about all the news I have for the moment. Firkušný is going to play the new *Invocation* for Piano and Orchestra[95] here in the autumn. We'll be away, but he'll surely do it again in Europe.

Charlie and I send our love and wish you an end to winter and the coming of sunny days! As I see it, the springs are getting cleaner and cleaner all the time!

Love,
Your Bohouš

---

[93] They were forced to spend the summer of 1956 in Switzerland, because Charlotte Martinů's authorisation of residence in France (she was now a US citizen) had expired.

[94] As Composer-in-Residence at the American Academy, i.e., as consultant to young American composers studying there on stipend.

[95] Piano Concerto No. 4, *Incantation*, written for Rudolf Firkušný. It was first performed in New York on 4 December 1956. On several occasions in his letters Martinů – whose command of English was always imperfect – referred also to the work by mistake as *Invocation* rather than *Incantation*.

LETTER 98
To his Family
[Schönenberg] 27 July 1956

My dear ones,

Thanks for your letter. I'm happy about the music school. As you described it,[96] it must have been lovely. So there'll be another generation of musicians! I hope they'll have a better life than we had – a life filled with war and other unnecessary things. I see you have constant visitors, and I know time passes a little more pleasantly for you that way. It's beautiful here already, and I rarely go to Basel because it's a shame to go to the city when it's so lovely outdoors. We had the fun of saving a blackbird – a young one – from death, and we took care of him for a while. He was a lot of fun for us, and he got so used to us that even when we let him go, he'd always fly to us from a branch, especially when he was hungry, and then we had to look for worms for him. He was with us for 14 days, and yesterday his mum found him and took him under her wing. It's beautiful among animals – better than among people – who would prefer to devour each other. We wondered how it was possible that after 14 days she found him and recognised him! So now we're alone again, but perhaps we'll see them again.

The Salzburg Festival has begun and my composition will be played around the 23rd of August,[97] I think, but I don't know exactly. I hope they'll invite us. Kubelík hasn't written, but I think that Universal Editions will let me know the date. If they don't invite us, I don't know whether I'll go, because it will be hard to find a hotel. Everything will be completely booked. The Sachers are already back from England and they also had miserable weather, and so they're glad to be home, but it probably won't be for long. He's conducting again in Zurich, and they're continually on the move – although if we had a villa like that, I wouldn't budge.

We speak German with the gardener here and we go to watch the deer. How they romp about! – it's a joy to watch them! – they have young ones now. The cherry season is already over – they've all been picked – and we had our fill of them.

Charlie sent you a letter and a photo – you might have got them already. I sent a photo to Mr Šíma.[98] He's probably away on vacation – but perhaps he'll get it.

I don't know where to have copies made here, so again you're going to have to wait for the *Hymn*.[99] I haven't heard from Mr Berkovec, and it's a mystery to me that he can't find me. Apart from this, my mail doesn't get lost, and it's only his letters that don't arrive, so I can't write back.

Mrs Ježková was in Basel and telephoned. They're in Europe with those men she's staying with. But they didn't stay in Basel – only an hour – so I didn't see her. They're probably in Italy by now. She'll surely send you a card.

I hope they'll give you the money soon. Go and see about it, won't you?

---

[96] Student concert of the Polička Music School at the end of the school year, at which works by Martinů were traditionally performed.

[97] *The Frescoes of Piero della Francesca* had its premiere there on 26 August 1956.

[98] Most probably the painter Josef Šíma: *cf.* note 192 on p. 70, above.

[99] For copying the score.

You haven't told me what Šebánek said or how he's doing. His letters are always a little puzzling. They certainly have fine weather for filming now[100] and perhaps the sun will stay around for a while. Again, people everywhere are complaining about the heat wave we're having.

Otherwise, there's nothing new here. Firkušný hasn't written – I don't know where he is. Rybka – if you remember him – gave his daughter away – and gave a big wedding party. Now, everyone is on vacation, and almost all our friends here are somewhere by the sea.

The two bags we sent haven't arrived yet, so I have a lot of correspondence as a result. We're looking for them. Miloš Šafránek is travelling in France – he has a lot of invitations. He surely likes it here. It's a shame I wasn't able to get together with him. Karel Novák wrote concerning Munch and says they might ask him to do *Fantaisies*[101] in Prague. They played it this week at the Tanglewood Festival and they're also going to do the *Field Mass*. Zouhar wrote and also Jan Novák. Everyone is in the countryside now. Zouhar has a lot of plans again. Maybe he'll tell you about them.

Well, I guess that's all that's new. We send you lots of love and our best wishes for happy times in the garden! You had a short spring this year, anyhow. Perhaps the good weather will stay now.

Love,

Your [102]

LETTER 99[103]
To his Family
[Schönenberg] 23 September 1956

My dear ones,

We're back again, and I found your letter from Prague. I see you met Munch at his concert.[104] It's a shame he didn't do *Fantaisies*. They really cocked it up in Prague.[105] I hope he told them. I couldn't speak with him much – only at the intermission. *Fantaisies* had a big success here.[106] They played it beautifully, and the orchestra gave me a big ovation. Charles was quite pleased with it, the hall was packed, and we were introduced to a lot of important people, like former Ambassador Bonnet,[107]

---

[100] That is, for the first film adaptation of *The Opening of the Springs* (for Prague TV) – *cf.* note 76 on p. 168, above.

[101] The Sixth Symphony.

[102] Martinů forgot to sign the letter.

[103] Charlotte Martinů added a lengthy postscript.

[104] Marie Martinů went to the Boston Symphony concert in Prague.

[105] Perhaps reluctance of the Prague organiser, perhaps his tactics: *Fantaisies Symphoniques* had been in the repertory of the Czech Philharmonic since February 1956.

[106] Martinů means in Paris, one of the stops on the European tour by the Boston Symphony in September 1956.

[107] Martinů wrote 'Bonet', an obvious misspelling. The reference is most probably to the Gaullist politician Henri Bonnet (1888–1978), a follower of de Gaulle from the time of the Second World War. He was

and so on. The reviews were fantastic – Šafránek has them all. He'll send them to you. I have the review from *Le Monde*, which I still need, but I'll send it later. There'll be more in the literary reviews – Šafránek will find them. I look forward to a letter from Mařka to hear how she liked it in Prague and what she found out. I heard from Brno, too, but they got some misinformation from our newspapers – I haven't sent anything new to Prague, and especially not that *Mount of Three Lights*. Again, somebody simply made it up.

We were going to go to Rome this week, but Universal Editions wrote to say they have to speak with me and that someone is coming here to make arrangements for the opera in Zurich,[108] so we put off our departure for a couple of days. We'll leave around the 3rd of October. It annoys me a lot – each day we lose in Rome – because everyone raves about it and how beautiful it is there. We had magnificent weather in Paris – almost too hot, in fact – but we enjoyed it. We didn't see much of our friends. On the way we stopped at Mt St Leger, where we always used to meet the whole gang.[109] It was nice. I strolled around Paris like I did when I was a young man, but my legs hurt me now, so I'll take a rest. It's a beautiful city. It's still full of people, and it's also quite expensive. Now I've got to see to my correspondence, which I've neglected, so as to have everything in order before Rome. I'll leave space for Charlie.

Love,
Bohouš

Our address in Rome is: American Academy, 5 Via Angelo Masina, Rome 28, Italia.

LETTER 100
To Vanda Jakubíčková
[Schönenberg] 25 September 1956

Dear Vanda

Once again we've gone astray in the world, and thus it's taken me a long time to answer. I enjoyed your lovely letter very much. It took me far back in time to our forests and to the memories they evoke. They leave me with a certain quiet sadness, thinking that perhaps it's all quite different now than I remember it. Nevertheless it's always precious to me to return to those times when we didn't yet know what life had in store for us. I often think back to our rencontre in London,[110] of that quiet street where I lived – as well as of London itself. I suppose you think of it sometimes, too. It seems like everything has somehow turned out differently than we had imagined and expected. Don't worry about your having been alone – each of us on this earth lives something of a solitary life. Perhaps it's we who have changed – perhaps it's the world. We simply have to accept those changes. Again I'm roaming

---

French ambassador to the United States from the official recognition of de Gaulle's governent in 1944 until 1954.

[108] Unnamed employee of the Vienna publisher Universal Edition, which secured publishing rights to *The Greek Passion*, not yet completed at this time. It was premiered, in Zurich, only on 9 June 1961.

[109] Members of the group of composers known as the 'École de Paris', an informal society of friends, foreigners in Paris, *cf* p. 18, above.

[110] In June 1938, at the festival of the International Society for Contemporary Music.

around the world from place to place, but you know where I'm drawn to most of all. Perhaps I can also look forward to my dreams coming true, and then we'll tell ourselves about all the things that gave us joy and sadness. Somehow, those feelings are always intertwined.

Now, about your sonnet. I thank you for sending it but, unfortunately, to set it to music simply wouldn't be possible. There's nothing to be done with it. A country fair is so special an event that no such adaptation could genuinely evoke it, and so we must take it for what it is – a country fair – with all that you depict in your lovely lyrics. No musical working of it could make of it what it already is. I'm sure you understand me. I'll keep your lyrics as a remembrance, and I thank you for your confidence. I'm sorry I can't do it. It would just be a vague picture, lifeless and artificial.

When you next take a walk through our forests – Liboháj[111] and such – think of me – and remember me to them!

With many fond memories and warm wishes I am

Your
B. Martinů

LETTER 101[112]
To his Family
[Rome] 16 December 1956

My dear ones,

Your letter came rather quickly. We thank you for your good wishes, and Charlotte and I wish you a happy holiday and all the best for the New Year and good health, most of all. Of course, the best is rather bad these days. We have to content ourselves that things aren't any worse, at least. But when a person is in good health, other things come right more easily. We'll be thinking about you. We'll probably have supper with the Vaněks,[113] although there's a holiday party and banquet here at the Academy. We're constantly going out somewhere.

How many Christmases have we already spent without you and always with the single wish – which for so long has refused to be fulfilled – to be together once again at home. And so again we have to shuffle along into the future and remain hopeful. How are you going to spend Christmas Eve? At least you'll give the house a good heating – I think it must be cold there. Again, the weather here has changed, and now it's beautiful – the sun is warm in the daytime and only in the evening does it get cool. Please extend our best wishes to everyone in the neighbourhood – our friends. I sent a card to Karel [Novák], but I'll also write him a letter for Christmas. Zouhar, Bureš, Jan [Novák] and a lot of others also sent us their good wishes.

This month went by so quickly that Christmas came as a surprise. It's already at the door and New Year's is only a step away. Who knows what it will bring us – let's hope something good – that there might really be Peace on Earth to All Men of

---

[111] Liboháj is a woodland in Polička where the young Martinů used to take extensive walks.

[112] Charlotte Martinů added a lengthy postscript.

[113] The family of Vladimír Vaněk; *cf.* note 9 on p. 35, above.

Good Will, although there's precious little good will in the world today. Write and let us know how you spend Christmas. Mr Maděra[114] wrote. I've got to respond to everyone. I'll tell you all the news next time I write, although there isn't much. I must leave a place for Charlie, who wants to add something. I think it's going to be a sad Christmas in the world this year.[115] Perhaps people will give some thought to these beautiful holidays and will reflect on what they're doing and how with each day they're drifting farther away from an understanding of the reason these holidays came to be and what the meaning of them is. We'll be thinking of you.

We send you our love,
Your Bohouš

If you have a photograph in profile, send it to Šebánek to give to the other sculptor. They say it was Diviš's last wish.[116] And let me know. I don't have any myself.

LETTER 102

To his Family
[Rome] 13 January 1957

My dear ones,

I'm writing this in answer to yours of December 30th. It's very strange that you haven't had any news from me in a long time, even though I wrote every week. So now I guess there are lots of things you don't know about. Thanks for sending Maruška's regards.[117] I sent her a card at your address. And thanks, too, for the greetings from Zdeňka Podhajská.[118] I'm always glad to hear something from old friends.

Now I have some news: I don't know if Bureš was in Polička, but I thought everything over again and realised that it isn't a good idea to struggle against the universe, even though it's as crazy as it is, and it will just be better to give the people what they look forward to, and to forget what I don't like.[119] In short, I'll send *Legend of the Smoke from Potato Fires*[120] home. Indeed, it's written for that purpose. I've written to Bureš to tell him to wait and perhaps he'll get it soon. As you know, they're going to do it in Polička, too, but probably not the first performance. That's Prague, you know – they won't let it out of their hands – like with *The Springs*.

---

[114] *Cf.* note 42 on p. 160, above.

[115] After the bloody suppression of the Hungarian Revolution in November 1956.

[116] A close friend of Martinů, the painter Alén Diviš (*cf.* note 25 on p. 99, above) died on 25 November 1956. No details are known about the last wish mentioned in Martinů's letter. Of a number of busts of Martinů, the one closest to this date is the relief bust by Josef Kadlec, which was mounted on St James' Church in Polička in 1957 (*cf.* note 176 on p. 186, below). Martinů's Czech reveals, though, that he is talking about a female sculptor, and yet it cannot be Irène Codreanu-King (1896–1985), who sculpted a bust of Martinů, probably the best yet done, shortly before the Second World War.

[117] Marie Pražanová.

[118] Zdeňka Podhajská (1901–91), dancer and dance educator, was a friend of Martinů in Paris around 1930.

[119] A response to the suppression of the Hungarian Revolution.

[120] The cantata *Legend of the Smoke from Potato Fires*, with a text by Miloslav Bureš, composed in 1956.

I'm curious if the performance in Polička on New Year's Day took place.[121] I got *The Springs* from Prague, but only one copy. It's nicely printed, and the translation is beautiful, but there's not a trace of the recordings. I don't know where they went astray. I think they didn't send them, because even if they stayed at customs, I would have received notification and, for that matter, nothing sent here to the Academy would be held up there. Strange, very strange! I wish I had heard them already in case we don't manage to catch it on the radio. And they're also curious about it here. The Vaněks like the poem a lot.

You have to come to an agreement about the *Legend* with Bureš, who will certainly want to do it at home, too. The Kühn Choir[122] is going to sing it and I hear they're fantastic. They have probably also recorded *The Springs*, so you'll know how they sang it and whether it was better than Brno. He probably did it with the children's choir, which always sounds lovely.

Now some other news:

In spite of the pain in my hand, I wrote some short pieces for the Prague teachers' choir.[123] Venhoda[124] is perseverance itself and doesn't let himself get discouraged and sent me a privately printed book with illustrations.[125] Some man from the Vysočina printed it and did the drawings himself. They are *Brigand Songs*, and I thought a little robber's blood would do them good – to revive the spirit and mitigate fear – that's why I wrote it for them. I wouldn't have had any peace from Venhoda, but otherwise I like him because he didn't get dismayed but hung on until he got it done. It's five *Brigand Songs* for male chorus – only chorus – without instruments. So they've got their work cut out for them.

Of course, I'm going to have to satisfy the others in Brno,[126] but I can do that later.

My hand isn't serving me well, especially for writing, but it's nervous fatigue and there's nothing to do for it except to rest, and I can't do that until I finish the opera, which will be soon now,[127] but even when that's done I won't be able to get much rest. In the evening I put hot compresses on it.

---

[121] He probably had in mind the public showing of the TV version of *The Opening of the Springs* which, however, did not take place until 9 February 1957.

[122] The Kühn Children's Choir was founded by Jan Kühn (1891–1958) in 1932. (The Kühn Choir Prague is a different ensemble, founded in 1958 by Kühn's son, Pavel (1938–2003).)

[123] First volume of the *Brigand Songs*, H361, composed in January 1957.

[124] The choral director Miroslav Venhoda (1915–87), in the years 1956–58 conductor of the Choral Society of Prague Teachers. His name is connected above all with the group Prague Madrigalists, a mixed chorus, for which he also arranged three of the *Brigand Songs*. During Martinů's lifetime, he introduced other vocal works by him to the Madrigalists' repertoire: *Primrose* and *Czech Madrigals*, H278, composed in 1939, and after his death the *Madrigals (Part-Song Book)*, H380, written in 1959.

[125] The *Brigand Songs*, the text of which was selected, calligraphed and illustrated by Metoděj Florian (1904–96), a painter, carver and composer in Stará Říše. His book *Brigand Songs* was published by the Prague Teachers' Chorus in 1957. This charming little book has on page 2 Florian's dedication to Martinů and contains the texts of the songs, which the composer set to music in the first volume of *Brigand Songs* (1957).

[126] The Moravian Teachers' Chorus, for which he wrote the second volume of *Brigand Songs* almost immediately after the first volume.

[127] *The Greek Passion*. He finished the first version in 1957 and the second version in January 1959.

Charlie was quite ill, and it got increasingly worse, but we hope she's past the worst of it now, but she must slowly begin to eat. At least she's more cheerful now. She's sorry that she can't go for a walk, but the weather isn't very good anyway. Today it actually seemed as if it were going to snow! There's lots of snow in the mountains. Maybe it will change in the next few days.

I assume you have already received our news of New Year – we stayed at home!

I don't know anything at all about Miloš [Šafránek]. I think I heard he's back already, but he hasn't written. Šeb[ánek] hasn't written either to say how it looks for his tour, but I think it's been held up again for some time, and that he'll stay in Prague.

Herberta Masaryková wrote, too. She's seeing a lot of Karel [Novák]. She mentioned *Juliette*. I can't imagine what became of the *Carols*[128] – they must have been lost somewhere long ago – or else they're at Vieux Moulin. I'm sorry about it, because it was all the songs that Mum used to sing. I looked for them not long ago but didn't find them. Don't wish for Miloš's reviews or anything, because he won't send them to you. He'd rather you sent everything to him. How far along he is on the book I don't know.

You wrote that Baby Jesus returns at the Czech Christmas! But I think maybe he changed his mind and put it off until a later time.

Not a trace of Firkušný, although he must be in Europe. If Šebánek goes to Paris, he'll get the address of that sculptor[129] at the Mihalovicis',[130] with whom he's also acquainted.

I wrote you about Diviš in two letters. You didn't get them.

Your Bohouš

LETTER 103
To Miloslav Bureš
Rome, 10 March 1957

My dear friend:

It was sad for me to hear from you of the death of your father. Please accept my sincere condolences. These are sad times in our lives and we can only say: Thy will be done on Earth as it is in Heaven. Your conclusion of *The Springs* is filled with it – with the old men and women who have departed and are departing – the journey of life.

Thanks, too, for *Wedding Suite*. There are some beautiful images in it. For the moment it's just a catalogue, some sort of collage, which has to be chosen and arranged from the verses in order to make a coherent whole. The theme is beautiful and I think you were rather counting on its being made into a film, which perhaps made you somewhat uncertain. We'll go back to it when I'm going to have more

---

[128] The ballet *Koleda* ('Carols'), H112, composed in 1917, of which the score is lost. It was a substantial work, consisting of a prologue and four acts; it was scored for soloists, female-voice choir and orchestra.

[129] Irène Codreanu-King; *cf.* note 116 on p. 175, above.

[130] Marcel Mihalovici (*cf.* p. 18, above) was married to the pianist Monique Haas (1909–87).

In Rome, 1957

time, and I'll present my suggestion. As it is, it's not suitable as a film, as it would be quite without a controlling storyline, nor as a performance in concert, which would depend on the way it had been adapted for film. We have to decide on either one or the other answer to the problem. Naturally, I'm for the concert version, and in that case a lot of repetition in your text would have to be cut, and it would have to be given order. Mind you, there's one danger in that, and that is that our wedding songs are in fact somewhat sad and rather sentimental, referring mostly to the mother and to the parting from her. To put it briefly, there is in them something left over from a patriarchal age, and the entire wedding in that concept appears, except for the dancing and the screaming and hollering and here and there a matchmaking joke, rather sad – for the most part a lament for the separation from the family. These are only my thoughts, which don't exactly have to do with your poem. And yet, if they're related in some way – in something that is your own – it's in a certain melancholy which colours your expression. I had an opportunity now with my opera[131] with its Greek wedding to see another approach to the wedding, which is actually thoroughly masculine and at the same time full of poetry that is as hard as a diamond. In so doing, I thought a lot about you and your writing – to the extent that I'm familiar with it – and even of some other good poems by Halas and Seifert,[132] where the feeling for the earth or nature, the mother or the family, somehow dissolves in lamentation and sadness, and in some way the positive aspect gets lost. It's the old truth about life to death and from death to new life. Perhaps you'll tell me it's easy for me to talk, but that wouldn't solve anything. As you know, I chose the texts of *Brigand Songs* and the choice was expedient. It was its harsh masculine element that determined my choice, even if that perhaps offends our so highly developed sense of social order, which has collapsed into disorder anyway. But there is in it rebelliousness and conviction.

Both of us have our eye on a certain goal about which we don't speak in our letters, but one day we'll talk about it properly. Now we had *The Springs* which made people sentimental and brought tears to their eyes. We played it here in the company of Czech friends. Firkušný was also here, and the effect was the same even on gramophone. Now we should do something again, at which people might clench their teeth if they couldn't do anything else. And that is your project about Man. Poetry is a luxury, and though when it comes from the heart it's like the earth – hard and merciless – yet it is what keeps us alive.

Leave me *The Wedding*. I'll give it some thought, and I ask you to think about what I'm saying to you today. The little songs somehow don't come to me. They're rather folkloric, and in that case genuine folksongs would be better. Don't be angry.

I hope that your case, about which you write, will be resolved to your satisfaction, and that if you need my intervention, you'll write to me.[133] It irks me that you put off

---

[131] *The Greek Passion*.

[132] The Czech poets František Halas (1901–49) and Jaroslav Seifert (1901–86), who won the Nobel Prize for Literature in 1984.

[133] Probably a reference to Bureš's problems in obtaining an Italian visa for his intended journey to visit Martinů in Rome.

With Miloslav Bureš in Rome, May, 1957

your tour until September, because I don't know myself where I'll be in September – whether I'll still be here or somewhere else.

I must ask if you know any other language than Czech.

Best regards,
Your
B. Martinů

LETTER 104
To his Family
[Schönenberg] 10 November 1957

My dear ones,

Your letter arrived and also the textbooks. I'm glad you found something – I don't understand why they're so scarce – everyone studied German at home. I was the only one who neglected it. They came in handy, and I see it's best to turn to you when I need something, otherwise it always takes months and then I get something I didn't ask for. You don't write anything about what Šebas[134] said and whether he

---

[134] Šebánek.

gave you any more suggestions. That's his forte. What is that diploma from Lidice?[135] I just got a letter from somewhere in Germany where they're going to play *Lidice*[136] and that there are some Sudeten Germans there who don't like it. I have to ask for a good translation. I'll send it to you. Dean Novák also wrote to me from Chrudim and sent me some of his poems for me to set to music and to have published. Just now I have other worries, but I'll write to him. I constantly receive little poems from somewhere. It could keep me busy for years!

We're still not over the flu, and it's beginning to be unpleasant, because we can't be in the company of others, so we're here all alone, and I have many, many things to attend to. We bought a good radio, so now maybe we'll be able to hear my works better when they're played somewhere. This week in Beromünster they're playing some Divertimento.[137] I think it's one of those little things that were printed in Czechoslovakia.

I'm glad the *Mount* was a success. It was a beautiful evening in Bern.[138] Perhaps you'll hear it on the radio. I hope they'll do it more often. You might have read that Kazantzakis died[139] – it upset us both very much. They wrote to me from Freiburg in Germany before we left for Paris that they were returning from China and that he had been in the hospital there. I answered his letter and when we got back I thought they'd already be in Antibes, and I wanted to write him, and just then they announced over the radio that he had died. It's a shame – he could yet have given us some beautiful works of literature – there aren't many such writers around nowadays. Everywhere there were articles in the newspapers. I've written to his wife – I don't know what she's going to do – I suppose she'll go back to Greece. I'm still quite sad about it.

I also confirmed to Venhoda the receipt of what he sent me, and he's already answered me. I still have to thank Mr Florian for the book he dedicated to me.[140] Again they sent me a package of scores from Prague. I don't really know what I'm supposed to do with them. I asked them so many times not to send anything except when I ask them to. I also got a letter from the record company.[141] It seems they're sending something – records, probably – but so far nothing has come.

---

[135] Diploma of the Society for the Restoration of Lidice. In the documentary film *Lidice žijí* ('Lidice Lives'), directed by Jindřich Ferenc (Czechoslovakia, 1957), which originated at the suggestion of the Society, Martinů's *Memorial to Lidice* was heard, with his agreement.

[136] *Memorial to Lidice*.

[137] *Divertimento* (*Serenade* No. 4) for chamber orchestra, H215, composed in 1932. Martinů's uncertainty is typical: with a few exceptions, he found it difficult for him to recall his early compositions; some he forgot about altogether.

[138] The premiere of *Mount of Three Lights*, Berne, 3 October 1955, with Die Haghe Sanghers.

[139] The Greek writer Nikos Kazantzakis (1882–1956), whose novels Martinů admired and to the ethos of which he felt close. The novel *Christ Recrucified* became for him the point of departure for work on his own libretto of *The Greek Passion*. At the time of his residence in Nice in 1954, he visited Kazantzakis in nearby Antibes and later exchanged a number of letters with him. For a facsimile edition of this fascinating correspondence, *cf.* Růžena Dostálová and Aleš Březina (eds.), *Řecké pašije, osud jedné opery. Korespondence Nikose Kazantzakise s Bohuslavem Martinů* ('The Greek Passion. Destiny of an Opera. Correspondence between Nikos Kazantzakis and Bohuslav Martinů'), Set Out, Prague, 2003.

[140] Metoděj Florian and the *Brigand Songs*: *cf.* note 125 on p. 176, above.

[141] From the Czech recording company Supraphon.

Iša Krejčí wrote. He wants to do *Theatre behind the Gate*.[142] It might be best if he sent my earnings to you in crowns.

I signed a contract with Éditions Max Eschig in Paris, mainly for some smaller chamber works. At least I'll get something from it for myself. I also received a handsome honorarium, but we had to spend it in Paris, because just now French currency can't be taken out of the country, so we bought a lot of things for the garderobe. We had to spend half a million francs.[143] Imagine! But it wasn't so difficult, because it's quite expensive there, and they just had the Auto Show, so everything was even more expensive, and yet we did well. We had oysters and lobster and some good wine, and if it weren't for the flu, it would have been ideal. And that's how we managed to spend it all! In other respects it's a shame the way things are in the world today. I wanted to give all my works to Prague but, as you know, I wouldn't get anything from it – everything would go to the bank.

We're sending you a plaque with an engraving of the Queen of Belgium, which I received when we were there two years ago. You'll like it. Apart from that, stop the celebrating! As you know, the cult of personality doesn't pay these days.[144] The parcel will have to wait until we go to town again, which I hope will be soon.

Well, I think I've told you all there is to tell. I have a lot of correspondence to attend to and little time to do it in, because the piano concerto[145] has to be done by January, and I lost a lot of time with the travelling and the illness.

Thanks for the German books! I hope they'll help me. I've got to get to them now that I'm involved with the theatres here and in Germany. The Webers telephoned, and I think they'll come for us next week and take us to Zurich, so I'll be able to get the opera ready.[146]

Much love from me and Charlotte,
Bohouš

LETTER 105
To Miloslav Bureš
[Schönenberg] 7 January 1958

My dear friend Bureš,

Charlotte and I thank you for your good wishes for the New Year, and we again wish you lots of good ideas for more poems and lots of confidence in yourself! I see you're continually troubled about your stay in Rome,[147] and to no purpose, for you know that we were glad to have you there, and I still take pleasure in the fact

---

[142] The composer Iša Krejčí (1904–68) was at that time engaged as director of the Olomouc Opera. He staged *Theatre behind the Gate* on 24 May 1958.

[143] 'Old francs'; the 'new franc' was introduced, at a rate to 1 to 100 of the inflated old francs, in 1960.

[144] Perhaps an ironic reference to Khrushchev's denunciation of Stalin in his 'Secret Speech' to the 20th Congress of the Soviet Communist Party in February the previous year.

[145] The Fifth Piano Concerto, *Fantasia Concertante*, H366, commissioned by Margrit Weber and composed in 1956–57.

[146] Agreement regarding the staging of *The Greek Passion* at the Zurich Opera.

[147] Bureš spent some time in Rome in May 1957.

that you at least saw another world and a beautiful one. As for my time, it certainly wasn't wasted being with you. I always have enough time for my work, so you didn't in any way put me out. On the contrary, it made me happy to be able to get to know you better. So there's no reason for your grim thoughts. That you ran about, as you said, like a scared rabbit, was natural. I was like that, too, the first time I was in Paris – it seems to be perfectly natural and rational. I'd be happy to see you again.

Preparations for the premiere of the opera are not going as smoothly as I would wish, but it'll turn out all right.[148] Trojan[149] sent me a letter and his gramophone records. I only sent him a card, because I just finished a new work[150] and I'm dedicating myself to my correspondence, which had piled up over a couple of weeks. Give him my regards! I'm sure he'll write some beautiful music for your lyrics!

I see that *The Springs* continues to make a career for itself, which is good, and I hope the other things will go well also. I'm looking forward to *Dandelions*. Unfortunately, we didn't catch the *Legend*,[151] so I'm still not familiar with it. I gave it to the publisher[152] and they have to talk with Kühn about it – how to make it sellable. The accordion and the flute are going to create difficulties.

As far as *Mikeš*[153] is concerned, I think you should, after a while, take another look at it. It seemed to me, based on the first impression I had when reading it, that the snowstorm scene isn't clearly enough depicted. I would very much like to read *The Lime Tree*.[154]

I heard about the celebration in Polička,[155] and I was glad to hear of it, even though I wasn't able to be there. Please, if you have any kind of relation with Artia,[156] ask if they got my letter. I inquired of them about some scores of Dvořák besides those they had sent me, but I haven't heard anything from them in a long time.

I think the translation of *Gilgamesh* would be difficult for you, because it's a musical translation which must be done according to the score. It's really work for an expert translator, and it will be especially difficult to translate into Czech.

Just now I'm reading Eisner's *A Cathedral and a Fortress*, a fantastic book[157] – you should read it. I think I've now answered everything that was in your letter.

---

[148] It is not clear whether the reference is to the as yet unfinished *The Greek Passion* or to *Mirandolina*.

[149] The composer Václav Trojan (*cf.* notes 144 on p. 136, above, and 66 on p. 165, above).

[150] The Fifth Piano Concerto.

[151] The work for mixed chorus *The Romance of the Dandelions*, H264, composed in 1957, and the cantata *Legend of the Smoke from Potato Fires*, both set to Bureš's poetry.

[152] To the State Music Publishing House of the time.

[153] The chamber cantata *Mikeš of the Mountains*, H375, was not composed until 1959.

[154] Bureš's retelling of folk tales and legends of the Vysočina *The Singing Lime Tree* (Krajské nakladatelství Havlíčkův Brod, Havlíčkův Brod, 1956).

[155] A second, independent, permanent Martinů exhibition was opened on 8 December 1957 at the Polička Museum, and a memorial plaque was unveiled with a portrait in relief of the composer. It is at the entrance to the tower of the Church of St James.

[156] A state-run publishing house in Prague.

[157] That Martinů should be reading a book (1946) by the writer and translator Pavel Eisner (1889–1958) about the stylistic richness of the Czech language is evidence of the breadth and depth of his interests in and his enduring ties to his mother tongue. Eisner, incidentally, was of German-Jewish origin and survived deportation to Terezín. *Cf.* also LETTER 115 on p. 197, below.

You said something to me in Rome about some very good comedy by Klicpera. I wonder what it was. I'm in touch with Šafránek, and he knows a lot about me.

Say hello to Kühn and his wife[158] and all my friends.

Be well and get a lot of work done!

Charlotte and I send our regards and wish you all the best.

Your B. Martinů

LETTER 106

To his Family

[Schönenberg] 30 January 1958

My dear ones,

I'm late with the news, but maybe you've already read something in the newspapers about the concert.[159] A representative of the Composers' Union[160] was here from Prague – sent expressly for the performance. It was a resounding success! The audience shouted and stamped their feet! Briefly put, it was a huge success at both performances – Thursday and Friday. They played it beautifully, and Sacher conducted magnificently. They're still talking about it today. I'll send you the reviews – Sacher took them with him. He's in Holland just now – so when he gets back. There was also a picture in the newspapers that they took of us on stage. Paul and Maja[161] are very pleased – they liked it a lot. So – it was a triumph! In February the *Sinfonia Concertante*, which I wrote many years ago in Paris and up till now has never heard[162] will be performed. It will be a different orchestra – not Sacher's – so there'll be some work to do again. After the concert, we were at supper and everyone was excited. I was presented with a bouquet of flowers at the podium and there was a bottle of French liqueur with it and, afterward, we both got a present from Sacher. I got a beautiful winter coat – sporty, speckled and warm, which is needed here now, and Charlie got a white sweater to keep out the cold. I even spoke over the radio – a shortwave station from Geneva – which means that it was transmitted all over the world!

---

[158] The choral director Jan Kühn (*cf.* note 122 on p. 176, above) and his wife, Markéta Kühnová (1905–94), singer, pianist, and choral director. Kühn presented the chamber cantatas based on Bureš's texts with his children's choir.

[159] The first performances of *Gilgamesh,* Basel, 23 and 24 January 1958.

[160] The musicologist Professor Antonín Sychra (1918–86), one of the most influential ideological leaders of Czech musical life in the 1950s, a rigid enforcer of orthodox Marxism-Leninism during the Stalinist era.

[161] Before her marriage to Paul Sacher in 1934, Maja Sacher (1896–1989; *née* Stehlin) had been married to Emanuel Hoffmann (1896–1932), the son of Fritz Hoffmann-La Roche, the founder of the pharmaceutical company that bears his name. The Hoffmanns were important collectors of contemporary art; in 1933, after her husband's early death (in an accident), his widow set up the Emanuel Hoffmann-Stiftung to continue their work in the promotion of contemporary art and artists. Paul Sacher's enlightened support of major contemporary composers – none more so than Martinů – was thus part of a wider cultural engagement.

[162] *Sinfonia Concertante for Two Orchestras,* H219, composed in 1932.

Now things are quiet again and I'm doing some work for Munch.[163] It's Hans Munch,[164] a relative, who's here – Charles is in Boston. Besides that, I go for therapy three times a week and they give me a massage and an electric shock treatment,[165] so I always have something to do. Just before the concert there was such a heavy snowfall that we were nearly unable to get up to Schönenberg, and the snow stayed, so it's beautiful now – a real winter like it should be!

Now to your letter. I don't think that Jan [Novák] has become arrogant. He had some serious problems with his apartment and got ruffled about it – I don't know how it turned out. He writes to me frequently. Eliška played the *Concertino*[166] but we didn't hear it. We had been invited somewhere. Miloš [Šafránek] wrote to ask if we liked the recording of the *Bouquet*,[167] but I don't have it. I guess he was upset that they had sent someone else here as representative. He wanted to come himself as my biographer, and the same holds true for Šebánek. I think he's going to Paris, and that he wants to organise something for me there, but that's a sort of illness! So just give yourselves enough heat that you don't catch cold. Winter is here and it seems it's going to be a long one this year. It's a shame that Mařka had to leave the hospital just when she was getting a good rest. Serkin[168] played the Sonata in Canada. I hear it was a big success – surely he'll also play it in Europe. I got the greeting card and it's lovely! It surprised me that it was from Jeník.[169] Thank him for me. The people from Wiesbaden apologised and still want to do *Juliette*,[170] so I hope I'll get the German translation from Prague and that they'll get a move on. Boosey and Hawkes hasn't said anything yet. Maybe they're too embarrassed. I'll remind them.

I don't have any news from Olomouc, although I wrote and asked them to send you whatever I had coming to me, but it has to go through the Theatre Union, and I have to acknowledge it. They're doing *Theatre behind the Gate* but I don't know when – maybe in Spring.[171] They're going to do *The Marriage* in Brno,[172] but I also don't know yet [when]. We'll find out everything in good time.

It surprised me a great deal that Žalmanka[173] was in Polička again. She leaves

---

[163] On the orchestral work *The Parables*, H367, written in 1957–58 for Charles Munch and the Boston Symphony Orchestra.

[164] Composer and conductor (1893–1983), cousin of Charles Munch. Born in Mulhouse, in Alsace, he studied at the Basel Conservatoire from 1912, played cello in the the Basel Symphony Orchestra from 1916 to 1918, when he joined the staff of the Conservatoire, teaching piano until 1932. He was the director of the institution from 1935 to 1947 and from 1935 until 1966 conducted the Allgemeine Musikgesellschaft in Basel.

[165] Treatment for the pain in his right hand, his 'occupational disease'.

[166] Eliška Nováková, wife of Jan Novák, and the Concertino for Piano and Orchestra, H269, composed in 1938. She devoted consistent attention to Martinů's piano works; for example, she first played the Sonata, H350, written for Serkin, in Brno on 3 December 1957, a day before Serkin himself.

[167] Karel Ančerl's recording of the cantata *Bouquet of Flowers*.

[168] *Cf.* note 57 on p. 163, above.

[169] Jan Jílek; *cf.* note 201 on p. 71, above.

[170] The opera of the Hessen State Theatre presented *Juliette* on 25 January 1959.

[171] 24 May 1958.

[172] 22 May 1960.

[173] *Cf.* note 203 on p. 71, above.

me in peace now, which I'm glad of. Don't worry about who's going to pay *Radio Journal*. It's not your worry – you don't have anything to do with it. They know I'm not going to pay it to them either.

I guess that's all for today. I'll send you the reviews and a big poster and another packet of letters and other documents if I can find time to hunt for them all.

I send you much love. Charlie is going to add a few words.

Your Bohouš

LETTER 107
To František Popelka
[Nice] 31 March 1958

Dear Mr Popelka,

What with my nomadic life I haven't had time until now better to express my thanks to you for your participation and your effort and the work which you devoted to the celebration of the recordings and of my birthday![174] Your thoughtfulness made me very happy, and I thank you for everything most heartily and with an apology that I do this so late. You not only made me happy, but also our family and many others from our town, and the memorial to me will always be associated with your name. Young Popelka's university essay in the *Proceedings* interested me a lot,[175] and I'm curious how he's getting on.

I wish you all the best and I remain,
with best regards,
your B. Martinů.

Many thanks, too, to the sculptor Kadlec![176]

LETTER 108
To his Family
[Schönenberg] 17 May 1958

My dear ones,

Your letter came, and I thank you for understanding and for not adding to my woes. You know with what a heavy heart it was I wrote to you of my decision.[177] And now there really remains nothing left to us but hope. Perhaps one day I'll be able to explain everything to you. My circumstances are constantly changing – one moment things are better and then overnight it gets worse again. But some little hope remains, although not immediately, but for some time in the future – that things in the world will be put right so that we'll be able to come home. But it

---

[174] *Cf.* note 155 on p. 183, above.

[175] 'Poličská léta Bohuslava Martinů', *loc. cit.* (*cf.* note 1 on p. 7, above).

[176] Josef Kadlec (1894–1959), native of Borová, near Polička, graduate of the Prague Academy of Arts, Architecture and Design. He worked in his birthplace and from 1945 in Svitavy, in the Pardubice region. Martinů had in mind the memorial plaque at the entrance to the St James Tower, which is Kadlec's work.

[177] Not to visit Czechoslovakia.

would only be to Polička and it wouldn't be at a time of those great festival-like manifestations – those official shows that no one can get out of – which could be detrimental to me in other parts of the world! The truth about a situation could get twisted on both sides – and it's never to our good! I thanked Prague Spring, of course, for their invitation. I know, though, that there are lots of people there who wouldn't be so glad to see me. I excused myself by saying I was here for therapy for my hand and that I couldn't interrupt the treatment which, as a matter of fact, is true. Otherwise, it seems to me from the letters I've received that not many people really expect me to be there, because it's already happened so many times that it was announced that I was coming and I never came that they don't believe it any more.

I wrote to ask them to send me a tape in case they're going to record *Gilgamesh*, which they'll surely do. I'm sorry I won't be able to hear it myself, but the performance here was beautiful.

I already wrote you to say that neither Munch nor Fournier will come. They're both ill. Munch sent me a telegram saying he can't come to Prague. He's in Paris and possibly will not go back to the States now to the festival at Tanglewood, which he directs.

The books already came. They were in eight cartons. And in them we also found programmes from America – from my early days. We'll send you a package again so you can enjoy them. It's all stored now at Mr and Mrs Reber's[178] – the place where we stayed when we came the year before last.

Otherwise, it's lovely here. We had a terrible heat wave, but now it's quite cool. The Sachers were in Denmark, so we haven't seen them for a long time now. We're working in the garden, and taking home asparagus. We're going to plant peas and radishes. I continue to go to the hospital but progress has been slow. Sometimes it's better and then it gets worse again. I can write well enough except that my hand gets tired. I should have a long time free without any writing, which I think I'll give myself in the vacation. We wanted to go to France, but it got mixed up in politics, and I don't know what will come of it.[179]

Miloš [Šafránek] has already completed his book and is now doing the final revision. Where it's to be published I do not know.[180] Šebánek writes often and perhaps will come to Paris. He's somehow out of sorts and sad, but who isn't nowadays? He says *Bouquet of Flowers* will be out on record soon. There's great interest in it here, and I'm looking forward to it, too, because I've never heard it. He also said you might be coming to Prague for *Gilgamesh*, but I think his news is out-of-date.

It's a lot of work with the opera,[181] and I don't know whether I'll be [able] to finish it definitively before the summer vacation, and I'm also not particularly in the mood for it, so it goes rather slowly. Zouhar also wrote and will be disappointed that I'm not coming. We had a visit from one of my pupils at Tanglewood. He came

[178] Willy and Charlotte Reber, Martinů's friends from Basel. Willy Reber (1922–95) trained as a surgeon and published on the psychology of war; he studied music (including a course of analysis of contemporary music with Martinů and a conducting course with Pierre Boulez, another friend); and from 1945 he developed as a major artist, producing some 2,500 paintings, exhibited only after his death.

[179] They did go to France and spent the holiday mainly in La Baule on the Atlantic coast, not far from Nantes.

[180] It was published by SNKLHU, Prague, in 1961.

[181] *The Greek Passion.*

from Italy on his way back and stopped by with his wife and little boy, and we talked over old times.

I'm glad that Fanouš is with you at home again. He's going to have to take good care of himself. It's fortunate that Maruška[182] takes such good care of you. I know it's a big help and it's very nice of her, because she surely has a lot to do for her own family. Morkes[183] needn't have paid you anything – it was a pleasure for me to do it for him. I don't understand why he's working in Svitavy. Did he lose the bakery?

I don't know if my situation might not get worse again because I didn't come. Maybe you will also feel it, but it will pass.

The [Czech] Philharmonic may be going abroad, but it seems they'll leave Karel [Novák] at home. He wrote to say that Talich is going to have some sort of anniversary on the same day they play *Gilgamesh*. There's a lot of interest in *Gilgamesh*, and they may be going to do it in Holland. Again, the chorus[184] will be the one that sang the *Field Mass* in Czech and also *Mount of Three Lights*. An elderly lady wrote to me to say she was so moved by the *Mount* that when she came home after a performance she knelt down beside the piano and prayed. It makes me happy to hear something like that, but the greatest happiness – to see each other – we again had to deny ourselves. Apart from that I haven't had much news from Prague. Perhaps everyone is expecting that I'll come and that they'll arrange everything personally.

Charlie is in the garden – she'll write next time. We think of you often. We send you lots of love.

Your Bohouš

LETTER 109

To Adolf Kurz
Nice, September 1958[185]

Dear Dolf,

Your letter and your reminiscences pleased me greatly. Thank you and thanks to all of you who think of me sometimes and recall the days of our youth. I have often wondered how you were received at home the time you went out on the joists of the tower. I can even remember quite well the sausages and that they cost 25 kreutzer! Now it seems like something out of a fairy tale. They were good too! Although I've traversed half the earth, I've never again found such good sausages! And what a great time we had eating them all! How happy I'd be to be able once again to go down those tower joists, although such sport is no longer made for us – our bones aren't quite as supple as they once were. I often wonder what happened to all of you – and how many of us are already gone! I don't think we'd fit at our little school desks anymore – but we can never forget them!

I thank you and all the other 'survivors' for your good wishes, and I once more

---

[182] Marie Pražanová.

[183] Vladislav Morkes (1901–78), a friend from Martinů's youth in Polička. Martinů apparently refers to a delivery to their home of a medicine that was difficult to obtain in Czechoslovakia.

[184] Die Haghe Sanghers.

[185] Date of postmark 9 September 1958.

wish all of you lots of good health. For myself I wish that I might once again be with you, so we could go to celebrate at 'The Corner' on the other side of seventy, which is pressing upon us.

With warm regards to you and to all,
Your B. Martinů

I'm sending you a bouquet of flowers![186]

LETTER 110
To Marie and Jindřiška Martinů
[Nice] 1 October 1958

Dear Mařka and Jindřiška,

I got a sad letter from Mrs Nebuda in Prague today. Now is the moment when you must take courage in both hands. I'm sure you already knew of Fanouš's hopeless condition. And we knew about it in spite of your refraining from speaking of it and expressing hope – but what was inevitable happened and Fanouš has gone from us forever.[187] He went back to Dad and Mum, where we will all return and perhaps will be together again. It must be a consolation to you to know that Fanouš got such good care, and I hope that he didn't suffer with that terrible illness. I'm afraid he no longer found much joy in the world. I was afraid of every letter that came from home – afraid that it would bring me this sad news, and we were uneasy in recent days – as if we sensed it. I'm so sorry that I wasn't able to see him again nor to accompany him on that last journey from his home. I think he's in a better world than we are. At least he had a peaceful old age and lived to a ripe age. He must have had a constitution of iron that his body was able to withstand so much.

We have all survived him, and it seems to me we no longer belong here. The world has changed a lot and now should belong to those who are younger. We've seen so much and lived though so much in our lifetimes – tragic and terrible things. So many of our friends are gone and only the memory of them remains. It seems to me as if I were once again watching from the tower and walking with you there where our loved ones lie. I'd like to return to the little house to give you as much peace as might be possible. It will be desolate there after his departure – desolate and empty – but you have good and sincere friends around you – like Maruška,[188] who has also had her share of the pain of life and who understands you and will give you reassurance. And you have us, who are thinking of you in these moments and are trying to give you courage so that you might come to know that this sad moment was inevitable. It's the lot of all of us – we abide here awhile and then we must leave. The Lord God has granted us that we remain just long enough in this strange world, but when it's over we must be grateful for what we had. So – be brave! Time tempers all. Your sorrow will be with you for a long time but, of course, nothing can cure it

---

[186] A postcard with a photograph of the flower market in Nice. Kurz's letter of 4 August 1958 and the postcard are preserved at the Martinů Centre in Polička.

[187] Martinů's brother František died of cancer in Polička on 23 September 1958.

[188] Marie Pražanová.

and you can only endure it in order that it not cost you your health. You know that you must respect your health, because it's a great gift. Perhaps I'm not cheering you up much with all of this, and I can't. It isn't in our power. But I'll feel better if you'll listen to me and will think about yourselves – that you have your lives ahead of you. Give our love to Fanouš once again when you go to the cemetery. People loved and respected him, and we can only say – perhaps he's better off in that new and unfamiliar world. We ourselves don't know when fate will summon us to him. Write soon and let me know that you've overcome the pain at least somewhat.

In my last letter, I asked you how you'll arrange matters after his departure, which I knew would come any day. I doubt that J[indřiška] will stay in Polička. She was used to city life, and our little town hasn't much to offer her. Might she go back to her family in Prague? Tell me everything you can about how you've decided to arrange your life from here on. I would urge you, dear Mařka – if it's possible – to stay with Maruška[189] for some time so the empty house doesn't constantly bring back sad thoughts and so you might have different surroundings and impressions. Maybe it will be possible. Maruška always cared so much about you and will be a big help just now. Charlotte and I both thank her for this.

> We think of you all the time,
> Your Bohouš

LETTER 111
To Miloslav Bureš
Nice, sometime in October 1958

Dear Bureš,

Thanks for your letter – for its sympathy and solace. Some things are inevitable and there's nothing left for us but to accept them.

I'm curious how they did *Dandelions*[190] and if they're going to record it. Let me know how the concert goes. Somehow you should push the undertaking forward so that *The Springs* will be recorded on long-playing records – eventually with other poems. There's interest in it and it should be taken advantage of.

I don't have the poem about Mikeš[191] with me. You say there's a possibility you'll go to Switzerland. We'll be back at the end of November (in case of cold weather sooner)[192] again at the old address in Schönenberg, Pratteln. It's near Basel. So let me know. You know I'd be happy to see you again.

As for *Mikeš*, I'll have a look at it as soon as I get back. That sort of narrative tone – descriptive – bothers me a little. To a certain extent it ties my hands as in the case of *Legend*,[193] where I had to follow the development of the plot and then adjust the music to it. I like poems where the poetry somehow completely dominates.

---

[189] The ailing Marie Martinů remained with Mrs Pražanová. After suffering a stroke she was admitted to Polička Hospital, where she died on 17 May 1959.

[190] *The Romance of the Dandelions.*

[191] Bureš's poem *Mikeš of the Mountains.*

[192] They left Nice on 6 or 7 November 1958, for Basel, where Martinů was hopitalised and on 14 November underwent an operation on his stomach.

[193] *Legend of the Smoke from Potato Fires.*

I mean without description but, rather, meditatively, as in *The Springs,* where the dynamism is intensified by its central concept. It's somehow outside of time, and here the music takes its place without being descriptive. I'm sure you know what I mean. Even the *Romance* is in that style even though it, too, is often descriptive, but everything is somehow in a haze, and the delineation of the plot is obscured. There is room in it only for poetry and, consequently, for music. In *The Legend,* there are places that tempt one to dramatic expression, and the action of the plot must be depicted, and a particular kind of accompaniment is needed. I'll write it all succinctly, because I would like some new choruses from you, and in the style of some kind of meditative poetry.[194] I'm sure you understand what I want to say. You see, it's the same for the composer as for the poet – as soon as the verse sings, the music sings independently of everything else, and your verses are like that. I don't want to suggest that you should do everything in the manner of *The Springs* – that's not what I mean. Briefly, it's like a folk song – free and immediate. So if you're in the mood, write some new verses and send them to me. I don't know whether I've expressed everything well. Let me go back to the example of the national song, where the second, third, and further stanzas perhaps require stressed syllables in different places, and yet the music continually repeats the melody of the first stanza and just as beautifully. Even if in later stanzas there are stresses that are misplaced, the text must be accommodated to the music. It is therein that the poetry resides.

You surprised me immensely by pointing out that several places at home have biblical names – like Damašek and Betlém.[195] It's tremendously interesting. Do you know anything more about how they got their names? All that interests me greatly, and I'm surprised that I didn't realise it sooner. You see how habit changes things?

As for the opera,[196] it's a good idea. What is a plot? I'll give you some advice for writing libretti: don't try 'to help' the composer with certain indications like 'dance', 'music offstage', and so on. He'll find it all himself. I mean don't write a scenario for him – it only confuses him. The most important thing is that everything should occur on stage actively in order that it be clear even without words – to be shown and not learned from a description. You have a tough job in front of you. Let me know how it goes. I rather set aside that Chekhov work.[197] Perhaps I'll get back to it.

Give my regards to Mrs Kühn and thank her for me. I'm still sorry it wasn't possible for me to meet them both – as well as Eisner.[198]

Write soon!
Best regards,
B. Martinů
17 bis Boulv. Mont Boron
Nice, AM
(only until the end of November)

[194] So far as is known, Bureš did not comply with Martinů's wishes.

[195] Communities of the district Pustá Rybná in the Polička township, the names of which are also the Czech words for Damascus and Bethlehem.

[196] Apparently Bureš's attempt to write an opera libretto, probably a response to the discussion which Martinů held with Bureš during his visit to Rome in May 1957. The composer returned to the subject twice more in his letters to Bureš.

[197] In a letter of 20 April 1956 (not included in this collection), the composer suggested to Bureš that they work together on the libretto for a little comedy based on Chekhov's short story 'Scandal'.

[198] *Cf.* note 157 on p. 183, above.

LETTER 112[199]

To his sister Marie
[Schönenberg] 11 December 1958

Dear Mařka,

We're back in our own home,[200] and I hasten to tell you the news, which I suppose you've been eagerly awaiting. We were at the hospital for a check-up again, and they told me I don't have to go there anymore. Now it's just a question of getting back the weight I lost. And that's going to go rather slowly, since I have to be careful about what I eat. So, it'll probably take another few weeks before I'll feel together again and be able to go down to the town. For the time being we only take a walk of a few steps around the house, and I still have to get a lot of sleep. So, slowly it's getting to be like it was before. I've received a lot of letters and greeting cards. Jindra[201] also wrote, but I'll answer them all later. Up to now, everything has quickly got me quite tired out, and so I'm only writing to you so you can have the most recent news and a better holiday. We sent some packages – this is because Charlie was in town. One is for Maruška and one is for you, so you'll have to divide them with her. It seemed to me we ought to somehow return the favour to her and not always merely thank her.

I suppose that winter is just around the corner where you are. We're having cool days here, and there's already snow in the mountains. I think it will go by more quickly for me now, when I'll be able to take care of some odds and ends here and slowly put my things in order. I still have to wait until I can get back to work. After the hospital, we were at the Sachers' villa for a couple of weeks, and they both took good care of us – that is, mainly of me, to see that I had good food and whatever else I needed, and here I'm allowed to eat more, and so we came back to our own home again and, slowly perhaps, I'll get into good shape again. I was so thin after being in the hospital that you wouldn't have recognised me if you'd run into me on the street. It was all a great surprise, but I'm thankful that at least it turned out as it did. I had one of the best surgeons in the world, thanks to Maja [Sacher], who arranged everything.

I'll leave some space for Charlie. I'm a little tired again. I send you and Maruška much love and with Charlotte wish you a joyous Christmas. I'll write again as soon as I recover. I'm sure it will go more quickly now and that in a couple of weeks I'll again be able to go to town and to take a walk in the forest at the back of the house.

We send you both our love. I'll write more soon.

Love,
Your Bohouš

---

[199] Charlotte Martinů added a letter on the reverse.

[200] In Schönenberg. After the premiere of *Gilgamesh* (*cf.* p. 188, above) Paul and Maja Sacher invited the Martinůs to stay in their guest house as permanent residents.

[201] His sister-in-law, Jindřiška Martinů.

LETTER 113[202]
To his sister Marie
[Schönenberg] 27 January 1959

Dear Mařka,

We're back from Wiesbaden. The premiere of *Juliette*[203] was glorious – a tremendous success! I had to go on stage alone about 15 times and by the time I got there from the loge there had already been about 10 curtain calls for the singers. In short, a great success! It was very beautiful and everyone was glad that we came. After the theatre, we were invited out, and I met all the members of the orchestra and all the singers. They had performed it superbly and it had been a lot of work for them, the conductor[204] told me. They had had seven weeks of rehearsal, and the more they rehearsed, the more they liked it! So *Juliette* has won again and I suppose will be again on some other stage in Germany. Talich probably reminisced and me, too. I recalled that wonderful Prague premiere[205] 20 years ago. Ever since that time I wondered if I would ever see it again. But it's no longer the charming *Juliette* that it was in Prague. The world has changed and now everything is different and people want something different. And so they played it here like a real dream – everything almost in the dark, and the horror emerged from it – such an oppressive dream, which we call a nightmare. Everything was sombre and filled with so much tension that it was almost too much to bear from start to finish. In short, it was a completely different *Juliette* than it was when we did it in Prague. It created fear, and people were completely startled. But they liked it here, and so we had a triumph with it. Michel, the tenor, was magnificent – both as singer and actor.[206] He made it into a great role. Everything was well-rehearsed. So we saw *Juliette* again, but in a different way than we had known it in Prague. Indeed, it was like a terrible dream. Nowadays, they make such magic with lighting in the theatre that it takes your breath away. Sets are changed without anyone realising it's happening and as if by itself into another setting because they do it mainly with reflectors, so you don't know that people are walking on the stage, but it's as if everyone were suspended in the air. It can't be described in only a few words, except by saying that people didn't want to leave the theatre.

I held up well, but I didn't wait for the next performance on Monday. We came back with Maja and the Rebers – Mr and Mrs – and one of their friends. Maja took care of everything and translated for me, because my German is weak. I was introduced to the Minister of Culture, and there were a lot of people there from the neighbourhood – publishers – including mine – Mr Vötterle, who is going to

---

[202] Charlotte Martinů wrote a letter of her own on the reverse.

[203] On 25 January 1959. It was only the second staging of *Juliette* since that in Prague in 1938.

[204] Ludwig Kaufmann.

[205] On 16 March 1938.

[206] Georg Paskuda (1926–2001), a German tenor with a reputation particularly for contemporary music, singing in works by (for example) Berg, Bialas, Hindemith and Reimann, though also gaining acclaim for roles in Strauss, Verdi and Wagner. Before Wiesbaden (1958–61) he had been engaged in the opera houses of Lübeck (1952–54), Bielefeld (1954–55) and Wuppertal (1955–58); from 1961 until his retirement in 1995 he sang as a lyric tenor in the Bayerische Staatsoper in Munich.

publish *Mirandolina*[207] – and everyone was enthusiastic. So we hope that *Juliette* will have a great career. The director of the festival in Amsterdam was also there. He had come expressly because he'd like to do *The Greek Passion* at the festival next year.[208] Kaufmann conducted – he knows a little Czech, and he also translated the work.

So everything turned out well and now I'm relaxing, because it was a real exertion even though it isn't so far from Basel. But we travelled in comfort in first class, and the hotel was first-class, too. Maja arranged it all, so that I didn't even have to change a single franc. Maja was excited about it and happy that she came with us. Paul was quite sorry that he couldn't come, but he had a rehearsal in Zurich, where they're playing my Sextet[209] this week. We might go to hear it. But we've decided not to go to Berlin.[210] It would just be awfully tiring. Mrs Weber appreciated that, although she was sorry. We'd have had a good time there – the Webers are quite fond of us. Mrs Weber got an engagement in Boston and will do a concert with Charles Munch next year. We still have *Gilgamesh*, which is supposed to be in Francfort in February – that will also be a gala affair! We reached an agreement with Prague, but I must wait now to see how it turns out. As we well know, they're good at making promises, but when it comes down to it, they sometimes don't come through. *Mirandolina* is now being copied. They want it to do at the festival in May.[211]

I think that's everything. A package arrived today. We didn't have to pay much for it – next to nothing. It's beautiful![212] Tomorrow we're going to Maja's to give it to her, and I'm sure she's going to be very happy. One doesn't see such beautiful things nowadays!

I'll write and let you know how she likes it, though she'll surely thank you herself. It was a good idea, and she's sure to be pleased by your thoughtfulness. They both care a lot about us – as if we were part of their family – and you only have to drop a hint and right away they see to whatever it is! Maja's glad we're not going to Berlin – she, too, said it would be awfully tiring.

My hand is quite a lot better, and I'm able to write quickly again – especially notes – apart from that, handwriting still gives me difficulty, but I write everything on the typewriter, anyway.

The mum of which Franta died? Could it be I didn't know her?

Just now I'm writing something for the Prague Nonet[213] – for nine players. I was told they're first-rate. The next time I write I'll send you something that can be shared.

We send you and Maruška[214] our love.

Bohouš

[207] Karl Vötterle (1903–75), founder of the publishing house Bärenreiter Verlag, from 1927 headquartered in Kassel. Bärenreiter published *Mirandolina* in 1959, and later a succession of Martinů works (some of them co-publications with Supraphon).

[208] *The Greek Passion* was not staged in Amsterdam until 1969.

[209] The String Sextet from 1932 in the composer's later version (H224a) with double-bass parts added; it was first performed by the Louisville Orchestra conducted by Robert Whitney on 7 January 1951.

[210] To West Berlin for the premiere of the Fifth Piano Concerto (*Fantasia Concertante*) on 31 January 1959, with Margrit Weber as soloist.

[211] *Mirandolina* was premiered at the National Theatre in Prague on 17 May 1959.

[212] Very probably a piece of handiwork by Marie Martinů.

[213] The Nonet, H374, for the Czech (not the Prague) Nonet, who performed it all over the world.

[214] Marie Pražanová.

In Nice around 1959. The dogs are certainly not his.

LETTER 114
To his sister Marie
[Schönenberg] 4 March 1959

Dear Mařka,

I don't know if you're expecting a letter from me – I think I answered your last letter. But maybe I didn't – so better I write. We both send our love to Maruška. I'm curious whether you came to any agreement with Jindřiška.[215] It appears you like it at Maruška's. It's probably more cheerful there than at forlorn Na Svépomoci.[216] It seems that spring has already returned to you – it's quite beautiful here, too, and we've been going for long walks in the forest. We don't often go to town nowadays.

P[aul] Sacher has a concert again this week, and we'll go on Saturday. We don't miss the city. It's quiet here and it's beautiful. I can't seem to get back the weight I'd lost – I remain at 65 kilos. That means I've only gained three kilos since Christmas! It's not much. Apart from that, things are fine. Most important is that we don't have to go on a lot of visits and see a lot of people. I'm at the piano and slowly I'm starting to enjoy composing again. *Mikeš*[217] will be finished soon, so Bureš will again have something to look forward to. It'll be a nice cycle of cantatas. He probably told you about it when he was in Polička. I'm writing another work at the moment – for sextet. We had an invitation from Braunschweig. It's in the north of Germany somewhere. The festival is in November, and they want something new. They want to present an orchestral work and two chamber pieces.[218] It'll last a whole week. We'll see some of our other friends from Paris there. It's sure to be lovely!

I still don't know anything about *Juliette*. It's already been played eight times.[219] The director[220] is coming here, so we'll have a chance to get to know each other. He was in Yugoslavia when we were in Wiesbaden. There's some interest now in *The Miracles of Mary*. A lady in Munich translated it to German, so it may be that that opera will again find its way to the stage.[221] At home, of course, they don't believe in such things anymore. It won't have a production there, nor will *Juliette*.[222] For them, it represents the Old World. But they're now busily rehearsing *Locandiera* – we call it *Mirandolina* now – in Prague for a performance in May. Meanwhile the world is falling apart again.[223] We're getting ready to go to Nice. One can get a rest there and

---

[215] The agreement most probably had to do with the future of the Martinů family home.

[216] Martinů is trying to convince his sister to stay at the house of Maruška Pražanová, not to return to her own house at Na Svépomoci.

[217] The cantata *Mikeš of the Mountains*.

[218] *Chamber Music* No. 1 for clarinet, violin, viola, violoncello, harp and piano, H376, first performed in Braunschweig in November 1959.

[219] That is, in Wiesbaden.

[220] Dr Friedrich Schramm, director of the Hessen State Theatre.

[221] It was not performed until 18 December 1966, in Wiesbaden.

[222] This scepticism was justified only in part: *The Miracles of Mary* was produced in České Budějovice and in Plzeň in 1968, in Prague in 1969 and in Brno in 1990, and *Juliette* in Prague in 1963, in Plzeň in 1978, in Brno in 1982 and in Prague again in 1989.

[223] Martinů may be referring to recent events in Cuba: just two months earlier, on 8 January, Fidel Castro had marched into Havana and soon after was named prime minister.

has guaranteed sunshine from morning till evening and the sea, besides. I think we both deserve it. We'll go at the end of March.

They say that *The Parables* had a great success in Boston and New York.[224] Firkušný wrote me to say it made a big impression. They sent me a tape recording from Louisville. They recorded *Estampes*[225] – so at least we'll be able to listen to that, too. It will be put on records in April. We listen to the radio quite often these days. They play my stuff a lot and all at once they're doing a lot in Belgium, too. They invited me to serve on a jury again, but I said no and thanked them, and I added that the Belgians are going to forget me, which is true because there was nothing of mine in their programming this year except the *Comedy on the Bridge*.[226] I guess they took the hint. We heard *Comedy* from Milan. They played it very well and sang it superbly, especially Cinderella. I'll send you the programme – when I put things in order again! Did you get the last package I sent? We sent it about two weeks ago. Rybka often writes. He wants to come to Europe on his vacation, but he's waiting to see what the world is going to look like. I think there will be fewer tourists this year. Everything is so uncertain. His son bought a farm somewhere in Vermont – in the north – so maybe they'll go there for the summer. They're copying *The Greek Passion*. They might be going to do it in Hamburg, but it's not certain yet.[227] Mrs Kazantzakis was in America and is also looking forward to it. He's enjoying a great success now. It's a shame he had to depart this life so soon.

That's enough for now. Send me some news from Polička!

Much love,
Bohouš

LETTER 115
To Miloslav Bureš
[Schönenberg] 15 March 1959

My dear friend,

Tomorrow I'll send a copy of *Mikeš*[228] to you in Polička. I'm going to think some more about the dedication. I'll surely have something else that I can dedicate to Maruška.[229] To dedicate it to Eisner[230] doesn't appeal to me. I didn't know him, even though I valued him highly. But it's as if in memoriam, which wouldn't suit our cycle – do you agree? You haven't told me the name of the soprano who sang The Little

---

[224] *The Parables* was premiered in Boston on 13 February 1959, with Charles Munch conducting.

[225] The orchestral work *Estampes*, H369, composed in 1958 to a commission from the Louisville Orchestra. The premiere followed in Louisville (Kentucky) on 4 February 1959.

[226] *The Comedy on the Bridge* had already been presented at the Théâtre de la Monnaie in Brussels in April and May 1957, but not in 1959.

[227] The first performance took place in Zurich on 9 June 1961, conducted by Paul Sacher.

[228] *Mikeš of the Mountains.*

[229] Martinů dedicated his *Madrigals (Part-Song Book)* for mixed voices, composed at this time, to Marie Pražanová; they were premiered in Brno on 15 June 1959.

[230] *Cf.* LETTER 105 and note 157 on p. 183.

Brezen15 59.

Mily priteli:
Zitra vam poslu kopii Mikse do Policky. S tim venovanim
si to jeste rozmyslim a budu miti jiste jinou vec kterou
budu moci venovati Marusce. Venovani Eislerovi se mi
nazamlouva, ja jsem jej neznal, pres to ze jsem si jej
cenil vysoko ale to je jako in memoriam, coz do naseho
cyklu se nehodi,nemyslite. Neodpovedel jste mi to jmeno
sopranu co zpivala Kralovnicku, ma-li vysoky sopran
chtal bych aby zase zpivala v Miksovi,ma tam znacnou
partii. Co se tyce tech Associaci,navrhoval bych pres
to kdybyste nejak mohl obejiti ta vemena,to by jen prospelo
aniz by to snad basni uskodilo. Pak tam je jedno slovo
ktere jsem musel protahnout ale v basni muze zustat,to
jest vzdmute, coz je velmi pekne ale zpivat se neda, stejne
sbor bude zpivat vzedmute, jak vite zpev se sklada ze
samohlasek a tak jsem dal do partitury vzedmute.
Tu prvnd sloku jsem musel vypustit,ale je mozno ji tam
doplnit pouhou recitaci na jednom tonu,takze basen by
zustala cela,ovsem trochu to zbytecne natahne komposici.

Ty zkazky co jste mi poslal jsou moc pekne ale nevim co
by se s nimi mohlo udelat.Ja bych vam radil abyste se
pokusil o neco, co nedovedete i kdyz byste to zkazil,
to je vzdy dobry pokus se dostat ven z urcite posice,byt
i oduvudnene, Kde i pri veskerem zdaru se to dostava do
urcite routiny. Vy jste semtimentalne velmi spjat s temito
krasnymi vzpominkami a to vam mozna vadi se od nich nejak
odpoutat a zkusit neco jineho. Nebot potentialne je ve
vas vice poesie nez ji ve skutecnosti uzivate. Vase verse
jsou radost sama a hudebne se tvori bez namahy, je v nich
necd co nelze definovat ale co nese celou atmosferu a
je to vyhranene a krasne, zadny text az dosud mi nedal
tolik uspokojeni a radost s nim pracovat. Vite ze kbydy
toho nebylo ze by cyklus nebyl povstal. Ja sam,jak se na
to divam, ze ,jak jsme rekli cely cyklus je z jednoho
soudku a to je pravda. Rovnez bych ale podotknul ze jsem
asi ten soudek vycerpal a ze bych musel nacit novy s
novym vinem. Ja myslim ze to plati i pro vas. My nekdy
pracujeme pro svoji radost ale nekdy musime zkusit neco
skoro proti nasi radosti, to je takovy impuls, ktery nas
nuti zdanlive opustit to co devedem a zacit neco co se
nam zda cizi a neprijatelne, nicmene na konec se objevi
ze to otevrelo nove horizonty a ze to pridalo i mnoho
k tomu co jsme dovedly. Je to takovy vnitrni boj.

Letter (115) to Miloslav Bureš from Schönenberg, 15 March 1959

Ted abyste mi porozumel, nechci abyste se vzdalil sveho
projevu, jez je tak blizky vsem lidem jak jsme videli
pri
   Studankach a abyste zcal psat basne jako vsichni ostatni,
i dobre. Chci jen rici abyste neustrnul na jednom bode,
ktery je myslim spise sentimentalni a ktery jste v celem
cyklu dobre obesel se vzacnym uspechem. hci jen rici
abyste se nenechal prilis zlakati , ted prave nevim jak
to rici. Ostatne jsem toho rekl uz dost a vyberte si z toho
take co potrebujete, ukousnete si jak z krajice.
ak se na mne nezlobte, ja vam to rikam protoze jsem sam
prosel takovym bojem, ono nas to stale tahne zpet k te
stare krase, vecne nasich zpevu a zvyku ale nekde na nejakem
miste to musime nejak zlomit abychom se tomu dostali jeste v
vice na kloub. A ve vas je toho vice nez si myslite.

Pozdravte vsechny u nas a napiste az dostanete Mikse.
Bude se vam libit.
                          rdecne vas

Queen[231] – if she's a high soprano I'd like her to sing in *Mikeš* – it's a sizable part. As for connotations, I would suggest that you somehow get around that word 'udder'. It would only help the poem and not harm it in any way. Then there's one word there which I had to stretch out, but it can stay in the poem – the word *vzdmuté*, which is very pretty but can't be sung. The chorus will sing it as *vzedmuté*.[232] As you know, vowel sounds predominate in the vocal score, so I put *vzdmuté* in the choral part. I had to cut the first stanza. It would have been possible to keep it if it were recited on one note. This way, the poem would have remained in its entirety. But, of course, it extended the composition by a little and unnecessarily.

The legends you sent me are very beautiful, but I don't know what could be done with them. I would advise you to try something that you're not good at. Even if you should fail with it, it's always good to try to get out of certain routines, even though we may be able to explain them to ourselves. With each success we can get into a certain routine. You are very much bound up sentimentally with these beautiful memories, and it may be that which prevents you from detaching yourself from them and from trying something new. The fact is that there's more poetry in you than you know! Your verses are joy itself and, musically, they take shape without difficulty. There's something in them that can't be defined but which creates a complete atmosphere, and it is unambiguous and beautiful. No text up to now has given me so much joy and satisfaction to work with. You know that if it weren't so, the cycle would not have come into being. I myself, when I look at it, see, as we said, that the entire cycle comes from one cask – and that's the truth. But I would also like to make it clear that I have perhaps drained the cask dry, and I would have to begin again with new wine. I think it's the same for you. Sometimes we work for our own happiness, but sometimes we have to try something that almost goes against our happiness. It's the kind of impulse which compels us to abandon what we're doing and to begin something new which seems to us to be strange and, for the moment, unacceptable. Nonetheless, we discover in the end that it has opened new horizons to us and that it has added a lot to what we had been doing before. It's something of an inner struggle.

Now, in order that you understand me, let me say that I don't want you to distance yourself from your own expression, which is close to the people, as we saw with *The Springs*, and that you would begin to write poems like the others – and good ones. I only want to say, in order that you not become fixed in one place which, I think, is rather sentimental and which, in the whole cycle, you got around well and with uncommon success. I only want to say, in order that you not let yourself become too enamoured of your own – at the moment I don't know how to say it! In fact, I've said enough already. Take from it what you can use. You need only nibble at the edges.

Don't be upset with me. I tell you these things because I too went through such a struggle. It always takes us back to that eternal beauty of our songs and of our customs, but somewhere – somehow – we have to part from it in order to go even deeper within ourselves. And there's more depth in you than you think!

---

[231] On the first gramophone recording of *The Opening of the Springs*, Květa Urbanová-Němečková, at the time a member of the Kühn Children's Choir.

[232] The meaning is the same – 'billowy' or 'swollen' – but the extra syllable makes the second one easier to sing.

Give my regards to everyone at home, and write me when you get *Mikeš*. You're going to like it!

With warmest regards,
Your B. Martinů

APPENDIX ONE
ADDRESSEES

I. Immediate Family

FERDINAND MARTINŮ (15 August 1853–12 October 1923), the composer's father, a shoemaker by profession, later also keeper of the tower of the Church of St James. From 1889 he guarded Polička against fire 'by day and by night' – a worthy occupation in a town some of whose inhabitants still remembered a devastating fire in 1845. From 1902 he was again down in the square in the service of the mayor's office and, at the same time, of the savings bank. As 'dramaturg' and prompter at the amateur theatrical club 'Tyl', he took his son Bohuslav to rehearsals and performances. He was highly regarded mainly as the capable instructor of the volunteer firemen's corps. The training he gave conformed to that of fire departments of neighbouring municipalities: theirs were unremunerated efforts for the welfare of the community. A grower of flowers and a breeder of birds, a mild and apparently a good-hearted person, gifted with an ability to accept tasks assigned to him in the unchanging course of his daily life with calm composure, he bequeathed to Bohuslav his own stoic view of life, his compassion toward all living things, and his sense of humour – even when he was stricken with cancer. His son loved him.

FRANTIŠEK MARTINŮ (2 December 1880–23 September 1958), the composer's brother, studied for some time at the Gymnasium Vysoké Mýto and after that studied decorating arts (the certificate of apprenticeship is dated 1 January 1903). In 1904–7 he studied at the Prague School of Industrial Arts, and at the same time (and until 31 January 1908) worked for the painter Antonín Häusler (1869–1938) in Vinohrady in Prague. In the reference that Häusler wrote for him one can read that he was 'employed in the atelier, where he was engaged in drawing and decorative composition and, as well, helped me with various kinds of decorative work as it had to do with frescos, graffitoes, church decorations, exhibition works and so on'. The reference accords well with the way in which František Martinů made himself useful at that time and later. For example, he restored the interiors of churches in Slezský Orlov, Pardubice, Želiv and Vyšší Brod, as well as paintings by Mikoláš Aleš and Karel Rašek in Makov u Litomyšle, and he also worked abroad. He lived much of his life in Prague, where he married, although it seems that he combined his residence in Prague with frequent stays in Polička. Apparently, he struggled with existential difficulties throughout his life, though his brother tried to find a permanent position and financial security for him with the help of his Prague friends and acquaintances in the 1930s and again after 1945. In about 1950 he settled down permanently in the Martinů family home in Polička with his wife Jindřiška.

JINDŘIŠKA MARTINŮ, née Palečková (15 July 1882–23 June 1965), lived in Prague all her life with the exception of her residence in Polička in the 1950s and early 1960s. She married František Martinů when he was about 40 years old.

KAROLINA MARTINŮ, *née* Klimešová (17 October 1855–10 March 1944), the composer's mother, was the real head of the family thanks, it would seem, to her energy, assiduousness, industry and her husband's submissiveness. Her marriage to Ferdinand Martinů (she was at the time already the mother of Karel, a son born out of wedlock) was, for her, the daughter of a well-to-do Polička family, a step down on the social ladder of the time. It was obviously one of the sources of her efforts to raise the status of the family, the crowning glory of which would have been the appointment of her son Bohuslav to a professorship at the Prague Conservatoire. His failure in his attempt to be appointed professor of composition in 1936 weighed heavily on her, as had his expulsion from the Conservatoire in 1910. Bohuslav, already independent of authority in his youth, politely respected her 'matriarchy' but in adulthood always made his own decisions. Karolina Martinů passed on to him his musicality and his awareness – perhaps already vicarious – of what was once a vital folk-tradition.

MARIE MARTINŮ (28 August 1882–17 May 1959), the composer's sister, was trained as a dressmaker and managed her own business, according to the recollections of those who knew her, in an accomplished way. Thanks to her knowledge of French, she was obviously better able than her Polička competitors to adapt her work to trends in the world of fashion. (To the façade of the Martinů home on Na Svépomoci, to which the family moved in 1923, her brother František affixed, not long after this date, a decorative and conspicuous sign 'House of Fashion'.) The well-read and culturally knowledgeable Marie was the main support in the Martinů family for her musically gifted younger brother. She believed in his talent with an almost awestruck certainty, in spite of her brother's appreciably delayed beginnings, and supported him in his arduous first efforts, not only morally. She followed her brother's career closely, for six decades, from its early days right up to 1959, the year in which they both died. For years she collected (to the extent that she was able and within the limits of her knowledge) documentation of her brother's creative work. She also cared for the manuscript compositions Martinů had left in Polička, and in 1930 she began to put aside in safekeeping her brother's letters addressed to the family or to her. She mediated relations between the composer and his friends in Polička and, eventually, even with leading figures of Czech and Moravian musical life. In 1957 she donated to the Polička Museum her collection of the correspondence and manuscripts received from Martinů, and numerous other written and pictorial documents. She was also a support of Charlotte Martinů, with whom she came to terms as early as the end of the 1920s, and was a counterbalance to the reserve which Karolina had adopted toward Charlotte.

II. Friends and Acquaintances

MILOSLAV BUREŠ (actually Jan Bureš, 6 November 1909–12 November 1968), journalist, writer of poetry and prose; a native of Polička. He graduated in 1930 from the Gymnasium of Science and Technology in Polička and for a short time worked as a teacher. From 1932 until 1937 he served as editor of *Severočeský deník* ('North Bohemian Daily News') in Liberec. Even in the years of the Nazi occupation he worked as a journalist. After the War he changed places of employment a number of times and in 1961 took a position in the culture section of the Prague periodical

Svobodné slovo ('Free Speech'). He had written poetry and had published some of his work since he was a secondary-school student. In spite of his disassociation for so much of the time from his birthplace and from the Vysočina (the Moravian Highland), to which he frequently returned, especially in the 1950s, he made constant and devoted use, in his collections of poems, of subjects, themes, images and the spiritual climate of his native region from as early, it seems, as the mid-1930s. The Vysočina also figures in several of his works of prose. Bureš and Martinů met during the composer's visits to his native town probably as early as the end of the 1920s, and especially, no doubt, in the '30s. As is apparent from the composer's letters to his family, he did not later remember Bureš very well from that time, perhaps because the poet was a generation younger. In 1955 Bureš sent the composer the manuscript of his poem 'The Opening of the Springs' (at that time it was entitled 'Song of the Spring'). It intrigued Martinů to the extent that he began almost at once to set it to music, with a number of changes to the original text. Beginning in 1955, these two natives of Polička maintained a correspondence, although with interruptions, and met twice more (in Rome in May 1957, and later in the Swiss town of Liestal in 1959, not long before Martinů's death). In the years 1955–59 Martinů wrote two more chamber cantatas based on Bureš's poetry (*Legend of the Smoke from Potato Fires* and *Mikeš of the Mountains*) and the cantata for mixed chorus *Romance of the Dandelions*. Bureš described his relationship with the composer and some aspects of his collaboration with him, clearly from his own perspective, in his commemorative volume *Bohuslav Martinů a Vysočina* ('Bohuslav Martinů and the Vysočina').[1] This collection of 24 of the composer's letters to him is a valuable documentation of Martinů's friendly, kindly attitude toward Bureš and his literary work and poetics. The letters have been preserved in the archive of the Polička Memorial Museum (now the Martinů Centre) since 1988.

Josef Hlavsa (17 March 1889–?14 December 1970), headmaster of the Polička Girls' School, a cultured and well-educated man, for many years an official of the local Sokol organisation. A capable cellist in local chamber and orchestral groups, for some time he also held the position of chairman of the local National Committee in Polička.

Vanda Jakubíčkova (actually Václava Jakubíčková, 25 January 1888–14 November 1968) worked as a teacher as a young woman in the primary schools of Polička and in communities in the Polička region, as well as in Nymburk, Vysoké Mýto and Letovice. In 1907 she passed the state examinations in French, in 1910 and 1915 the teaching examinations, and in 1923 the state examinations in English. From 1924 or 1925, she taught Czech childen living in London at a remedial school. She worked in London until 1947, when she returned to Polička. She then taught English, especially at the Gymnasium in her hometown. During the time she was employed in London she had furthered her impressively broad education: she passed the so-called supplementary examination at the University of London, where she also studied European history from 1925–27, and from 1931–34 comparative religion and Bible studies. She also served as a volunteer social worker in poor districts of London, was an active political writer in the magazine of British Czechs

[1] Krajské nakladatelství (Regional Publishers), Havlíčkův Brod, 1960.

Krajan ('The Countryman') and in the British press, lectured on Czech literature and folk art, and participated in the setting-up of a Czech exhibition. As is obvious from the letters Martinů sent her and from the numerous references to her in his letters to the family, he held her in high regard, and in the second half of the 1930s was hoping for her literary collaboration in his efforts to promote *The Miracles of Mary* in England. He undoubtedly already knew Jakubíčková in his early years in Polička – the oldest preserved written communication from the always correct Martinů to 'Miss Vanda' is dated 1922. They met for the last time in London in June 1938. Martinů was there at the time at the festival of The International Society for Contemporary Music, at which Vítězslava Kaprálová conducted.

JOSEF KAŇKA (29 June 1868–10 January 1944), bookbinder, stationer and postcard-designer and -publisher. He was born in Roudnice nad Lábem and permanently settled in Polička in 1887. From 1886 and until the prohibition against Sokol in 1939, he served as leader of the local association, and carried out his duties with remarkable enthusiasm and devotion. As leader of the eastern Bohemian Pippichova regional association, Kaňka was financially supportive of the young Martinů (and not only him) at the time of his study at the Conservatoire, perhaps even from funds which Karel Till, president of the Polička Sokol, provided. As becomes clear from the letters which Martinů addressed to him, Kaňka was also a moral support for him. It was hardly by chance that Martinů took part in his early years in cultural programmes of the Polička Sokol Association. Thanks to the considerable number of postcards that Kaňka produced, the topography of Polička during the time of Martinů's childhood and years of adolescence can still be seen in some detail. Some of Kaňka's postcards even give information about the life and appearance of the inhabitants of the town, shortly after 1900, sometimes with humorous hyperbole.

ADOLF KLIMEŠ (8 May 1880–15 July 1946) was for a number of years in the First Republic mayor of the town and director of the tax office, and one of Bohuslav Martinů's friends and patrons in his early years. It seems that Klimeš recognised the importance of Martinů's creative work for the reputation and prestige of the town even before the composer made a name for himself in Europe.

ADOLF KURZ (6 May 1890–21 August 1968), a fellow-pupil of Martinů in their childhood. He learned to be a butcher and for years ran a small business inherited from his father in a building at Palackého náměstí (Palacký Square) No. 20. He contributed a letter, which Martinů addressed to him in September 1958, to the Town Museum (now the Martinů Centre) in Polička.

FRANTIŠEK POPELKA (23 March 1908–27 May 1989), a native of Polička, an accountant by profession, and a broadly cultured man. He knew Martinů socially from the time of a holiday stay in Polička in the 1920s and maintained relations with the Martinů family until the time of the death of the composer's sister and the departure from Polička of his sister-in-law Jindřiška. As an accomplished violinist, he played Martinů's chamber music in Polička from the 1930s to the 1970s as first violinist of the Polička Quartet, as a frequent solo violinist, and as player in various chamber ensembles, and in the 1980s especially in a string trio with Miloslav Svoboda and Jan Zároba. He initiated the representation of Martinů at the exhibits of the Polička Museum as early as the 1930s, and for decades systematically assembled, at first as a volunteer and from 1968 as an employee of the Museum, Martinů documents and published works as well as photocopies and manuscripts of his compositions, and thus laid the foundation of the wealth of Martinů resources in the Polička Museum. In 1945 he organised the first independent exhibition devoted to the composer at the Museum. At his instigation and through his participation, the square in front of the Church of St James was given the name of Martinů in 1945, the composer's family dwelling was restored to its original condition in 1947 and after that made more accessible, and in 1957 a plaque memorialising the composer was placed at the entrance to the church tower. In the 1960s Popelka organised concerts, performances of operas, and a lecture series, 'The Polička of Bohuslav Martinů', by which the people for the first time became better acquainted with the life and work of their fellow-townsman. He introduced a series of lectures and informal discussions of Martinů's work and published numerous articles about the composer. He was co-author of the book *Martinů a Polička* ('Martinů and Polička'; Panton, Prague, 1990). He published privately the composer's memoirs (1945), letters which Martinů addressed to him (1977) and a thesis entitled *The Composer's Lectures on Musical Theatre* (1983), and he also supervised the Museum's Martinů publications. He was one of the initiators of the founding of the music school in Polička (1948), contributed to its orientation towards Martinů's work, and in 1949 was instrumental in getting Martinů's agreement to using his name in the name of the school. At his suggestion, Miloslav Bureš in 1955 offered Martinů his poem 'The Opening of the Springs' for a musical setting (Bureš had originally thought of Václav Trojan). In spite of all the personal difficulties it created for him, Popelka did all this on behalf of Martinů and his work – even in the first half of the 1950s, when town and regional authorities were dependent on the hostile attitude of Communist regime towards the composer and his music.

MARIE PRAŽANOVÁ (18 June 1897–12 December 1982), a resident of Polička, wife of the sawmill-owner Ladislav Pražan (19 June 1889–8 March 1979), a friend of the Martinů family and especially of the composer's sister. She got to know Martinů during one of his visits to Polička (after 1928). She helped the Martinů family to cope with the difficult years of the Second World War and unselfishly looked after the ailing Marie Martinů in the late 1950s. After Marie's death, she painstakingly took care of the written and iconographic documents relating to the composer and his work, especially the collected letters of Bohuslav and Charlotte Martinů to his family in Polička. In June 1978 she donated these materials to the Polička Town Museum. Even before that, Martinů scholars like Miloš Šafránek, Jaroslav Mihule, Zdeněk Zouhar, Harry Halbreich and Michael Henderson had the opportunity, as her guests, to make use of these documents. It was at Marie Pražanová's instigation that the composer's sister wrote some charming reminiscences of life in their dwelling in the tower of the Polička church in the time of Bohuslav's childhood, which were later published – together with the memoirs of the composer's mother – by the Polička Museum. In 1958 she took the initiative for the restoration of the composer's family dwelling. In 1959 she gave Martinů the suggestion for the composition of a musical sonnet, *Greetings* in a few bars which is dedicated to the children of the Polička Music School that bears his name. The composer, although he did not see her again after 1938, was well-informed, through his sister, of her care for the Martinů family. As a token of gratitude, he dedicated to her the *Madrigals* he composed in 1959.

VÁCLAV KAREL RIPPL (3 May 1896–21 March 1950), one of Martinů's closest friends from early childhood, representing the third generation of the Rippl dynasty of booksellers and stationers dynasty in Polička. He was a graduate of the booksellers' trade school in Prague, where he also got to know numerous leading Czech publishers and booksellers. For years he served as deputy chairman of the Association of Czech Booksellers. His activities were centred in his native town. His bookstore attracted those interested in literature and was the centre of informal 'literary Thursdays', when Polička book-lovers, including Gymnasium students, met at Rippl's to peruse the latest shipment of books. Some of them soon after made a name for themselves in literature: Bohuslav Březovský, Miloslav Bureš and Jan Vladislav. Prominent persons who visited Polička and the Vysočina (for example Václav Lacina, Petr and Jaroslav Křička, Arne Novák, Zdeněk Otava, Emil Mikelk and Arno Nauman) also helped to give the bookshop a good name as, of course, did Martinů on his visits from Paris. In 1924 he also began to manufacture paper. Rippl took part in the public life of the town as a member of numerous organisations (among them the Palacký Museum Association), and for years he was a member of the town board of representatives. In his letters to Polička, Martinů spoke of him familiarly as Vašík, sometimes Vaš.

In LETTER 73[2] Martinů expresses his sorrow at the death of his friend Václav K. Rippl. But he was acquainted also with Rippl's father, Václav J. Rippl (21 August 1858–8 March 1951), to whom he sent greetings on his 90th birthday in 1948.[3] This Václav Josef Rippl was a founding member of the Polička Sokol and an active member and later honorary member of the Tyl amateur theatre club.[4] In 1882, he assumed the management of the bookstore and the stationery store, when he took it over from his father's widow after the death of his own father, Josef Jan Rippl (1824–69), who had founded the company in 1851 and also worked as a publisher.

The composer's mention of 'young' Rippl in his letter to the family of 29–30 May 1951[5] refers to Václav Rippl (b. 1925), an expert in the paper industry, author of a number of specialised articles and co-author of several textbooks. He is the elder of the two sons of Václav K. Rippl.

BOHUSLAV ŠMÍD (26 November 1895–27 February 1982), one of Martinů's Polička friends. In 1919 he successfully completed the building engineering examination and, after working in the studio of Prague architect Pavel Janák, settled in Polička in 1920. There he brought into being, as creator of projects and head of a contruction company, a number of apartment and specialised buildings which, in the period between the Wars, markedly determined the look of Polička outside the town wall. Among his works are, especially, the spacious Masaryk School, the reclamation of the south shore of Synský Pond, the surgical pavilion of the Polička Hospital, and

---

[2] *Cf.* p. 132, above.

[3] *Cf.* POSTCARD 6 on p. 122, above.

[4] Martinů recalls his energy in his letter of 11 March 1948 to the periodical *Jitřenka*: LETTER 66 on p. 124, above.

[5] LETTER 77; *cf.* p. 138, above.

the Villa at No. 483, a prized example of one man's interpretation of functionalism in architecture. From 1950 Šmíd was compelled to work outside Polička, but he continued to work in his profession until his eighties. His friendship with Martinů dates from 1920 or 1921. The fact that from 1923–34 the Šmíd and Martinů families were almost next-door neighbours on Na Svépomoci furthered their friendly relations. The Martinůs spent several days with the Šmíds in 1932 in Potštejn in the Podorlické Hills. In the spring of that year, the Šmíds bought a piano from Bohuslav Martinů for their children; it had stood idle for a long time and Martinů was trying to sell it. (Today, thanks to the generosity of Šmíd and his heirs, the instrument is part of the exhibition of the Martinů Centre in Polička.) The two friends met for the last time in Polička in the summer of 1938, though the friendship of both families continued until the deaths of the composer's brother (1958) and sister (1959).

'Božánek' and 'Sonička' in Martinů's correspondence are the children of Jarmila and Bohuslav Šmíd: the engineer Bohuslav Šmíd (born in 1924) and Soňa Šmídová (born in 1927; her married name is Kytlicová). In 1932 Martinů wrote four short, untitled piano pieces for them (H221 in Halbreich's catalogue), with the dedication: 'to Božánek and Sonička Šmíd as a keepsake of the holiday in Potštejn from Boh. Martinů in Polička'. The piece was published in 1992 by the Prague publisher Tempo and by Bote und Bock in Berlin.

EDUARD VENCOVSKÝ (14 February 1900–15 March 1991), Gymnasium teacher. After graduation from the Prostějov Gymnasium in 1919, where he became friends with the poet and playwright Jiří Wolker (1900–24), an early member of the Communist Party of Czechoslovakia, and later Ivan Sekanina (1900–40), another leading leftist, he studied at the Philosophical Faculty and from 1922 at the Natural Sciences Faculty of Charles University. From 1926 to 1955 he worked at the Gymnasium of Science and Technology in Polička, where he became one of the most respected members of the staff. In 1938 he was elected mayor of the town. In the critical days after the Munich Agreement, when Polička was occupied by the German army, he undertook a number of firm, well-considered and ultimately successful steps in protest, which had as their aim the freeing of predominantly Czech Polička from German occupation. In 1941 the German occupying authority removed him from office. From 1939 Vencovský had been a member of the illegal military organisation Obrana národa ('Defenders of the Nation') and, from October 1943, a member of the Národní výbor ('National Committee'), which was also illegal. After May 1945 he served for several years as First Deputy Minister of the Local National Committee (the name given to the local authority after World War II). During his tenure in Polička, he came to be a scholar of the natural history of the Polička region, acquainting the public with his knowledge in articles which made a case for a number of nature reserves in the area. He also published the valuable study *Nástin geologie a geomorfologie poličského okresu* ('An Outline of the Geology and Geomorphology of the Polička District', published in the collection 'Poličsko', Krajský dům osvěty, Pardubice, 1958), and in 1968 his 'Mé vzpomínky na Jiřího Wolkera' ('My Recollections of Jiří Wolker') were published in Olomouc in *Zpravodaj Wolkrova Prostějova* ('Reporter from Wolker's Prostějov'), No. 1, 1976, pp. 7–8, (republished by Pavel Marek (ed.), *Jiří Wolker ve vzpomínkách současníků* ('Jiří Wolker in Recollections by his Contemporaries'), Melantrich, Prague, 1990).

III. Organisations and Institutions

JITŘENKA ('Morning Star'), the Polička periodical, appeared as a weekly publication from 10 July 1872 until 15 December 1949, when the last issue in its 77-year existence was published. It appeared with remarkable regularity and continuity. In the beginnings *Jitřenka* was linked to the printing and publishing activities of Václav Vetterle and his son Josef. In December 1885 it passed into the hands of the Popelkas, a family of printers, in the succession of František Ladislav, František, Jindřich and Jan. From summer 1948 it was published by the Polička regional board of education. The periodical went through a remarkable evolution from being predominantly educational-cultural and *belles-lettriste* in style, when it counted among its contributors Adolf Heyduk, Jakub Arbes, Alois Jirásek, Tereza Nováková and (in its early years) Josef Svatopluk Machar and Jiří Karásek, gradually becoming a periodical focused largely on the region and its interests, all the time reducing the space devoted to *belles-lettres* and instead featuring articles devoted to the history of the town (sometimes from local sources from the Middle Ages up to the nineteenth century), its folklore and traditions, ethnography, the dialects of neighbouring communities, and personalities connected with the town by descent or origin. Time transformed *Jitřenka* into a chronicler of the modern history of the town, a valuable and often the only source of information about its citizens and about those for whom Polička had once been their home, including Bohuslav Martinů. *Jitřenka* first gave prominence to him in issue No. 17 of its 34th year (1905), in a review of his first public performance – the violinist was at that time fourteen years old – and continued to follow his artistic career and the course of his life with attentiveness and empathy, especially after 1912 and until *Jitřenka* was silenced in 1949: the double issue Nos. 13–14 and issue No. 15 in 1948 carried a lengthy article by František Popelka dedicated to the composer's career and his work. On 1 December 1948 (Nos. 19–20, p. 122), *Jitřenka* published a remarkable letter from Bohuslav Martinů addressed to it.[6] In January 1991 *Jitřenka* was re-established as the monthly magazine of the town of Polička under the editorial direction of Zdeněk Vojtek and largely oriented toward cultural history. The magazine regularly features articles on the work and life of Bohuslav Martinů.

The Polička **MUSIC SCHOOL** began its activities in 1948, with the name The Music Institute of the Town of Polička; its first director was Jaromír Chalupský. A well-trained pianist, choirmaster and conductor, he soon proved himself to be an excellent administrator as well, and attracted to the faculty several graduates of the Prague Conservatoire. The young people around Chalupský brought a new impulse to the musical life of Polička, and some of them, from the first years of their engagement there, recognised the importance of Martinů's work for Czech music, an awareness expressed in their concert activities and especially in the repertoires of their pupils. In 1949 Martinů agreed in writing – not without first informing himself of the details – that his name should be bestowed upon the school. From then until the mid-1950s the School and the Association of Parents and Friends of the Bohuslav Martinů School of Music made it the centre of local Martinů activity, among other things as organiser of a number of 'semi-legal' evenings in honour of

---

[6] *Cf.* LETTER 66, p. 123, above.

Martinů. In view of the ban on the composer's work by the Communist regime, such events could be, of course, only of modest scope. Nevertheless, they contributed to the continuity of the Martinů tradition in Polička and acted as implicit criticism of the timidity and short-sightedness of local and regional authorities. The tradition, given shape in the fertile soil of the music school by its first group of teachers, endured those difficult times and continues to this day. All of the school's young pianists – even the very youngest – played pieces from Martinů's *Loutky* ('Puppets'), and all the pupils heard and became quite familiar with Martinů's music. In the 1980s the Polička branch of the Bohuslav Martinů Society co-operated closely with the School of Music. On 16 June 1988, there was 'solemnly conferred upon the school the honorary name' People's School of Music Bohuslav Martinů, thanks especially to the efforts of Dr Václav Holzknecht. The name that had been added to the name of the school in 1949, and which it had been denied by the irremediable narrow-mindedness of the educational bureaucracy, was finally restored.

APPENDIX TWO
MARTINŮ
AS CARTOONIST

La vie champêtre.

For several decades Martinů availed himself of a form of self-expression which has received scant attention in the literature on the composer: he drew cartoons. Although it is not obvious from the correspondence with his family in Polička, Martinů was strongly interested in the visual arts all his life. He numbered the major Czech painters Jan Zrzavý,[1] Josef Šíma[2] and Alén Diviš[3] among his close friends (all of them spent a part of their lives in France), and was also well acquainted with some of the best-known painters of the twentieth century, among them František Kupka and Pablo Picasso. The American composer David Diamond, a good friend of Martinů from the 1930s onwards,[4] once told me of a visit Martinů paid, at his suggestion, to the French painter Léopold Survage,[5] a close friend of Amedeo Modigliani as well as of the Russian painters around the avant-gardists Mikhail Larionov and his wife Natalia Goncharova.[6] Asking Martinů about his opinion on Survage's work, Diamond received a very interesting answer: 'It really didn't interest me. There was no colour counterpoint in it'.[7]

In his own drawings, of course, Martinů was not attempting to make a substantial contribution to the arts. He simply liked to draw funny cartoons, either for himself or for some of his closest friends, especially Stanislav Novák.[8] In these sketches he portrays himself with a mouse-like nose – although there is no obvious connection between this self-stylisation as a mouse and his early ballet *Who is the Most Powerful in the World?*,[9] which has a family of mice as the main characters.

Martinů often used his drawings to comment on some awkward situation in his life, such as an almost empty concert hall during a benefit concert for Czech legionnaires in Polička in 1918, or his 'Battle with Piano, a Tragedy in 4 acts', a commentary from around 1920 on his unsuccessful attempts to

[1] *Cf.* note 35 on p. 42 and note 77 on p. 49, above.

[2] *Cf.* note 192 on p. 70 and note 1 on p. 153, above.

[3] *Cf.* note 25 on p. 99, above.

[4] Diamond (1915–2005) had lived in Paris from 1935 to 1939.

[5] Survage (1879–1968) was a French painter of Russian-Danish-Finnish origin. Martinů most probably knew the set-design and costumes he created in 1922 for the world premiere of Stravinsky's opera-buffa *Mavra* at the Paris Opera.

[6] Larionov (1881–1964) and Goncharova (1881–1962) met in 1900 and both left Russia in 1915, eventually settling in Paris and becoming French citizens.

[7] Conversation with Aleš Březina, Rochester, New York, April 2000.

[8] *Cf.* note 13 on p. 22, above.

[9] *Cf.* p. 18, above.

master the keyboard. He also reported on his journeys, planned or recent, first to neighbouring villages and to Prague and later also to Italy, England and France. A special category among the drawings are his ironical reports of visits to concerts and the theatre, such as one of Wagner's *Siegfried* showing the eponymous hero with an ox, Dvořák's 'New World' Symphony conducted by a conductor dressed as a native Indian warrior holding an axe in his left hand and a spear in his right, Debussy's *La Mer* performed by an orchestra consisting of water-nymphs and -goblins, or Smetana's symphonic poem *Wallenstein's Camp* performed by a group of miserably dressed soldiers.

The 'golden period' of these cartoons was the 1910s and '20s. In the decade before the Second World War they became less and less frequent, with one significant exception from the very end of 1930s – they featured prominently in his love-letters to Vítězslava Kaprálová.[10] After her death in 1940, Martinů stopped drawing cartoons. At the end of the war, when communications with Europe once again opened up, his best friend, Stáňa Novák, died in Czechoslovakia and thus Martinů lost the favourite recipient of his cartoons.

In the last twenty years of his life he used his drawing skills only for sketches of set-designs for his theatre works, meant not so much as inspiration for the designers as a help to his own imagination while he was composing his operas. Most of his drawings are deposited at the Martinů Centre in Polička, and many of them have been used for LP and CD covers of recordings of Martinů's music. This collection – which presents a cycle of drawings from 1911 entitled *Decline and the other things* – is the first extensive publication of any of these drawings in an English-language publication.

Aleš Brězina

---

[10] *Cf.* note 210 on p. 72 and LETTER 39 on pp. 76–77, above.

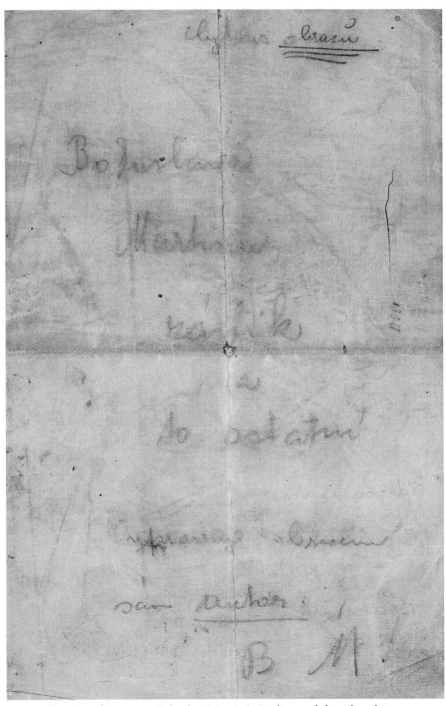

*'A series of cartoons. Bohuslav Martinů: Decline and the other things.
As told in pictures by the author himself. BM'*

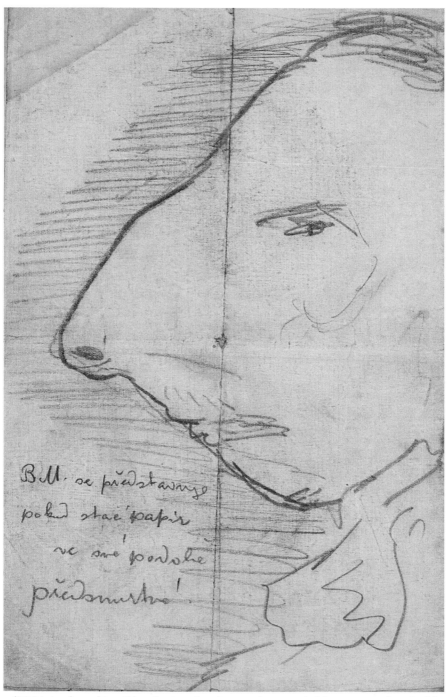

'*BM introduces himself, as long as there's enough paper, in his pre-mortal outlook.*'

Top: 'The after-life of the so-called artist Bohuslav Martinů.
Picture 1 BM takes his own life'
Bottom: 'BM finds himself in a coffin. (His friends raised money
in order to celebrate the memory of this great man'

'*The last journey of BM*'

Top: 'BM tries to conquer Heaven'
Bottom: 'First impressions in Heaven [Angel:] "What's up, then?" BM stares at new
acquaintances'

Top: 'BM is reminded in a polite manner that he has to take his hat off'
Bottom: 'BM makes himself at home'

Top: 'Morning [by clock]. [Winged sexton:]"Danse macabre".
The awakening of BM'
Bottom: 'BM before the court of judgement'

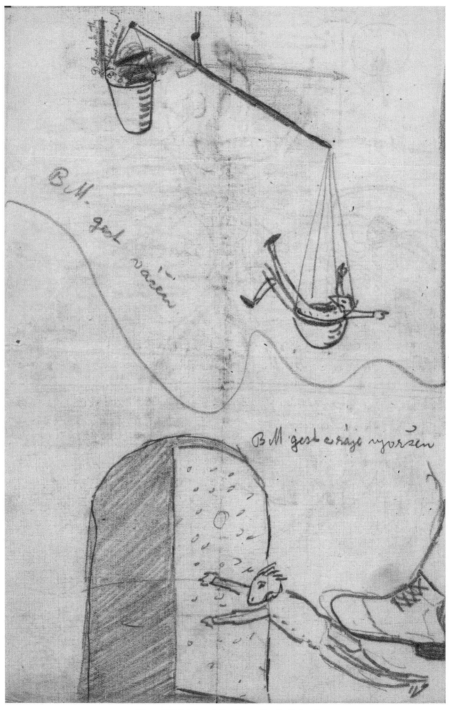

Top: 'BM is weighed in the balance'
Bottom: 'BM is expelled from Paradise'

Top: '...and rendered unto Hell'
Bottom: 'BM as cinders'

'The End'

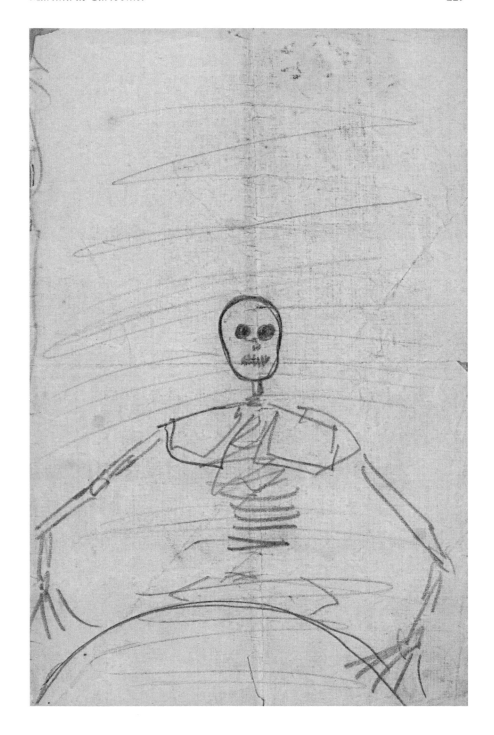

Index
of Martinů's Works

General
Index

A number in italics indicates an illustration.

Also available

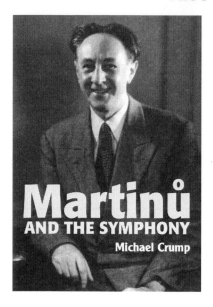

Martinů and the Symphony is the first book on the Martinů symphonies to appear in English, and is by far the most comprehensive work in any language on the subject. Each Symphony is examined in turn, the analyses revealing what makes each creation so individual and yet also part of a close-knit family of works. Aspects of his melodic, harmonic and instrumental style are scrutinised in detail. The path to symphonic mastery in Martinů's early orchestral works is examined in unprecedented detail, and a study of the late triptychs rounds out this appraisal an enthralling symphonic and orchestral legacy.

ISBN 978 0 907689 65 2 ~ 512 pages ~
Royal octavo ~ 199 music exx.

Press comment

'an engaging book that should do much to enhance the esteem of a unique and treasurable corner of the symphonic repertory'

Music & Letters

'a sequence of magnificently enlarged programme essays that will surely resonate with the composer's admirers and also provoke wider interest [.... Crump's] passion is infectious'

Times Literary Supplement

'Crump's comprehensive investigation of Martinů's symphonic legacy is a particularly welcome occasion. [... his] musical descriptions provide a personal perspective that acts as a counterweight to the more formal analysis. This dual approach seems perfectly suitable, and indeed reflects the music of Martinu itself.'

MLA Notes